"*Walking the Tycoons' Rope* offers a Peeping Tom-like view of Hong Kong's most well-known tycoons and their unlovely world. Shudder-inducing glimpses into familiar personalities, business dealings, family relationships and value systems turn this book – like all well-documented train wrecks – into truly compulsive reading … This excellent memoir has enduring social history value." – *South China Morning Post*

"The insider's guide to understanding Hong Kong's tycoon scene." – *Hong Kong Tatler*

"Robert Wang … has a gift for picking out the most relevant, interesting and entertaining anecdotes … *Walking the Tycoons' Rope* is a surprising and unlikely page turner." – *iTV-Asia*

"A cautionary tale of greed and ambition and also a fascinating look back at a Hong Kong that no longer exists – that tantalizing, Westernized city of dreams for mainland immigrants who managed to escape the Spartan world of communism under Mao Zedong … Its publication could not be more timely, coinciding as it does with a growing resentment among ordinary people toward the tycoon class in Hong Kong, which now has the largest wealth gap in the developed world." – *Asia Times*

# WALKING THE TYCOONS' ROPE

*How ambition drove a poor boy
from Ningbo to compete with the richest
men of Hong Kong and Singapore*

Robert Wang

BLACKSMITH BOOKS

*To Elaine, my perfect wife*

ISBN 978-988-16138-1-3

Published by Blacksmith Books
5th Floor, 24 Hollywood Road, Central, Hong Kong
Tel: (+852) 2877 7899
*www.blacksmithbooks.com*

Published April 2012
Reprinted November 2012

This is an autobiography. The names of some of the characters have
been changed to preserve anonymity. The telling of the events relies
on memory which may mean that some names, organizations,
places and incidents may not be totally accurate and some of the
names and likeness of the story may have been changed and parts
added to entertain; any resemblance to actual persons, living or dead,
events or locales is entirely coincidental.

Front cover photo: the Suntec Board
Back row: Chow Chung Kai, the author, Tony Yeh and Li Dak Seng
Front row: W.H. Chou (deceased), Lee Shau Kee, Run Run Shaw,
Frank Tsao, Li Ka Shing and Cheng Yu Tung

# Contents

*Foreword* . . . . . . . . . . . . . . . . . . . . . . . . . . . . . . 7

Part 1: Reunions . . . . . . . . . . . . . . . . . . . . . . . . . 15

       Ting Kuan – my father's story . . . . . . . . . . 32

       Sau Chi – my mother's story . . . . . . . . . . . 39

       Ting Hai (Siaw Ko)   my aunt's story . . . . . 58

Part 2: Hong Kong . . . . . . . . . . . . . . . . . . . . . . . 87

       The Walled City . . . . . . . . . . . . . . . . . . . . 93

       Growing Pains . . . . . . . . . . . . . . . . . . . . . 100

       The Lost Generation . . . . . . . . . . . . . . . . 114

       Puppy Love . . . . . . . . . . . . . . . . . . . . . . . 126

       Rich Friends. . . . . . . . . . . . . . . . . . . . . . . 136

Part 3: Student Days . . . . . . . . . . . . . . . . . . . . . . 141

       Meeting Aunt Diana . . . . . . . . . . . . . . . . 144

       The Ritz Hotel, London. . . . . . . . . . . . . . 146

       Golders Green . . . . . . . . . . . . . . . . . . . . . 149

       The Report. . . . . . . . . . . . . . . . . . . . . . . . 160

       The French Connection . . . . . . . . . . . . . . 164

       The Holiday. . . . . . . . . . . . . . . . . . . . . . . 166

       Western Rain and Eastern Sunshine. . . . . . 180

Part 4: The Practice . . . . . . . . . . . . . . . . . . . . . . . 203

       Shanghai Parties. . . . . . . . . . . . . . . . . . . . 223

       City in Jitters . . . . . . . . . . . . . . . . . . . . . . 229

       The Tycoons' Club . . . . . . . . . . . . . . . . . . 242

       Singapore. . . . . . . . . . . . . . . . . . . . . . . . . 267

       The Crescendo. . . . . . . . . . . . . . . . . . . . . 277

       The Establishment . . . . . . . . . . . . . . . . . . 297

       Alive in the Crocodile Pit. . . . . . . . . . . . . 308

       The Perfect Storms. . . . . . . . . . . . . . . . . . 323

       The Comeback. . . . . . . . . . . . . . . . . . . . . 354

*Epilogue* . . . . . . . . . . . . . . . . . . . . . . . . . . . . . . 373

## Author's note

I would like to express my thanks to the people who helped me with this book. My thanks are due in particular to Michael Dalton, my erstwhile partner, who edited the text chapter by chapter as I had completed it, putting right matters of grammar, syntax and language; without his help this work would not have been possible. And to Gillian, my daughter, for reading the manuscript and giving me timely and appropriate comments.

I am grateful to John Berry who advised me as the book evolved, did the initial editing and wrote the synopsis and to Philip Nourse for reading the manuscript and giving me useful advice.

On page 156 some lyrics are quoted from Simon and Garfunkel's *El Condor Pasa (If I only could)* and on page 304 there is a poetic interpretation by Mike Garofalo of Chang San-feng's original text.

I owe a huge debt to Carol Cole for her masterly editing skills. She has a mind for detail and guided me through the book with comments and anecdotes to ensure the story flows smoothly.

Royalties of this book will be donated to Ningbo Charitable Foundation Limited.

# FOREWORD

I am delighted to have the opportunity to contribute a foreword to this remarkable autobiography of Robert Wang, solicitor and entrepreneur extraordinaire.

This is a fascinating story, spanning a period of over a century, from the days of his great-grandfathers to his parents' and Robert's own life; through the upheavals of China's recent history to the calm and stability of life in colonial Hong Kong; turbulent years in the run-up to 1997, to the highs and lows and continued success of Hong Kong after sovereignty was returned to China. All in all, Robert's life seems to bear an uncanny resemblance to the graph of Hong Kong itself.

In order to appreciate the difficulties encountered and the scale of Robert's success, one must understand the historical, political, economic and cultural contexts in which the events took place.

From my observations of Robert over a period exceeding thirty years, I notice Confucian traditional values are ingrained in him and are very influential in his management style and decision-making: filial piety, industry, tolerance, harmony, humbleness, loyalty and observation of the hierarchical order. Of the last, I must say he was not strong, and it was this weakness that caused his fall from grace in Singapore.

Robert's character is inexorably shaped by the environment in which he grew up: arriving as a toddler at the clock tower of the Star Ferry, living through the harshness of life in the colonial Hong Kong of the '50s and '60s, and enduring much discrimination as he tried to escape from the throes of poverty. All these made him the character he is: enterprising, determined and ambitious.

Robert was, I believe, extremely fortunate in that, shortly after he commenced in practice, he consulted a Mr Liu Tian Oung ("T.O."). T.O. was undoubtedly "a scholar and a gentleman". He was many years Robert's senior, a graduate of Tsinghua University in Beijing. So talented and successful was T.O. that he had been tipped to become Minister of Finance of the Central Government of China before his move to Hong Kong. T.O. clearly recognized Robert's potential and unostentatiously took him under his wing. For the rest of his life, he discreetly tendered advice to the young solicitor, introducing Robert to businessmen influential in Hong Kong. Robert appreciated and acted upon the guidance that his mentor wisely gave him.

It was through T.O. that I met Robert. When I joined his firm – Messrs Robert W.H. Wang & Co, Solicitors & Notaries – in 1979, Hong Kong was still a British Crown Colony. The administration was run by the British. The civil service, the judiciary, the disciplined forces and, more importantly, most of the major corporations, banks and trading houses known as "hongs" were of British origin or British-controlled. T.O. advised Robert to recruit an English solicitor to generate business for the practice from the important British-controlled sectors of Hong Kong's economy, and that is where I came in.

This was a move I have never regretted. For me, and I believe also for Robert, it was the start of an exciting voyage. We sailed through placid seas, steaming ahead at full speed, but we often had to cope with turbulent waters. There were good times and there were difficult times but throughout we kept the ship on an even keel. Robert was always master of the ship, the skipper and the navigator, while I was the master's mate for the next twenty-seven years.

In the early 1980s, at the start of our journey together, the Hong Kong economy was booming. I remember the first day I started work, Robert said to me: "You will find life in Hong Kong is not like a single day." I puzzled over this enigmatic observation but soon came to understand what he meant. In contrast to the work of a solicitor in the UK, where I had practised for twenty years before joining Robert and where everything was so predictable, in Hong Kong you never knew what type of work would be on your desk the next day. It was exciting and rewarding.

"You only have to open the window and money flies in," Robert said one day. Or as two of his tycoon associates and clients observed: "There's so much money lying on the ground, I really don't have time to bend down to pick it up" and "Money falls like manna from Heaven".

That is how it was until 1983 when Margaret Thatcher, the then Prime Minister of the United Kingdom, commenced negotiations with the Chinese Government over the future of Hong Kong after the expiration in 1997 of the lease of the New Territories. These negotiations proved to be protracted and difficult and produced panic in the streets. The local people quite understandably imagined that the Red Army would march in and that the Communist Party would take over Hong Kong, destroying its booming economy. These fears triggered a "brain drain" with mass emigration of talented and enterprising people to Western jurisdictions, largely to Vancouver and Toronto.

In order to stem the brain drain, the British Government introduced a "Right of Abode" scheme under which local Chinese Hong Kong residents with the appropriate qualifications could apply for British nationality. This was designed to give comfort to key businessmen and their families and to stabilize the economy in the run-up to 1997.

For Robert and his local partners, whose numbers were growing as the legal practice prospered, the question was: What would happen to the legal practice in 1997 and what would life be like under Communist rule? Robert needed a bolt-hole not only for himself and his family but for all his local Hong Kong Chinese partners, key employees and, possibly, key clients, if things went wrong after 1997. Could the firm relocate as a successful going concern to a safe haven? With the help of T.O., he identified Singapore as a suitable destination. It was culturally compatible with Hong Kong, politically stable and, more importantly, the former British colony had retained the English Common Law legal system, as in Hong Kong.

However, the major problem was the fact that no Hong Kong lawyers, let alone firms, were allowed to practise in Singapore. This technicality did not deter Robert. He would need all his determination and audacity if he were to overcome this seemingly insuperable barrier.

Robert initially lobbied the Attorney General of Singapore but made no headway there. He approached ministers and business people of influence and eventually met with the Deputy Prime Minister, Dr Goh Keng Swee, who asked Robert to make his proposals in writing. Ultimately, the Prime Minister of Singapore, Lee Kuan Yew, must have been impressed by Robert's tenacity as he summoned Robert to meet with him. At the end of the day, Robert single-handedly persuaded Lee Kuan Yew and the Government to amend their Legal Profession Act to enable suitably qualified and selected Hong Kong lawyers to be allowed to practise in Singapore.

In 1985, Robert was the first Hong Kong solicitor to be admitted. He established the firm of Robert W.H. Wang & Woo, Solicitors & Attorneys. This would enable Robert and his partners to relocate to Singapore and continue the legal practice there in the event of adverse conditions in Hong Kong after the handover of sovereignty to China. This was undoubtedly a momentous achievement, but even more noteworthy feats were to follow.

Robert followed up with a paper he submitted to the Singapore Government entitled "Scheme for Eminent Entrepreneurs". Again it was his initiative that gave birth to the Corporate Special Holding Status Scheme (CSHS) introduced in Singapore in 1983 which allowed an approved entrepreneur to nominate one person for permanent residence in Singapore for every S$1 million invested there from among those who were closest to him – family, business associates and his trusted lieutenants.

The brutal repression of demonstrators in Tiananmen Square in 1989 renewed the fears of Hong Kong citizens as to the future of Hong Kong under Communist China after 1997. By 1989, the generation of the most successful business leaders in Hong Kong would all be in their sixties or seventies or even older. They were unlikely to emigrate to countries such as Canada. Singapore was ideal: friendly, sympathetic, multicultural and predominantly Chinese. The CSHS was originally intended to benefit up to 25,000 families from Hong Kong. In fact, the demand was so great that Singapore actually granted approval to 50,000 qualifying families.

Among them would be many of Hong Kong's leading Chinese businessmen. Robert had the genius to see that, if he was able to bring together a group of these top entrepreneurs and syndicate them with the object of making substantial investments in Singapore, they would have an extraordinarily formidable company. He set about this project with vigour, bringing together some twenty investors including seven of the wealthiest and most successful Hong Kong tycoons – between them holding some forty per cent of Hong Kong's market capitalization. The company registered in Singapore, Suntec, did not go unnoticed.

As the spokesman for Suntec, Robert found himself engaged in discussions with tycoons from all over the world, internationally recognized household names, all looking for some beneficial association with this new international powerhouse.

Suntec was an enormous success. It won the tender for a greenfield site of 11.7 hectares in central Singapore. The development they undertook was the largest private development ever in Singapore. I.M. Pei, the famous Chinese-American architect, was engaged to design Suntec City.

During this period, Robert was commuting between Hong Kong and Singapore supervising the legal firms in both cities, looking after his business interests in Hong Kong and attending to the business of Suntec in Singapore. By 1995, the transfer of sovereignty of Hong Kong from Britain to China was rapidly approaching and Robert deemed it time to relocate to Singapore. These were exciting times for him. He had achieved his ultimate objective – a lifestyle of the rich and famous. He was literally rubbing shoulders with the wealthiest and most successful tycoons in the world, heads of government, kings, prime ministers, leading politicians and international businessmen – dizzy heights. In the company Robert was keeping, it could not all be plain sailing. There was bound to be rivalry. Factions developed and plotting followed. Although Robert had brought the tycoons together, he was by far the youngest of the directors of Suntec and had no permanent close allies.

Traditional Chinese values came into play and were respected. "Tolerance of others" was perhaps only superficial. "Loyalty to superiors" was important, as indeed was "respecting the hierarchical order". Robert had to learn how to dance on a shifting carpet. In 1985, when he had initiated the "Scheme for Eminent Entrepreneurs", these people recognized his usefulness. However, once they were firmly established in Singapore, he was dispensable. He was caught in the crossfire from in-fighting between the tycoons.

Things came to a head with Robert's unfortunate mismanagement of the projected prestigious Singapore Hong Kong Club. Robert committed a faux pas which in Western culture would be regarded as extremely trivial. The retribution brought about by this was quite extraordinary. The situation could not be retrieved despite all his efforts. He was humiliated and felt obliged to return to Hong Kong, his tail between his legs.

This was like Noah and his ark but with a very unhappy ending. Robert had perceived the flood coming which he imagined would drown Hong Kong and all its capitalist entrepreneurs and tycoons in 1997. He led them two by two to the ark, sailing to dry land: Singapore. Then, once they were on dry land, these seemingly ungrateful beings turned this Noah out. Happily for Robert, however, Hong Kong was not submerged in 1997. The fate that many feared in the 1980s did not come about. Hong Kong survived and Robert was able to return to his true home and rise like a phoenix from the ashes.

However, despite the smooth handover of sovereignty of Hong Kong on the 1st July 1997, other significant events impacted adversely upon Hong Kong's prosperity and on the fortunes of Robert's legal firm.

With the benefit of his training and experience as a lawyer, fortified by his spectacularly successful excursions into the world of high finance and international business, and as an older and much wiser man than the young man who took the tycoons into Singapore, Robert now lives a contented life in Hong Kong focusing on entrepreneurial activities on his own account. He has now adopted the *modus operandi* of his much-admired late mentor, T.O. Liu.

Robert's achievements have been momentous by any standards, and are made no less so by his fall from grace in Singapore. The story of his journey is truly inspirational, and a lesson on what can be achieved without wealth or privilege but by sheer hard work, determination and courage. He may have written an epilogue to his story, but I feel sure there is another chapter yet to be written.

Michael Dalton

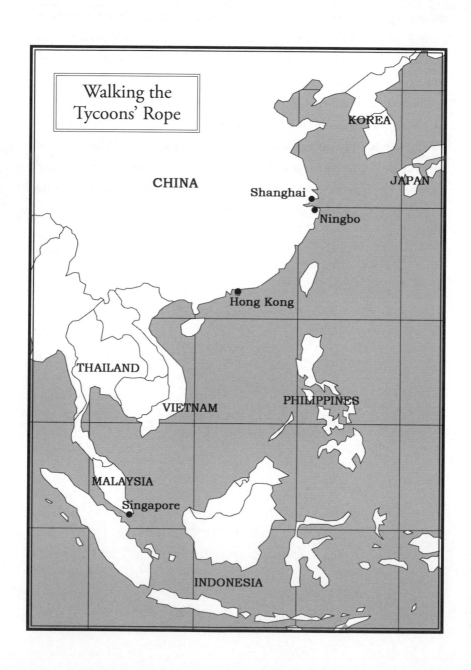

Walking the
Tycoons' Rope

KOREA

CHINA

JAPAN

Shanghai

Ningbo

Hong Kong

THAILAND

VIETNAM

PHILIPPINES

MALAYSIA

Singapore

INDONESIA

# PART I

# REUNIONS

"Where is Ningbo?" a foreigner asked his tailor in old Shanghai. "Shanghai more far," the tailor replied.

Ningbo lies south of and separated from Shanghai by the Hangzhou Bay, at the mouth of the mighty Yangtze River.

I was born on the island of Zhou Shan which is located across the harbour from the mainland. The city of Ningbo is just a short ferry ride away. Zhou Shan is also known as Ding Hai, which means 'serene waves'. Zhou Shan means 'mountain of sampans'. It sits to the south of the bay. It is the largest island in the archipelago of some one hundred islands known as the Zhou Shan Isles, which is listed as one of the world's four largest fishing grounds. It is famous for its sea products.

Zhou Shan achieved some historical fame after the Opium War. As compensation for China's humiliating defeat, Britain asked for the island. The corrupt and inept Qing Government considered the island to be too important – China would be cut into two halves by the Western powers if it were ceded. China therefore refused. Instead, it paid war compensation of US$6 million and ceded 'that barren piece of rock' known as Hong Kong to Britain. Today, the first British embassy on Chinese soil still stands on the island.

Zhou Shan is close to Japan. The inhabitants of the nearby Japanese islands share common cultures and traditions – for instance, the way rice cakes are made. A bowl and a hammer are used. Two people work in tandem: one hammers while, between strokes, the other flips the dough into the bowl. The only difference is that, in Japan, the utensils used are made of wood while in Zhou Shan they are made of stone. The Japanese islanders look more like natives of Zhou Shan than from the mainland of Japan.

Apart from fishing, the island lacks resources and therefore can ill afford to support a population of any great size. The harsh environment has created a people who are known throughout China for their hard work, trustworthiness and ingenuity. In business, the practice of 'my word is my bond' is strictly followed. Its people are high achievers, always striving for excellence.

'Giving a dinner is easy; inviting guests is difficult' is a saying which illustrates how high its people aspire. A disproportionate number of Ningbo's businessmen make it to the top. They become tycoons and earn such nicknames as 'king of textiles', 'king of banking' and 'king' of this and that.

I was born in dramatic circumstances during a time when China was ravaged by war and in chaos. Law and order had all but broken down. That night, in the spring of 1944, my mother was in an advanced stage of pregnancy – my birth was imminent and expected that same week – when the household was raided. Three teenagers broke into the two-storey house. After tying up and robbing the family on the ground floor, they proceeded upstairs where my mother lived with my grandparents. My father was away in Shanghai where he worked as a police detective. My grandparents were tied up and made to kneel by the knife-wielding young thugs and told that if they did not surrender money and valuables they would harm my pregnant mother. My mother had a small diamond ring on her finger, something she treasured greatly as it was given to her by my father when they first started courting. Despite my mother and grandparents giving them all they had, the robbers were far from satisfied. They demanded more. One of them had my mother in a stranglehold and placed the knife on her throat. My grandmother, in tears, reached out and gripped the arm of the knife-wielding robber, begging him not to harm my mother. As my grandparents pleaded for mercy, my mother managed to twist the ring off her finger and, during a moment when the attention of the gang members was distracted, hid it by placing it in her mouth.

Meanwhile, my grandmother's move enraged the attacker and, in the ensuing struggle, my mother was hit on the head by a hard object – probably the handle of the knife. It knocked her to the ground. She choked on the ring before she swallowed it. Her face turned green. She lay on the floor rolling around, moaning and groaning in pain. Blood oozed from her head wound. In the glaring eyes of all present that night, she suddenly went into labour and the birth progressed quickly after her waters broke. The speedy succession of events took the would-be robbers by surprise and filled them with fear. The teenagers panicked and bolted, probably thinking that my mother was about to die there and then.

That was how I was born, at home and delivered by my grandparents. Shortly after I was born, the family left Zhou Shan to join my father in Shanghai.

In Shanghai it is said that 'without Ningbo there is no market'. It is an illustration of how much the market is controlled by Ningbo people who are clannish and strive to improve each other's lot, not dissimilar to the Jews who live in the West. Indeed, people from that part of China are often called 'the Jews of China'. It was drummed into the head of every native that our homeland was poor and if one was to make good in life he must never forget to return to repay his native land. Hence, over the years, if one saw a good bridge or road in Ningbo, one knew it was not built with money from taxes but was paid for by yet another native of Ningbo who had made it big outside and returned to benefit the land by 'building bridges and repaving roads'.

This obligation becomes the sacred duty of every son of the land. No matter where he is, he always remembers that one day when he succeeds he must return to the land, like a fallen leaf going back into the soil to enrich the root of the tree. Deng Hsiao Ping, China's paramount leader, once described the sons and daughters as 'Ningbo Bong'. (Phonetically

the word 'bong' in Chinese has a double meaning: 'a gang' or 'assistance').
Deng was talking metaphorically. He appealed to businessmen of Ningbo
origin, wherever they were but particularly those in Hong Kong, to give
a helping hand to Ningbo's modernization programmes.

≈≈≈≈≈

When Shanghai was liberated in 1949, the Red Army soldiers paraded
triumphantly through the streets. As a boy of five, I was dressed up in a
uniform complete with a red scarf around the neck – the standard issue
to all families with children in the neighbourhood. The children were
asked to line up on both sides of the streets to welcome the soldiers. They
were told to bang a small drum tied to the waist to welcome them as they
paraded into the centre of Shanghai.

At that time, our home was a 'stone cove' *lung tong* house, so named
because of the stone thresholds at the entrances in the narrow alley-like
streets. In a *lung tong* house, one crosses a small courtyard, in the middle
of which is a stone well. Accommodation is spread over two levels: the
kitchen and sitting room on the ground floor and the bedrooms on the
upper. A *lung tong* house has no modern facilities to speak of: water is
drawn from the well and the toilet is a wooden bowl that is used in
privacy and placed outside the main entrance every night. The nightsoil,
commonly called 'fragrance of the night', is collected in the small hours
of the morning and is sold to farmers as fertilizer.

My grandparents originally rented it but when my father made good
as a '*pao-da-tien*' – a detective who was supposed to 'guarantee he knows
everything' – he bought the house for five sticks of gold. I don't know
where my father got the money from. He could not have afforded it on
his meagre salary and he was known to be a kind, upright and honest
man – not the usual corrupt kind one would expect to find in the police
force. As a child, I used to hear stories about my father helping detainees
by giving them food, water and cigarettes while they were detained by

the police. While most of them were common criminals, others were political prisoners – Communists and their known sympathisers.

As a child the house seemed big to me but, when I returned as an adult, it looked small. Recently, it has been demolished to make way for Xin Tian Di, the famous night hub of Shanghai, a hip area where bars and restaurants abound. Today's Hotel 88 is where the old house once stood. The stone well however still remains from the original house and is displayed in the foyer.

My father knew he would be a wanted man if he stayed In Shanghai after the Communists arrived because of the time he had spent in the police force. He left the force in 1948 and joined a company solely for the purpose of escaping the advancing Communists.

In the autumn of 1949, hot on the heels of civil war in China, my mother took us to Hong Kong. I was five at the time and my sister was three. My father had already settled there a year earlier. He was part of the withdrawal plan of his then employer, known in the market as the 'king of eggs', a clansman from Ningbo, who had moved his cold storage business lock, stock and barrel to Hong Kong before the arrival of the Communists.

My grandparents were at the train station to see us off. It was a sentimental occasion. Everyone seemed to be crying when the whistle was blown and the call was made for boarding.

"Sau Chi, it's time to board," said Sou Yue, my grandmother, as she wiped tears from her face. "Please take good care of Bo Bo."

She made no mention of my sister. Bo Bo – meaning 'double precious' – was my nickname. I was always her favourite.

With my grandmother, I could get away with murder. She would bend to my every whim. For example, when I wanted to build a tram system in the sitting room, not only did she allow me to strip decorative wooden beams from the walls but she also helped me cut the wires from electrical appliances. The beams were laid on the floor as tracks and the wires were tied together to resemble an overhead cable. The tram was a chair that was placed sideways on the tracks. The overhead cable was connected to

the tram by means of a stick tied to the chair. "Do, do, do…move away,"
I shouted excitedly as I sat on the legs of the chair and pulled in the air
with my clenched fist to resemble the action of the conductor pulling the
tram whistle.

Carrying my sister in one arm and holding my hand with the other, my
mother boarded the train. My grandmother started to cry even louder.

"I want Grandma." I turned my head and shouted again, "I want
Grandma. Let me go." I cried as I tried to twist free of my mother's grip.
"Let me go. I want to go to Grandma."

"My Bo Bo," my grandmother cried uncontrollably. "My heart is
broken. Grandma loves you. When will I ever see you again? Oh, An
Chai, you go and get Bo Bo back for me. I can't stand the thought of Bo
Bo leaving us. How am I going to live without my darling Bo Bo? Go
quickly!"

The whistle blew for the final call and the doors were slammed shut
one by one.

Grandfather suddenly jumped on board. "Leave Bo Bo behind," he
commanded as he snatched me away. "You can take my granddaughter.
You can't take both of my grandchildren away at the same time."

"You can't do that," my mother screamed. "I beg you. Please let us
stay as one family. How can I answer to my husband, your son, in Hong
Kong, if I leave Bo Bo behind? Please be reasonable… please… please."

In the midst of the ensuing commotion, there were tears and screams
as my mother fought desperately to fend off the intruder. But she was no
match for my grandfather. I was taken off the train and reunited with my
grandmother. In fear, I clutched her legs as tightly as I could. The train
began to move.

Thinking that I was safe in their hands, Grandfather asked me to wave
goodbye to my distraught mother who by then was hysterical. The train
began to pick up speed.

Suddenly, at the last minute, my mother passed my sister to a passenger,
a total stranger who had witnessed the incident. She instinctively took
the girl under her care. My mother jumped off the moving train, took

my grandparents by surprise and totally unprepared and, grabbing me, jumped back onto the accelerating train and slammed the door, all in quick succession. Before my grandparents could react, the train had moved away from the platform.

≈≈≈≈≈

The journey to Hong Kong was fraught with danger. Under normal circumstances, it would have taken three days. But, after the defeat of the Japanese, China was in the grip of a civil war that was being waged between the two rival factions – Communist and Nationalist. The journey was constantly interrupted by aerial bombardments. The Nationalist army was retreating to Taiwan while the rest of China fell into the hands of the Communists.

The train had to traverse a vast coastal region, the control of which was all but certain. It was guarded by soldiers, and machine guns surrounded by sandbags were mounted on the roofs of the coaches.

One day into the journey, the train suddenly came to a grinding halt, jerking many passengers to the floor. It had happened before.

"Air raid! Air raid!" shouted a voice. "The train will be bombed. Leave the train immediately and run as far away as possible."

In confusion, passengers scrambled for the doors, pouring off the steps like cascading water, on top of each other, and ran like mad away from the target into the safety of the surrounding fields. A fighter plane swooped down from the sky and fired rapidly at the train. Clap… clap… clap… clap… the machine guns exchanged fire. Then a bomb was dropped. It exploded near the train, making a deafening sound and sending a cloud of thick smoke into the sky.

"Run… Bo Bo, run!" my mother shouted, still carrying her crying and panic-stricken daughter in her arms. "Run as far away from the train as you can. But make sure you stay close. Lie on the ground and don't move until I tell you to."

From the safety of the distant field, I saw the lone plane circle and swoop down to launch another attack. A fresh round of gunfire was exchanged. Then the plane turned, pulled up and disappeared into the distance.

When the attack was over, bodies of soldiers, many of them dead, could be seen sprawled on the sandbags. Those who were still alive were covered with blood, either their own or their fallen comrades'. One by one, the injured soldiers were lowered down from the roof and given medical treatment. The dead bodies, soldiers and passengers alike, were buried in a shallow grave that was dug beside the track. We all remained silently in the field waiting for the signal to board the train again.

When the 'all clear' was finally given, there was a frantic rush to get back on board. The train moved, gaining speed. Carrying my sister in one arm, Mother and I had to run frantically to catch it.

The attacks and consequential stoppages had meanwhile created a sense of camaraderie among the passengers, and people hung half out of the end coach with arms outstretched, shouting for my mother to run faster. My sister was literally thrown to a passenger and Mother pushed me forward. A passenger managed to catch my hand and lift me off the ground while my mother managed miraculously to find another outstretched arm. She stumbled, fell, managed to find her feet again, clutched tightly onto the arm and climbed back onto the moving train. The scene resembled a Hollywood movie!

≈≈≈≈≈

We arrived safely in Hong Kong. Father had waited at the Kowloon-Canton Railway Station clock tower but, when we did not show up two days after the scheduled time, he left the station, exhausted and saddened at the thought that his family must have perished.

Hungry and bewildered by the strange new environment, Mother took a handout of $5 from a passenger and went to a nearby store where, unable to speak the local dialect, she pointed at the bread and handed the note to the shopkeeper. She returned to the clock tower, where we waited in the care of a passenger, with a basket full of bread. We had arrived.

Our first taste of Hong Kong was good.

≈≈≈≈≈

I was a man in my early thirties when I returned to Shanghai again in 1978, a successful solicitor – senior partner of a prominent law firm with offices in Hong Kong, Singapore and London, an honorary fellow of Queen Mary College, my alma mater, and the Institute of Advanced Legal Education, both of London University – and recently elected chairman of the Ningbo Association in Hong Kong. I was amongst a delegation of dignitaries who were invited by the government to see Shanghai shortly after China had opened up to the outside world. The visit had been organized in a style that is called, in the Chinese custom, 'beating a triumphant return in fine clothes', a traditional ritual reserved for the favourite sons who returned after successfully passing the imperial examinations.

A welcoming party was on the airport tarmac when the plane landed. A red carpet was rolled out and a band was in attendance, playing loud music as schoolchildren in colourful clothes and carrying flowers were singing, dancing, waving and chanting repeatedly: "Welcome, welcome, many welcomes."

Amid much fanfare, the delegation was ushered into a waiting room while the entry papers were processed. It was apparent from the beginning that the local government had gone to great lengths to plan and prepare for this occasion.

It was the time when China was waking up from its prolonged hibernation under Communism. The sky was still grey and so were its people. Shanghai was lifeless. The bamboo curtain had effectively shut

China off from the outside world. This was not the place for a young man.

We were whisked away to the city in a convoy of cars – including a couple of the prestigious Red Flag limousines – and checked into the Jian Jiang Hotel, the best Shanghai could offer at the time. On the way to the hotel, I noticed the roads were completely devoid of motorized traffic. Cyclists had to dismount on both sides of the road to wait for our convoy to pass. There were hundreds of them, all dressed in the same drab Mao uniforms. It was drizzling and it seemed as if it rained the whole five days we were there.

The rain matched the atmosphere that prevailed in Shanghai: dark, grey and miserable.

"I swear next time I'm in Shanghai, I shall bring my own lightbulbs," I complained to those around the table at the coffee shop at the Peace Hotel, the only place where anything close to nightlife existed.

"This is a horrible place," I remarked. "There is nothing to do here after dark except listen to this dreary old men's band. I tell you, they are really bad. Look at them. Everyone is at least sixty years old. I'm sure they have been playing together since the liberation. One would expect them to play more in harmony. Yet, listen to this rubbish. They play so out of tune that it's embarrassing. And look at this place. It has no life and it's dark and dingy. I can hardly see you from where I am. The people are dressed so drably in the same Mao uniforms. And where else on earth do you see such miserable colour sense… yuk! Blue tops and green trousers? How awful. It offends my artistic integrity. If I'd only brought my own lightbulbs, I could at least read after dark instead of coming here to listen to this cheerless crap!"

"Shut up, Robert," said Aunt Diana. "Be grateful. See how they have rolled out the red carpet for us. Count your blessings and stop complaining."

"Yes, relax and enjoy yourself," added Sau Chi, my mother. "The band is taking a break. Now, drink up and get the bill so we can leave. Tomorrow's going to be another long day."

"Ting Kuan, you must buy a house for my elder daughter in Zhou Shan," said my aunt Ting Hai to my father in a voice so loud that everyone present could hear. "She is applying to have her registered abode moved back to Ningbo from Tibet, to which, as you know, she was banished during the Cultural Revolution – on your account."

I noticed Aunt Diana turn her head the other way to avoid eye contact with her cousin. The two had hardly spoken to each other during the last two days and were behaving like strangers. There was something rather unusual, as if they shared a secret that no one else knew.

"On my father's account?" I came to my father's defence almost instinctively. I never quite understood this aunt of mine. I had no memory of her as a child. She gave the impression that she was resentful and even vengeful, as if she had a score to settle with my father. She was always on my father's back, picking on everything. "Are you mad? What's got into your head? This doesn't make sense. It sounds like blackmail. What on earth has my father got to do with your daughter being sent to Tibet? Why must he redeem his sin? What sin? You know, my father was in Hong Kong throughout the Cultural Revolution."

"Robert, mind your words," said Father. "Show some respect. Aunt Ting Hai is your elder."

"It must be the Cultural Revolution," I mumbled to myself. "Yes, the Cultural Revolution has distorted her mind into thinking so illogically."

"Had it not been for our overseas connections, my daughter would not have been banished to that godforsaken part of China and have to endure all those years of hardship in Tibet," Aunt Ting Hai continued defensively. "You are our only overseas connection. I suffered on your account. Therefore, you must pay back, Ting Kuan."

I was speechless; flabbergasted that anyone could think in such bizarre logic.

"I am sorry," my father replied quietly. "When I am back in Hong Kong, I shall arrange the money. Let me know how much it will cost."

"What?" I retorted. "Will you give in to her blackmail, just like that? Are you in your right mind, Dad? Shouldn't you rather say that you will consider her request and reply later? You're not exactly wealthy."

"No, my mind is made up," said my father. "I shall find the money when I am back."

I paid the bill and left in disgust.

"Why did you do that, Dad?" I asked my father on the way back to the hotel.

"Do what?" he asked.

"You agreed to buy a house for her daughter in Ningbo," I reminded him.

"Oh, you mean the house," he said. "My sister has suffered too much. Our family owes her a huge debt."

Shortly afterwards my father bought the house and gave it as a present to his niece. She successfully applied to have her abode switched back from Tibet to Zhou Shan in Ningbo.

The delegation of dignitaries was in town at the invitation of the government which wanted investments from Hong Kong to start off the open-door policy that China was introducing at the time. A hectic programme of talks and dinners with the top leaders coupled with sightseeing and other leisurely activities was organized. When our official business had finally been completed, our family business began.

A room at the old French Club, which was just across the road from the hotel, was booked as the venue for the first family reunion. The same menu for a table of twelve was quoted to us in three different prices: Y600 if Aunt Diana booked because she came from Singapore as an 'overseas Chinese'; Y400 for me because I was from Hong Kong and as such was a 'compatriot'; and a mere Y300 for a local as a 'comrade'.

No fewer than eight tables of relatives turned up for this first reunion.

It is difficult to describe how happy I was with so many of these relatives I was meeting for the first time – over four generations of them. It seemed as if everyone had a story to tell and, as we ate, we chatted happily and often emotionally and I could see tears on the faces of the elders among us, recounting and reminiscing about the past, oblivious to the occasional rats we could see scampering among the exposed pipes in the ceiling.

Aunt Ting Hai pulled me to one side. I felt kind of sorry that I had been unkind to her and was eager to be reconciled. After all, she was my aunt, my father's sister. I was glad that she took the initiative.

"Bo Bo, how old were you when you went to Hong Kong?" she asked me.

"Five."

"Ah… five. You know, I was abandoned by my mother, your grandmother, when I was that age," she continued. "I was left outside my grandfather's house in Zhou Shan. He was very, very rich when he died and Aunt Diana's father, my uncle, took over as the head of the House of Tai. I cried for three days but he would not let me inside. Later, an old servant took pity on me and I had to work as a servant in my own grandfather's house. I toiled from daybreak every day and was even badly treated by my very own sister.

"She had already been staying in the house a long time before me and had been raised as a Tai girl. She despised me and beat me often. I had to comb her hair every morning. There was a gap as wide as heaven and earth between us. Yet, we were sisters. She was treated as a princess and I as a servant. I did not return home until I was sixteen, when my parents forced me into a loveless marriage. My husband died early and I was widowed. It is not easy for a widow to raise her children. My life is still harsh. I am glad that life treats you well."

I listened with my mouth wide open. Like a jigsaw puzzle, the pieces were beginning to fall into place. No wonder she and Aunt Diana acted as if there was a huge secret between them. No wonder my father felt so guilty towards this sister. I knew my grandmother was a Tai. So was Aunt Diana. I was overtaken by a sense of guilt. I shouldn't have spoken those harsh words to Aunt Ting Hai. I wished a hole in the ground would swallow my shame.

"Wow… I don't believe it," I remarked. "You mean Aunt Diana is your own sister?"

"No, Diana is the eldest of the natural children of my uncle. But what others don't know is that her older 'sister', Ting Chi, was not her natural sister but is, in fact, my older sister."

"Does anyone know this?" I asked.

"No, Diana certainly doesn't, nor do any of her siblings. They all think Ting Chi is their oldest sister."

"Does my father know?"

"I don't think so. He was too young at the time. But my parents could have told him. I don't know. I am old now. I do not have many years left in this world. I want you to keep this secret between us only. I will tell you the whole story before I die. But, whatever I tell you, please keep it secret. Don't tell anyone else – not even your own father. But after I die you can tell whomever you wish. Can you promise me this?"

"Yes." I nodded. My head was spinning. I still could not believe what I had heard. "Yes, I promise you, Aunt Ting Hai. By the way, I am sorry, really sorry, for the way I behaved towards you the other day. Please forgive me."

≈≈≈≈≈

The next day, John Castle, a friend from London on the trip, joined me to explore the Shanghai streets together. No sooner had we left the hotel than we began to regret it. The two of us stood out like sore thumbs in a sea of homogeneity. In the streets, local kids followed us, laughing, mocking and jeering. One actually asked if he could touch John's hair, never having seen blond hair before. In the local market, which was more like a gathering of a few farmers trying to sell produce from the countryside, a farmer was selling pork from a pig he had slaughtered earlier in the day. We noticed a woman waiting and waiting until everything except one last piece of meat, mostly bone and little flesh, was left unsold.

"How much is this piece of meat?" she asked.

"Fifty cents," replied the farmer. "You can see. This is my last piece. It is lean."

"What is lean about it?" the woman remarked. "It is all bone. There is no meat. I will give you forty cents."

"Forty-five cents – not a cent less," demanded the farmer.

John and I watched in fascination. By the time we left, the woman was still waiting and continuing to haggle, hoping that the farmer would change his mind and she could get it at her price!

≈≈≈≈≈

Locals were not allowed to enter the hotel unaccompanied. While we were out sightseeing during the day, the relatives had to wait outside at the gate. Later, in the suite, they all marvelled at the facilities in the bathroom:

"Can I use the bathroom?" asked one cousin.

"Of course, be my guest," I replied.

"Can I take a bath in the tub?" he asked. "I have heard of a bathtub but have never seen one, let alone used it before."

"Take this towel and use the tub to your heart's content," I said as I tossed the towel at the young man.

From that day on, it seemed as if everyone, young and old, among the relatives wanted to use the bathroom. There was always a long queue as they gathered in the sitting room chatting while 'spitting watermelon seeds'. These seeds are roasted with salt and dried under the sun. The seed is placed vertically to the upper and lower front teeth and then split open to get to the 'meat' inside. The habit of eating these seeds is as common as eating potato chips in the West.

This first reunion was followed by other reunions over the years. Every time I am in Shanghai, I marvel at how the city has been transformed from a dreary Communist backwater into a thriving, modern metropolis

– full of life, zest and optimism. The city is quickly regaining its status as the 'Paris of the East'.

It started with the flyovers which instantly gave the city a modern look from above. For years the whole city seemed to be a huge construction site. New buildings sprang up like mushrooms. Old buildings were spruced up. Lights returned to the streets and suddenly, like burning charcoals bursting into flame, the city came alive. It was as if someone had waved a wand and magically transformed the city overnight.

≈≈≈≈≈

In 1992, I was there again for another reunion and was driving down Shanghai's tree-lined boulevards and through acres of landscaped gardens to the Garden Hotel. I could not believe my eyes – it was a splendid hotel rising up some thirty floors and everywhere I saw elegance and luxury befitting its five-star status. And what is spectacular is that its base is still the original historical building of the French Club.

In sharp contrast to the original venue for our first reunion, the same room had been transformed. It was now full of grace and elegance with its chandeliers set amid the spectacular art deco embellishments of the 1920s.

Not only had the room changed but also the fortunes of my relatives – they looked affluent and, it was apparent, awash with a mood of optimism. It was different from the earlier reunions. China has changed. It was a new world!

≈≈≈≈≈

In 2006, I returned to Zhou Shan. My father had passed away by then and, with the help of local government officials, I found the village where my ancestors once lived and where my father had been born. Au Shan was a picturesque fishing village. The sea was calm and as placid as a lake.

Modernization had hardly touched the village and life had changed little
– it was as if time had stood still.

The only difference was that there were now a couple of newer concrete
buildings. The toilet was still a gap between two planks of wood in a hut
built on stilts, as it had been for thousands of years. Everyone I met there
had the surname Wang, being related one way or another to the next
person.

In the village, I met an elder. He had been at school with my father. He
must have been in his nineties but remembered my father well. When he
saw me, he embraced me and burst into tears.

"Oh my God, Ting Kuan has come back to life," he said. "I am so
pleased I have lived till this day. My good friend Ting Kuan has returned
to Au Shan." He embraced me with tears rolling down his cheeks.

There in Au Shan, my ancestral homeland, I had found my roots.

≈≈≈≈≈

Our most recent reunion took place during Shanghai's World Expo
in 2010. The city had changed beyond recognition and had not only
caught up but also in many ways surpassed Hong Kong. Shanghai is
now prosperous and its inhabitants are happy. Its streets are teeming with
people and the shops are full of customers. There is a buzz about the city.
Its inhabitants spend lavishly and freely. Chic places and people abound.
Restaurants are filled with diners, many of them young expatriates from
different parts of the world. Nightlife is colourful. Xin Tian Di, where
my grandfather's old house once stood, is full of revellers. There is gaiety
and laughter everywhere. It is a world apart from what it had been at
the time of our first reunion. No one then could have predicted that
Shanghai would change so dramatically. It is where the old meets the new
and the East meets the West, just like the old days.

As the band played, relatives gathered for tea in the swanky lobby
of the new Peninsula Hotel on the Bund. The lifestyle of my relatives

has improved, often beyond recognition. Not only are they no longer poor but many of them now drive expensive cars, own properties and appear to be successful and rich – some very rich – by any standard. The gathering has however dwindled in size as the younger ones no longer view meeting relatives from overseas as novel and exciting – they have better things to do.

As we boarded the bus, we lamented the passing of so many of the older generation over the years – Aunt Ting Hai, Aunt Diana, my father and others.

The bus took us to the French Club and the same room where the first reunion was held. Now the process is repeated every year when we have our annual family reunions.

The annual reunion is always a happy occasion – something I look forward to even though its appeal to the younger generation has diminished over the years. Each reunion serves to foster the bond that was once lost – them in Shanghai and us in Hong Kong and, in that sense, we were always a lost family. Now we have not only discovered each other but also, in the process, have got to know ourselves better – who we are, where we came from and where we are headed. We are together as a family again.

Some of the stories told to me are incredible. They do not happen in the world we live in today. Yet they happened this way in a past era. It is my privilege to be the custodian of our family history and to record the stories as they were told to me – by my father, my mother and my aunt – during the reunions. These are the most memorable episodes that members of my family could recall.

## Ting Kuan – my father's story

The inhabitants of Au Shan in Zhou Shan plied the sea for a living; they were gone for weeks, months and sometimes years, often never returning. Catches were sold at markets along the South China coast. It was once said that "no people in the world have made so great an advance in the art of fishing but have yet made so little progress" - this aptly describes both the industry and the ingrained stick-in-the-mud attitude of the Ningbo fishermen, so set in their ways.

"My ancestors have been fishermen for as long as can be remembered. My grandfather went to sea and never returned. No one knew what happened to him. His name was Wang Pon Ann. He married a girl from the same village. Her name was Li Li. Together they had two children. The son, my father, An Chai, was nine, and the daughter, An Li, was eight when Grandfather disappeared.

For as long as the children could remember, there was never enough food for all of them to eat. At the best of times, the food supply was erratic. Sometimes the family had more, other times little, and most times there was nothing but plain rice. Their family accepted it and had to live from hand to mouth depending on the luck of the father and what he could bring back each day.

Once, at dinner, the children were given a bowl of rice each. There was nothing else, not even preserved fish.

"Dad, I need salt fish," An Chai said.

"There is no more salt fish," said his father. "And we can't afford it."

"But, Dad, one hangs at the door," An Chai reminded his father. "Why can't we eat it?"

"That fish is reserved for a special occasion," said his mother.

"Can you hang the fish in front of us?" asked An Chai. "I want to look at it while I scoop rice into my mouth."

His mother saw no reason why she should refuse. The preserved fish – a mackerel – was removed, taken inside and hung from a horizontal beam.

"You are allowed to take just *one* look at the salt fish… just once," said his father. "Then you finish your rice."

Instead An Chai looked at the fish with each alternate scoop of the rice.

His father slapped him across the face.

"Why do you hit me?" cried An Chai.

"Why do you eat so much salt fish?" his father retorted.

The whole family burst into laughter.

Despite the abject poverty, there was much laughter in the household. All in all, it was a happy family.

My grandmother was a pretty woman despite being the daughter of a farmer. She had fine features and a well proportioned body. By all accounts, she was attractive in her youth.

That day, on my grandfather's birthday, my grandmother, Li Li, gathered her two children at home. Home was a stone hut, which the family shared with animals, by the seaside. The livestock were kept separately behind makeshift fences at one side. The rest of the room was used as living quarters. Li Li's parents-in-law and two of her husband's brothers came. The dinner was unusually rich by normal standards. There was meat, fish and vegetables. It was rare for the family to have meat to eat. Indeed, only the rich people on the island could afford it. Most fishermen had to make do with whatever they could catch on the day. Meat was reserved for special occasions such as weddings and festive celebrations.

Early in the morning, Li Li had slaughtered the only pig. She took the meat to the market and managed to sell all the meat except for a trotter, which she kept for dinner that night. She then bought fish and vegetables from the market. The pork was stewed in soybean sauce. The fish was steamed and the vegetables wok-fried. It had been a long time since our family had so much food on their plates. Normally the family ate rice and things preserved in salt such as eel, jellyfish, mud snails, yellow croakers, sea cucumber and other sea products.

That evening something unusual was in the offing. Everyone ate in silence; no one spoke. It was as if our family was eating its last dinner together.

"An Chai and An Li, I want you to listen and listen very carefully to what I have to say," Mother said. "Your grandparents and two of your uncles are here tonight. Let them be witnesses. It has now been nine months since your father went to sea. He has not returned and there is no news of him." She began to cry. "You know I am a woman. With Father gone, I have to look after this family. We have no income. Although your two uncles have brought us food almost every day, we as a family cannot live on their handouts indefinitely.

"Like your father, your uncles are also fishermen. They are poor like us. Your two uncles have barely enough to support their own families and they have to look after your grandparents at the same time. We used to contribute to the upkeep when Father was around. Now they have to shoulder the additional burden. Our plight has made a bad situation worse for them. I can well appreciate the hardships they are suffering on our account. But, without the help your uncles are giving us, we will starve. *Leung tow ng doa ngon* – there is no shore in sight at both ends. There is no way out.

"This cannot go on forever. Something needs to be done and done quickly. This is the reason why we gather here tonight. We have to find a solution and make sure we all survive through these bad times. Things have come to a head…"

She could hardly continue. Her sobbing gave way to hysteria. She paused to steady herself. "Let me finish this miserable life in front of all of you," she said.

She threw herself, head first, against the wall. It was lucky that one of the uncles managed to stop her in time. His action softened the force of the impact. Already her forehead was bleeding. As the uncle grabbed her by the waist, her legs were still kicking in the air as she struggled to be free.

"Let go of me. Let me go…" she screamed.

"No, Mother. No, Mother… please don't," the children pleaded in unison.

"Think of the children, I beg of you. Think of the children… think of Pon Ann," said her father-in-law. "He is in heaven looking down at us now. He does not want you to die like this. Please… please…" He went down on his knees and begged her to stop.

Her mother-in- law quickly went down on her knees too.

"*Shienpo* (bride)… oh, *shienpo*," she said as tears rolled down her cheeks. "My dearest daughter-in-law, why is fate so cruel to you? Since marrying into this family you have not enjoyed one single good day. You have been such a wonderful daughter – a good wife and mother. You have taken good care of the children. You are responsible. You have made great sacrifices of your own in order to keep the family together. Oh… why is my son so useless? And now he has disappeared. No one knows where he is. But I know he has perished and is now in heaven. Oh, *shienpo*, how can we ever repay you?"

"If you must go, let Mother and I follow you and we will go to the Yellow Stream together," Pon Ann's father proclaimed as he too tried to throw himself at the wall. The children grabbed him by his arms and pulled him back. By now, everyone was crying. An air of utter despair filled the room.

"Pon Ann is at sea," Li Li continued. "He has been away for over nine months. He should have been back months ago. The sea must have swallowed him. He has perished at sea. There were at least two typhoons last summer. He is gone, I know he is gone. Why else would there be no news of him? He would have sent a message to us if he was still alive. He loves this home and he loves his children. What am I going to do? Tell me, please tell me."

"Let us talk. Let us find a way out," Pon Ann's father said thoughtfully. "*Tin mo chut yan chi lo* – there is always a road ahead designed by heaven. My dear wife, you are the children's grandmother, please speak. You are always the strong one."

There was a momentary silence.

"*Matopei*," my father's grandmother finally said. She was always a pillar of strength in the family. Her views were respected not only by family members but also by friends and relatives. She spoke with authority.

"What is *matopei*?" An Chai asked.

"It… it means 'selling the stomach'…" said Father's grandmother hesitantly. She wondered how best she could explain this to the children. Then she said, "I must be open about it now. The children must know. So must all present here today. We must take this action together as one family. We must accept the consequences together. No one shall regret it. No one has to bear this awful burden alone. We stand or fall together as one family. We shall bear the burden together. Li Li is innocent just like the rest of us. There shall be no blame on her no matter what happens. We stand tall. We are all victims of the same circumstances."

"You want to kill Mother? How can you sell her stomach? I forbid it… We must not allow it," An Li, the younger of the two children, wailed.

"Don't cry, child. Let me explain," his grandmother said in an authoritative tone. "In Zhou Shan, there is a custom that has been established since the beginning of time. When the family is hard-pressed by the absence of the husband at sea, for instance, local customs allow the wife to seek employment outside as a surrogate mother, bearing another man's child, a man who can afford to pay her for the service. It ensures her survival and that of her children. The two parties bind their words with a contract. It is normally good for three years.

"During this time the wife shall bear a child for the rich man. At the end of the contract period she will return to her own family. The child shall be left behind with the man and be brought up by his family. This practice is prevalent. When the wife finally returns home, she will be accepted back into the family. There is no social stigma attached to her behaviour. She suffers no shame. Yes, no shame. I want you children both to understand. She will not be discriminated against at home nor will she be looked down upon outside the family. She will not be cursed.

"Do you understand? No questions will be asked. We as a family shall condone your mother's actions. She sacrifices her dignity for the sake of the family so that you children can live. She does it for survival, understand? Even if Father returns, your mother is expected to honour the contract and serve out the term. Father must forgive this behaviour. So must all of us. Both of you must also forgive your mother. Do you understand, children?"

Everyone nodded.

"Yes, Grandmother, yes, we understand," said An Chai. An Li looked puzzled. She was too young to understand. Nevertheless, she also nodded.

"Good. Then tomorrow I shall get Ah Ming, the marriage broker, to find a suitable family," said their grandmother.

Thus Li Li was 'rented out' to be the third concubine of a rich merchant on the island. The man was old enough to be her grandfather. He desperately wanted an heir to succeed him. His wife and concubines could only satisfy him with daughters; he had seven of them. However, Li Li did not give him a son either because he was too old to beget. Having served the full term of three years, she returned home to care for her own children.

# SAU CHI – MY MOTHER'S STORY

❝I was my father's favourite as a child. His name was Yee Ting and my mother was called Ah Boo. Both of them came from Zhou Shan. My father was a successful businessman. His company, Ling Kee, was well known as a supplier of top-quality building materials. In fact, he was so successful that he was known in Shanghai as 'King of Building Materials', a title he carried with pride.

This name helped to dignify the part of his character that he actually wanted to hide – his life as a philanderer. My father was a lecherous man. He loved women – anything that moved in a skirt – of all ages, shapes and sizes. He was a familiar figure on the Bund – the Embankment – where most of the building materials found their way into Shanghai.

The Bund has many historical buildings that line the Whampoa River, a main tributary of the mighty Yangtze. It was initially a British settlement before it evolved into an international settlement dominated by the British. The buildings once belonged to hongs, big banks and trading houses mostly from Britain. When the Bund was a financial hub of East Asia, these buildings – such as the Shanghai Club, the Masonic Club, Sassoon House, the HSBC Building and the Jardine Matheson Building – housed the headquarters of major companies and institutions that operated in China. The buildings are of various European architectural styles: gothic, renaissance, neo-classical and art deco. Shanghai has the largest collection of art deco buildings in the world.

My father had extensive dealings with operators at the piers, on the steamships and sampans, and with coolies who plied their trades there. He was gregarious and generous to a fault to the people he dealt with, particularly the women he loved. He was a true character, mostly well liked by those who came into contact with him – from those coolies to the compradors of big British hongs at the Bund. A comprador was usually a commission agent. He took a cut of the wages paid to the labourers. The British manager would deal with him and him alone because he spoke English. In turn he would deal with the mass of labourers. That way a comprador would shield the manager from the unpleasantness of having to deal directly with the workers. It also reduced the chance of confrontation with the local workforce.

Ling Kee, my father's shop, was the largest along the stretch of Avenue Road, now Beijing West Road, that catered to the trade. It was a hub for building materials, local or imported, of all shapes and descriptions. Our shop sold mostly wholesale to tradesmen. The mark-ups were reasonable and the quality guaranteed. Business was brisk – it was the envy of the trade. I was my father's lucky charm. From the time I was born, Ling Kee's business began to take off and it grew from strength to strength. In the eyes of my father, I simply could do no wrong.

To say that he was an unusual man would be an understatement. There was something about this diminutive man that marked him out as larger than life. Despite his five-foot stature, he was popular with women. Whether it was his success, or his generosity, or his sharp wit and dapper sense of dress, or simply a combination of these, somehow women were attracted to him like bees to honey.

He was swarthy and well spoken. A first-class wit and a sweet tongue that could entice a bird from a tree made up for what he lacked in height. He was avant-garde, smart and generous to his women. He was always attired in a three-piece pin-striped suit of the finest materials, complete with a silk pocket handkerchief. His short hair was crisply cut, immaculately greased and parted in the middle, a style that earned him another nickname – Mr. Suez Canal. He was a good businessman, like his compatriots from Ningbo. No wonder women threw themselves at him. He was seldom seen without a cigar dangling from the corner of his mouth. He wore thick round-rimmed glasses. He spoke near-perfect Japanese. Having studied in Tokyo as a child there was 'something Japanese' about him – whether it was his demeanour or mannerisms, there was something sweet and sour about him. He was either loved or ignored but seldom hated by anyone who knew him, such was the man's charisma.

But my father was no gentleman when it came to business. He was shrewd. They used to say that if you shook hands with him you had better check to see if all your fingers were there afterwards. My father was a rare breed. He earned himself a formidable reputation.

Among his many pastimes, his favourite was womanising It was as if everything he did was for one purpose only: his women. He certainly had his way with them. He was as generous to them as they were to him. It was a perfect trade-off. He had the money and the charm and they had what he wanted – sex, with which he was obsessed. To him, all things rotated around it. Thus he was a playboy through and through. He was also terrified of his wife to whom he was submissively respectful.

He hid his instincts well; on the surface he was a perfect husband but beneath it he was a raving sex maniac. It was an open secret, known to everyone except my mother – or, perhaps, she was just so clever that she pretended not to know – that he was consorting and sleeping with numerous women, many of them serving as his concubines simultaneously or at different times.

When I was young, my father took me everywhere he went. He often used me as a front to disguise his amorous meetings.

"I am going out for a walk. I am taking Sau Chi with me," announced Father, loud enough that the staff as well as his wife could hear him. As we got close to the *lung tong* (alleyway) his pace quickened and, carrying me in his arms, he hastily made a turn and headed towards the 'house'. Inside, he placed me in the centre of the room and let down the canopy bed curtain. Then he and his mistress would fondle each other, thinking that I was too young to know what was going on.

These secret rendezvous continued a few times a week, always in the afternoons, until one day, unbeknown to my father, his little girl was old enough to talk. I let the cat out of the bag and told my mother.

It was early afternoon. No sooner was lunch eaten than I noticed a young girl in a *qipao* – the traditional dress for ladies – walk past the shop. Wearing heavy make-up, she wiggled, turned and winked at my father. Father nodded faintly in acknowledgement. Then he announced that he was going out for a walk and took me as his alibi. As usual, at the house I was abandoned to the floor to play on my own while the adults climbed onto the bed with the curtain dropped. As Father and I left, I memorized the exact location of the *lung tong* and the house. I then pulled the rug from under my father's feet by telling Mother what was going on.

Next day, as usual, Father announced that he was going out for a walk, except this time he chose to go on his own. Mother had summoned some of her friends to lay an ambush. The friends gathered together at a nearby teahouse. At the signal, they came at my mother's beckoning. The party set off from the shop carrying with them sticks and brooms.

"Now, Sau Chi, you lead the way and show us where Father took you yesterday," Mother said.

Our party arrived at the alleyway. I pointed with my little finger at the 'house'.

"You speak," Mother said to a woman in the raiding party as others in the group took their positions behind her.

The woman knocked on the door.

"Who is it?" the mistress asked.

"The dress that you sent to be altered," the woman replied.

"What dress? I have not ordered any dress to be altered. Go away, I am busy."

"But this is number five, isn't it?"

She continued knocking on the door. The mistress became agitated. "You fucking bitch. I am going to kick your ass. I told you I did not send anything for alteration. Can't you take 'no' for an answer?"

As she spoke, she pulled open the door in anger. She was scantily clad in a thin gown. No sooner had the door swung open than the party charged inside with all the might they could muster, knocking the mistress to the ground. Then, sticks and brooms rained down on her while she curled up to protect herself from the onslaught. The party then moved quickly into the bedchamber. There my astonished and frightened father was found crawling into a corner, naked except for the bedsheet he used to cover his lower body. Fear – sheer fear more than embarrassment – showed on his face when he saw his angry wife come storming into the chamber. She grabbed him by the ear as he tried desperately to cling on to the sheet he had used to cover his body.

"I can explain, I can explain," my father shouted, but his pleas fell on deaf ears.

He was dragged out to join his mistress in the courtyard. There they were taunted, jeered at and humiliated as a crowd of neighbours who had gathered at the door cheered on.

"You tart. It is finally payback time for you," said a neighbour jubilantly. She obviously bore a grudge against this young woman. The onlookers applauded. It was such a show.

My father was fuming when he found out it was I who had revealed his secrets and had taken my mother to wreck his dreams. Once back at home he vented his anger. He hit me repeatedly. It was the first time my usually loving and doting father beat me.

Whether it was a jealous lover or a hitman hired by a business rival, no one knew. It happened at the time of the Moon Festival which is one of the most important festivals in China and which is celebrated on the 15th day of August, according to the Chinese calendar, when the moon is full. It is also the day when summer ends and autumn begins. I was about twelve at the time and my father took me for a leisurely stroll along the Bund after dinner. It was a clear night. The full moon was reflected in all its glory on the calm waters of the Yangtze.

All along the Bund, large red lanterns decorated the many European buildings. It seemed as though the whole of the street was lit up. The air had just turned dry and crisp. The temperature was pleasant, the first sign that the long hot summer was drawing to a close. People were in a celebratory mood. There was laughter everywhere. A sea of red candles burned brightly along the stretch of the embankment where families picnicked in celebration of the festive occasion. It was the best Autumn Festival Shanghai had seen for years. We held hands and chatted happily as we strolled.

Then, without warning, an attacker appeared wielding a long knife.

The knife came down on my father's back and blood oozed out from where it landed – on his right shoulder. It narrowly missed his head. I screamed. As father staggered forward, the assailant was poised to attack him again. I instinctively pushed my father aside and the knife missed him. Father fell to the ground. I do not know where I got the courage from but I threw my own body over my father and shielded him, crying out frantically at the same time.

The attacker, a man in his twenties, was taken by surprise. He hesitated. Meanwhile, people nearby shouted and rushed forward to our rescue. They were obviously surprised by the heroism of such a young girl and instinctively rallied to protect me from harm. The assaulter panicked and ran off, dropping the weapon on the way.

My heroic act was reported in the newspapers the next day. I was hailed as the child whose bravery saved the life of her father in what was described as the ultimate in heroism.

The attacker was never caught. From that day onwards, my father would not go anywhere unless he was accompanied by a bodyguard – a tall, heavy-set Sikh man with a turban on his head who was at least six-foot-five tall and weighed more than 250 pounds. The contrast in the height and build of the two men made them an easily recognizable, formidable, and somewhat comical, sight to behold.

Given the opportunity, my father could not gloat enough to his friends and associates. His beloved daughter had saved his life at the Bund that night.

≈≈≈≈≈

It was 1939 when Japan invaded from the north. For months, trouble had been brewing and rumours were thick that the Japanese army would soon enter Shanghai. Fear among its citizens reached fever pitch as people frantically sought ways to get out ahead of the war. It was a foregone conclusion that, when the soldiers arrived, there would be a bloodbath and many would die.

"I won't go, I won't go," I shouted as I lay on the floor, rolling, kicking and screaming.

"You spoilt little bitch, what are you doing?" my father said. "Don't you know how difficult it is for me to get one ticket, let alone tickets for the whole family? I had to coax, bribe and flex my muscles to get these tickets for tonight's ferry. We will only be away for a little while. The city has the jitters. The Japanese army will be here any time now. God knows what would happen to us once they get here.

"You have heard how the army committed atrocities against us. They may arrive as early as tomorrow and their rampage will begin. How dare you tell me that you won't go! You are crazy. Can't you hear the sound of gunfire? Soon they will crush our defences. Do you know what is going to happen? There will be fighting and the streets of Shanghai will be covered with blood and littered with dead bodies. Tomorrow – yes, tomorrow – all hell will break loose.

"We are not leaving Shanghai for good. We can return once the crisis is over and the situation returns to normal. We must go. Now stop crying and get dressed. We have to leave immediately."

I stood firm, refusing to give way – I am prone to seasickness and the very thought of getting on a boat rattled my nerves. I was stomping on the floor, fists clenched, yelling and crying. I would not leave, no matter what Father said.

"Get Ah Mok and Ah Kee. Ask them to bring a blanket," he shouted.

Soon the two shop assistants arrived. Together they rolled a blanket around me. Then I was carried shoulder-high to the waiting car.

En route to the Bund, the streets were filled with refugees. With family members in tow, they carried whatever worldly possessions they could lay their hands on. Their numbers clogged the streets. The traffic was moving slowly. Rumours spread that the full force of the Japanese army had assembled to the north of Shanghai and was preparing for a final assault.

Panic-stricken refugees wandered the street aimlessly, not knowing where to go. The Japanese were cruel and brutal towards the race they sought to conquer. The Chinese were treated as a sub-species of humanity – an inferior race, no better than animals, which they could trample on at will.

It took us hours to complete a journey that would normally take less than twenty minutes. At the pier, I was carried over the plank, still in the blanket, to the waiting boat as the rest of the family hurriedly followed behind. We finally settled down in the hull of the boat. My energies were sapped and I was subdued. The events of the day and long journey had completely consumed me. After eating the rice cakes which my mother had brought along, we settled down for the night. At midnight sharp, the anchor was winched, the siren sounded and the boat was ready to set sail up the Yangtze River to Wo Shek where my mother's brother lived.

"Stop sail, stop sail!" a man cried from the pier. Lanterns were flashed as he waved frantically at the boat. "Stop sail, stop sail," the man continued to shout.

A crowd of curious onlookers gathered along the pier and passengers moved to the port side of the boat to find out what was happening. The captain rushed out to check the situation.

"The Japanese have mounted a blockade upstream just twenty miles from here," the man continued breathlessly. "Heavy guns are mounted on the shore. Orders were issued that no one was allowed to pass. The last ferry was fired on and sank. There were many casualties."

The engine was switched off abruptly and the captain aborted the sailing. Later, it was announced through the boat's speaker system that the scheduled ferry was cancelled until further notice. The earliest estimated time for the next sailing would be at least twenty-four hours later, when more was known about the situation. Passengers could either remain on board or leave the ship and return before midnight the following day. Their tickets would remain valid. Father chose to disembark and head home.

Back at the shop on Avenue Road where we also lived, no one knew where I was at breakfast the next morning. My anxious parents searched everywhere. I could not be found.

"That bloody bitch!" Father screamed. "I shall wring her neck when I lay my hands on her. I swear I shall."

As the hours ticked away, my father's impatience grew in tandem with his fury. I was nowhere to be found despite exhaustive searches. Anger gave way to anxiety as night fell. Then it was all too late. By midnight the ferry would have sailed without our family.

Meanwhile, news had arrived that the Japanese army had broken through the city defences and were slaughtering and plundering along the way. No one was spared – Chinese soldiers, civilians, not even women and children. Women were raped before they were killed. The killing had reached a frenzy and the city was gripped by fear.

By late evening, my parents were truly worried.

"Has Sau Chi fallen prey to the soldiers and been raped or killed?" Mother asked anxiously.

A mixed feeling, more of sadness, anxiety and fear than anger, prevailed as the family sat together. No one was in the mood to eat the dinner laid before them that night.

Knock… knock…

"Someone is knocking on the door," said Mother. "Open the door, open the door quickly."

"Wait, it could be soldiers," Father said. "Blow out the candles and keep your voices down… shh… shh." He gestured with a finger across his mouth.

The door creaked as it slowly opened. A silhouette appeared in the dim light of the street.

"Sau Chi, is that you? Is that you, Sau Chi?" Mother asked excitedly.

The slim figure of a girl appeared.

"Light the candles, light the candles," Father shouted.

As the candles were lit, my face appeared. I looked exhausted, pale and frail. I was tired and hungry, having been in hiding in the cockloft in the building next door with nothing to eat all day. My eyes were red and I was nervous, not knowing how I would be punished. I knew I had lost my family the opportunity to escape Shanghai ahead of the Japanese. Meekly and slowly, I approached the dining table where the rest of the family had gathered.

"You… you bloody fucking bitch!" Father shouted. He broke into a rare display of obscenity as he lunged forward and grabbed me by my hair. A mixture of anger and relief had taken control: angry because the boat had left and relieved because I was back. His fear vanished, only to be replaced by renewed rage. I had driven my father close to insanity. As I was wrestled to the floor, I lay still.

"Stop! Stop! At least we are together as one family," Mother cried as she shielded me from more beatings.

"What has gotten into the head of this girl?" Father cried in despair. "I dote on her. She is my favourite among all my children. Yet, this is how she repays me. She wants us all dead."

"It is payback for all the sins you have committed," Mother wailed. "Yes, those sins have come back to haunt you. She is your punishment. You have spoiled her rotten from the time she was born. You never allowed anyone to raise their voice to her let alone punish her in other ways. The girl needs discipline, can't you see? She is the fruit of the seed that you have sown. Look what she has done to our whole family. Why? Why did you have to spoil her? I ask you why?"

"Don't just blame me. You spoiled her too," Father remonstrated. "I spoiled her because she brought good fortune to my business ever since she was born. Also, don't you forget, she saved my life. How can I not love her? How could I not give her everything she wanted? Yes, I have spoilt her and spoilt her rotten. But I do not deserve this treatment from her in return. None of us do."

"Repent!" Mother's wailing grew into hysteria as she rolled on the floor. "Repent for your sins... all the bad things you have done in your life. You will be cast to hell and burn in eternity."

In the midst of all the commotion, the manager of the shop hurried into the room.

"What is it, Ah Chong? Can't you see that we are busy?" Father shouted.

"Boss, you will want to hear this news... the... the new... news," Ah Chong stammered. He was so excited that he could hardly finish the sentence. "The ferry... the ferry..."

"Calm down... what about the ferry?" asked Father. "The ferry left. You don't have to tell me. I know it left without us. Now just get the hell out of here. We have unfinished family business to deal with."

"The ferry that you were supposed to take tonight... tonight... was attacked by the Japanese. It came under fire. It capsized and sank just two hours after sailing. Those who fell into the water were machine-gunned. There were no survivors."

Father was tongue-tied. Silence followed.

≈≈≈≈≈

My memory of the incident is fresh – like it happened yesterday.

It was a hot day. We had finished dinner. The air was still, oppressive and stifling. The family gathered outside the shop to talk with neighbours. Almost everyone had a paper fan in their hand – the only reprieve from the unpleasantness of a hot and humid Shanghai summer evening. Summers in Shanghai are hot, but the summer of 1937 was the worst.

From afar a patrol of soldiers appeared. Rifles on shoulders, the soldiers marched. The patrol had been a familiar sight during the past week – like clockwork, the soldiers appeared at the same time. They were much feared as they were prone to abuse passers-by at random, punching and kicking at the slightest provocation and at times for no reason. As the soldiers approached, we withdrew into the shop and stayed there with heads bowed as a sign of respect for the Imperial Japanese Army.

Bang, bang! Two gunshots rang out through the thick air, breaking the silence. A soldier fell to the ground. Blood was oozing out of his head as he lay in his own pool of blood. The fallen soldier lay so close that I could see his mouth move. He was gasping for air.

The soldiers were well trained and must have been drilled for this contingency. A circle was formed around the dying soldier. Bang, bang, bang… shots were fired indiscriminately at all angles and at anything that moved; not even stray dogs were spared. Pedestrians fell on top of each other as they ran for cover. After what seemed to last forever, but in fact was no more than a few minutes, the street was strewn with bodies – dead and injured men, women and children; some were neighbours known to us for as long as I could remember.

As the commotion subsided, the soldiers checked the bodies that lay in the road. Those found to be still alive were shot again. Then they began to round up suspects at random. Anyone who happened to be on the same side of the road as the sniper's shots came from was forced at gunpoint to the middle of the street. There they were bayonetted or shot to death. The killing intensified as more soldiers arrived.

As I lay on the shop floor I was gripped by fear, trembling and crying hysterically. Father crawled over to me. He cast his body

over me – to protect and silence me. His timely action saved the
lives of others at the shop, as my crying would otherwise have
attracted the attention of the trigger-happy soldiers who showed
every determination to avenge the death of their fallen comrade.
By a stroke of good fortune, no one at the shop was shot except
for one – Ah Mok was hit by a stray bullet but his injury was not
serious.

The soldiers rounded up all the men at the scene and took
them back for questioning. At the station, my father had to squat
with others in rows in a large room. One by one they were taken
by guards to an adjoining room for interrogation. Anyone who
was perceived to be anti-Japanese was taken to the courtyard
and summarily executed. Screams rang out from the tortured
prisoners and shooting was heard throughout the night.

By the morning, the Japanese had grown impatient and wanted
to deal with the rest of the prisoners wholesale. Accompanied by
an interpreter, an army corporal entered the room.

"Tell them," commanded the corporal. "Within an hour
everyone in this room will be shot."

The interpreter translated his words to the cowed prisoners.
Some thirty of them remained.

"Does anyone have anything to say before he dies?" the
corporal continued.

The silence that followed was eerie. No one volunteered to
speak. Everyone was resigned to their inevitable fate: being taken
out into the courtyard and executed.

Minutes passed.

"Yes, I have a question." A man broke the silence.

Everyone in the room looked at him in disbelief.

"Stand up and speak," shouted the corporal.

"Yes, I have a question," he repeated this time in Japanese as
he stood up.

The corporal was visibly surprised by the impeccable Japanese the man spoke. "Ask," he commanded.

"Can I leave?" the man asked, again in Japanese.

The corporal hesitated for a moment. Then he gave a please-go-if-you-so-wish hand sign.

My father left quietly. Other prisoners stood up and followed suit. One by one everyone left. Apart from the sound of footsteps, there was no other noise.

The name of the corporal was Gorou Saito – fifth son of the Saito family. Corporal Saito befriended my father but not because he spoke the language. It was because, more importantly, my father was perceived to be a Japanese sympathiser – just the kind Saito's senior officer wanted him to recruit as a collaborator. Not only was my father able to speak near perfect Japanese, but he had also spent a number of years in Tokyo as a child when my grandfather was a school teacher there. Corporal Saito came from Tokyo. The two shared much in common and had much to talk about as they reminisced over their childhoods and the places that were known to them. They often met and drank. And when the sake went to their heads they sang Japanese folk songs and danced together until both were so drunk that they would embrace and cry.

Not only were they friends but also they found a use in each other – one was the ear and the eye while the other cushioned the friendship with a power base. The two fitted like pieces in a jigsaw puzzle. Thus a friendship developed between them.

"The people in my neighbourhood have asked me to approach you to see if you can help them to get provisions," said Father.

"What do people in your neighbourhood need most?" asked Corporal Saito.

"They need food and daily provisions such as salt, cooking oil and soap," he said.

As if by magic, the very next day a truck appeared in the neighbourhood bringing the much needed food and provisions which were distributed to the inhabitants.

Throughout the Japanese occupation, and through the good offices of my father, the inhabitants benefited. His kowtowing to the Japanese became a lifeline for them. It kept many of them alive. It was never forgotten.

"Lin-san, I wish to introduce my superior, Lieutenant Kobayashi, to you," Corporal Saito told Father one day. "He is not a rough man like me. He is refined and well-educated. He is a senior officer in the Imperial Army. He wants to hear the suggestion you've made to me on how our troops can be entertained. He likes your idea but wants to hear from you first-hand."

Lieutenant Kobayashi was indeed a refined officer. He listened politely as Father made the proposal that a local theatre should be allowed to reopen and show films from Japan for the soldiers' viewing pleasure. He had been asked by the owner of the theatre earlier to speak to the army chief. Of course, the owner wanted permission to reopen the theatre not only to the soldiers but also to the public.

Soon Father assumed the role of godfather and go-between. Anything the locals wanted from the occupying army, they went to him. Anything the Japanese wanted from the inhabitants was also channelled through him. He became a community figure for the neighbourhood, attracting both admiration and hatred; perhaps more of the latter than the former. For many he was the collaborator – a hated symbol of Japanese imperialism – against whom they conspired.

My father benefited from the relationship with Corporal Saito. During the Japanese occupation he became extremely rich. His bread and butter business – building materials – flourished and his go-between role brought him wealth beyond his wildest dreams. It was the crescendo of his life.

But the 'fireworks' did not last. Soon, 'poof', the big let-down – the anti-climax – came. The pillaging, philandering, power and greed had all but consumed him and ruined the family and, when it all came crashing down, it had the force of a tsunami destroying everything in its path.

Almost as soon as the war ended, and even before the Communists arrived, the clandestine resistance movement working with the advance party went on a witch-hunt to purge those who had collaborated with the Japanese and to exact revenge. They rampaged through the city looking for known enemies. None were spared. The collaborators, Communists, gangsters and those who had opposed the Nationalists were all rounded up, tied up and put on public display, each wearing a tall hat made of paper that depicted the crime he had committed and on his chest a tag with his name written on it.

My father was in hiding. They found him at the home of one of his many mistresses. He was tied up and dragged out of the *lung tong* and taken on a lorry to the kangaroo court that was assembled in a public square. It was surrounded by hundreds of spectators who jeered and cheered as lorry after lorry full of culprits arrived. The prisoners were taken before a panel of 'judges'.

One by one, the name of the prisoner was read out. He was made to kneel before the judges. His name and the crime he was accused of were read out. The prosecutor then invited those who gathered to give testimony. Drama unfolded as the crime was recounted, with the accuser in some cases working the crowd to near hysteria, gesturing, pointing fingers and shedding tears over years of grievances and hatred against the accused. The accused was not given a chance to defend himself and throughout the proceedings he was taunted and publicly humiliated. Then, when judgement was passed, he was asked if he had anything to say. Most would keep silent, resigned to the fate that awaited them – imprisonment or summary execution. In the latter case, the name on the tag worn on the chest would be crossed out by ink. His fate was sealed. In due course he would be taken to the hillside and executed by means of a single bullet fired into the back of the head.

As evening fell my father was tried. We watched in horror. The verdict was a foregone conclusion. Surely a collaborator of my father's magnitude would be found guilty and face execution.

"Traitor Lin Yee Ting, this court finds you guilty of the crimes you are accused of," declared the judge. "You are to be taken to face immediate execution."

With those words, a man approached Father and repeated the same ritual that he had done many times. He crossed out the name 'Lin Yee Ting' on the tag on my father's chest. He was loaded onto the waiting truck.

My mother fainted at the verdict. Family members cried and wailed – a familiar scene that had occurred throughout the day as each death verdict was declared.

Then a strange thing occurred. There was uproar from among the spectators too afraid to speak up earlier.

"Lin Yee Ting is a good man," one man shouted. "He is not a traitor."

Someone else joined him. Then, one by one, more voices were heard until they united to form a chorus. It seemed like a whole section in the wall of the spectators began to follow suit. A hundred people began to chant in unison. "Lin Yee Ting is a good man. He is not a traitor."

The chanting continued unabated for a few minutes. Then they clapped hands and stomped the ground while the chanting went on.

"Lin Yee Ting is a good man. He is not a traitor."

An even stranger event took place. Men began to step forward – at least thirty of them, one after the other. They were the men whose lives my father had saved from Corporal Saito when death for them was certain.

The emotion stirred up by the scene was infectious. Soon it seemed as if everyone in the square had joined the chants.

"Lin Yee Ting is a good man. He is not a traitor."

The judges looked at each other in disbelief, bewildered by what they were seeing. After conferring with each other, one pronounced loudly: "Remove prisoner Lin Yee Ting from Truck One and put him onto Truck Two."

A sigh of collective relief took place – Truck Two meant imprisonment for the prisoner and, in my father's case, it meant 'execution suspended pending reconsideration'.

Outside the detention centre a crowd gathered – the thirty survivors, their family members and the neighbours who had benefited from the wartime distributions that kept them alive during the worst of times. Their ranks were swollen by other supporters. A hundred-strong crowd kept an all-night vigil. Many of them held candles.

The next day Father was released. He was carried shoulder-high by the supporters and returned home triumphantly as a hero.

It was a narrow escape for him and he was lucky to be alive, even though he lost everything when the Communists arrived and Shanghai was liberated in 1949.

My father went through many hardships in the following years.

≈≈≈≈≈

It was 5 a.m. on a cold winter morning in 1967 when the youths arrived waving Mao's Little Red Book. The Cultural Revolution was at its peak. Father was dragged from his bed. The Red Guards went on a rampage, smashing whatever symbols of capitalism they could lay hands on. Nothing was spared: furniture, pictures, artefacts, radios... even his thick-rimmed glasses were tossed and ground into pieces underfoot. He was asked to kneel on the balcony while the ransacking continued. All the while, verses from the Little Red Book were recited to him. Then he was asked to get dressed. He was taken to a political meeting that morning. There he was repeatedly denounced as a capitalist and his many 'crimes' were recounted before a large crowd. When he was allowed to return home he was made to kneel on the balcony again.

After days of abuse, he 'jumped' from the upper floor into the street below. No one knew how it happened – was he forced or was it his own doing? Both of his legs were broken. He never recovered and lost his will to live. He died shortly afterwards, penniless and in ill health, branded as a capitalist during the Cultural Revolution.

# Ting Hai (Siaw Ko) – my aunt's story

**"**When my father was young, he worked as a clerk in an import-export firm in Zhou Shan, a joint venture between a British firm and my maternal grandfather, Mr. Tai. As a true Ningbonese, my father was honest and hard-working. Often he performed beyond the call of duty. Thus he was so well liked by my grandfather that he gave the hand of his eldest daughter, Sou Yue, to him. The couple married following ancient rites. Clad in a red embroidered *qipao* (a mandarin gown), the bride had her face covered by a matching veil and, under a large sign depicting 'Double Happiness', the couple worshipped heaven and earth, presented tea to the parents and the ancestors amid brightly lit red candles. The marriage was celebrated at the House of Tai, the ancestral home of the Tai family. It was a solemn yet splendid occasion. Together they had three children, two daughters and one son.

With so many disparities in the couple's backgrounds, not to mention the fact it was an arranged marriage, it was doomed to fail from the beginning. My father was of low birth. He came from a family who were mostly illiterate. They were local fishermen who lived from hand to mouth. My mother, on the other hand, came from a family of wealth and influence. She was a woman of good upbringing as shown by her bound feet. She walked with a wiggle like the wind blowing on the leaves of a willow tree. She was educated, graceful and polished. There was a distinct air of aristocracy about her. She was the eldest daughter of a most distinguished family on the island. As such, she was accustomed to the full trappings that wealth could bring.

She never ceased resenting that she was forced into marrying a man of such low birth. She looked down on her husband and loathed all things associated with him, including the children they had together – the daughters in particular. To say that the couple lived in disharmony is an understatement. In truth, she took little or no interest in the marriage, nor the welfare of the family nor, least of all, in the upbringing of the children.

Following an old Chinese custom that sees females as inferior to males, she treated her daughters as a liability, something to be got rid of as soon as possible, much the same way as she herself was treated by her own parents. Girls are considered to be 'outsiders', not part of the family. The family torch is passed down to its sons who are expected to carry on the good traditions of the family. They can be relied upon to support the parents when they grow old. The prejudice is deep-rooted, especially in old China.

Gambling was her way out of the unhappy marriage. She became addicted. She was a compulsive gambler through and through. The couple quarrelled often. Money was always short.

The meagre income that my father earned was hardly enough to support the family's livelihood, let alone her gambling habits.

She was addicted to a game called 'Fan-Tan'. The game is simple: squares from 1 to 4 are marked on the table. The croupier reaches for a large handful of small white buttons which he conceals by using a rice bowl that is turned upside down. When all the bets have been placed, the bowl is lifted, revealing the heap of buttons inside. Then, with a bamboo stick, the croupier removes the buttons, four at a time, and places them neatly in rows on the table for all to see, until the final batch is reached. If there are four of these buttons left behind in the batch then the number 4 wins, three for 3, two for 2 and one for 1. The odds can be 1:3 in favour of the winning bet, less the banker's commission which is five per cent on the bet.

Sou Yue was so proficient in the game that she often boasted that she could count the remaining buttons as soon as the croupier took a handful of them, even before they were laid out and counted on the table.

In the beginning her habit was fuelled by the money she managed to obtain from her own family but that source quickly dried up when her father died and the brother alone inherited the family fortune.

Against this background, one day she took her first daughter, Ting Chi, shortly after her birth, to her maiden home. By that time the household had been taken over by the eldest son of the family, her brother. He and his wife had no children of their own. He accepted Ting Chi as if she was the first-born of his own family. It was a secret known only to a few. In fact, Ting Chi herself had no idea that she was adopted. The couple later had children of their own who all looked upon Ting Chi as their big sister. She was much admired and loved by her siblings. At home she was addressed as 'Big Missy' not only by her brothers and sisters but also by the servants. House of Tai still kept a large contingent of servants even after the father died.

Thus, Ting Chi was brought up as a Tai girl in this great big compound house. The status of the owner of the house was marked in carvings on a large stone at the entrance. The size of the stone reflected the status of the owner. The House of Tai was the largest and the most prestigious. Having crossed the threshold, one found oneself in the first in a series of three courtyards. The first was the largest and was referred to as 'the grand courtyard' and was used as a place where the household entertained guests. Set at the back of the courtyard was a stage. It was decorated mainly in gold with elaborate and intricate carvings and embellishments. During festive occasions, tables were set up around the stage. The halls on the two sides and the courtyard could easily accommodate a hundred guests. There they would eat, drink and listen to operas. Tai Junior was known to throw the most lavish parties in town and the family entertained often.

When I was four, my mother took me to her ancestral home and asked to see her brother.

"Brother, you have met Ting Hai before. She is my second daughter," said Mother. "She is a good girl, gentle, happy and obedient although a bit shy. She is also very loving and affectionate. I know she will bring you and your family great joy and happiness, just like her sister before her. She has never given us any trouble and will not trouble you either.

"It pains my heart no end to have to give away my dear Ting Hai as well. But really we can no longer afford to keep her. My husband earns so little that there is hardly enough to feed the family. As you know, my husband is in and out of jobs since the day he left your employ. Jobs are scarce on the island. Besides, we are heavily in debt. I must ask you, dear brother, that you also take Ting Hai under your wing like her sister before her, and raise her as your own daughter. She is a good girl. You will not regret it.

"Also, that way she and her sister can be together. At the moment they don't even know they are sisters. This is shameful, really shameful, isn't it, brother? Tomorrow, my husband and I will leave for Shanghai. It is easier to get work there. This is the only way out for us. We have discussed the matter and, after soul-searching debate, have reached a decision. We can afford to take only one child with us. It has got to be our son, Ting Kuan. Please help me. This is the last favour I shall ever ask of you, good brother. Please do this, if not for me, for the memory of our parents."

The brother did not respond immediately. He was deep in thought.

"I am sorry. I cannot help you any more," he replied. "I have already accepted Ting Chi into my family and raised her as one of my own. I now also have three other children. They all look to Ting Chi as their big sister. No one knows that she is not our natural daughter. I cannot risk the secret getting out that Ting Chi is not their real sister. Think of the disappointment in my children if they knew. Taking on another daughter of yours is out of the question.

"Also, let me speak my mind. You have only yourself to blame for the predicament you are in. With due respect to you, you are neither a good wife nor a good mother nor, indeed, a good person. You are a pathological gambler. The gambling habit in you has driven you completely out of your senses. Where do you spend your time every day? Don't tell me. I know. You deserve none of my sympathy. I loathe you for what you are and what you do. You bring shame not only to your own family but also to mine.

"Tell me... tell me, how many times have I bailed you out before when you could not repay your gambling debts? How many times have you promised me that you would not gamble again? I am sick and tired of your lies. I don't believe in your promises any more. I have absolutely no confidence in you. Zero confidence. You do understand, don't you? Now, go home or I shall summon my servant to sweep you out with a broom. I am not your brother. Get this into your thick head. Now leave immediately."

Mother was totally surprised by this reaction from her brother. The outburst was blunt and merciless. Yet, he spoke the truth and it hurt her. For a moment she did not know how to respond. There, in the guest room, she stood silently, head bowed. She felt greatly insulted. She was indignant.

"How dare you say you are not my brother? If you are not my brother, why on earth are you in this house? Let me remind you. This is the ancestral home of the Tai family. I am a Tai just like you. Why am I not given a share of this house and the fortune our father left behind? Why wasn't I given a decent dowry when father paired me off with this good-for-nothing husband of mine? Instead, I was given just a few pieces of mother's jewellery. They were junk… nothing but junk, not enough even for me to buy a decent roof over my head.

"Yet you inherited this big house in all its splendour, including all these servants. Tell me, how many of them are there to serve you? At the last count there were sixteen. You inherited all of Father's possessions and businesses. Yet, you heartless bastard, the first thing you did, even before Father's corpse went dry, was find an excuse to kick out my husband – my husband who Father was so fond of that he gave my hand to him and forced me into this marriage that I despise so much. Now I am stuck with this man. He has no job. How do you expect us to live? You heartless bastard… We shall die together."

Mother fought back her tears as she tossed herself at her brother. With her bound feet, the brother easily wrestled her to the ground.

"Ah Mok… come, Ah Mok," he shouted. Ah Mok was the housekeeper. He was in his fifties, having served two generations of the Tai family, from father to son. Notwithstanding his age, Ah Mok was sturdy, strong and heavily built.

"Yes, Master," Ah Mok answered in his husky voice as he arrived hurriedly in his long Chung-shan attire.

"Kick this bitch out of this house," the brother commanded.

"Yes, Master," Ah Mok said. He gently ushered my mother to the door.

"Ah Mok, don't you touch me! I command you," she yelled. "Don't forget that this house belongs to my family. You are our servant. I am a Tai, just like he is. Don't push me or I shall summon the curse of my parents upon you."

Mother screamed as Ah Mok pushed her towards the door. There she was unceremoniously booted out of the house, all the time with me in tow.

It was a misty morning. A thick layer of fog had descended upon the street. Bewildered and lost, Mother did not know what to do next. Her pride was completely destroyed and her ego hurt. Then a thought crept into her mind. She decided there and then to gamble at the expense of her own daughter.

"Ting Hai, you wait here," she said. She pointed to a spot by the side of the stone lion statue. "Don't move, no matter what happens. Mother will soon come back to fetch you. Do you hear me?"

She hugged me and kissed me on the cheek. I was stunned by the events of the day. I sensed something unusual was happening although I didn't know what it was. Mother turned her head quickly so that I could not see the tears gushing from her eyes. As she walked away, I screamed and gave chase.

"Please don't leave me behind, Mother, please…" I grabbed her by the hem of her coat and pleaded.

"Child, I am just going away for a short while. I have to run an errand. Be a good girl. Just wait at the door; Mother will be back in a short while… okay? Be my good little girl. Just stay there. Don't go away. I will be back for you."

Mother lifted me with both hands and took me back to the spot by the side of the statue.

"Stay, child, stay. Mother is just going round the corner to buy you a bun to eat. She will soon be back. Understand? Stay where you are and don't move. Otherwise I shall lose you. You don't want that to happen, do you? Just stay and don't move away from this statue, no matter what happens. Do you understand?" Then she left.

"Mother, Mother…" I cried as I watched the back of my mother disappear down the mist-covered street.

Mother never returned. She had no intention of coming back for me. I was not part of her plan. Her plan was simply to unload me on her brother quickly that morning. She had no choice. My father was at home waiting for her to return. The family planned to leave soon after I was ditched. They were running against time. The family had to leave that morning, before the debt collectors came to the door.

Mother knew there could be no turning back. The consequences would be dire not only for her but also for the rest of the family. There was no way she could pay off the gambling debts she had run up this time.

For days now, ruffians had been sent by the owners of the gambling den in town and had been hanging around the house demanding payment for what was owed. She had been giving one excuse after another to delay them. Now they had issued an ultimatum: these gangsters promised to return that afternoon. If the money was not there then she could expect the worst. She was at her wits' end. She knew she could no longer expect help from her brother. Leaving town was the only choice. She had planned the escape down to the last detail for days now. She must stick to her plan. She must not let her brother's reaction distract her. Everything must go as planned. All other options were now closed.

The family had to travel as lightly as possible carrying only their personal belongings, mostly clothes and whatever valuable items they could gather. The couple would only take their son, not me. I was supposed to be given away to her brother. She never expected that he would be so cruel as to refuse her request and do so in such a blunt and hurtful manner.

She had abandoned me at the ancestral home. She was certain that eventually, after his rage had subsided, her brother's attitude would soften and there would be a change of heart. I would then be accepted into his family and be brought up as a Tai, just like my older sister, Ting Chi, before me. Therefore, she thought, no matter what happened, she simply had to follow her plan. One day, if my father made good, she would return triumphantly to reclaim her two daughters. She was like a cat on a hot tin roof as she hurried home.

"Did everything go smoothly?" Father asked.

"Yes. Ting Hai is in safe hands. We can leave now. How much time do we have?"

"Our ferry is at noon. We should leave."

"Okay, let's go."

None of the neighbours were there to bid the family goodbye. They knew what fate had befallen them. Coming out to say goodbye would only embarrass the fleeing family. Deep down, most neighbours were happy to see them leave anyway. The family was nothing but trouble. The couple quarrelled often and the children were neglected. They looked unkempt, underfed and dirty. The husband was either busy at work or looking for work. The wife, everyone knew, was a compulsive gambler. She spent more time at the gambling dens in town than at home. She abandoned her children to the street. She was also quarrelsome and unpopular. She niggled at the slightest provocation. They all knew that she was from a rich family. For years, the neighbours had put up with her condescending attitude. She was snooty and aloof. She behaved as if everything was beneath her, her own family included, except for the son she obviously loved and doted upon… if ever she was at home. She was altogether an unpleasant person; the sort, given the choice, the neighbours would rather ignore than befriend. Besides, for days on end now, the people who were there to collect the debts disturbed the neighbours.

The street was deserted and covered by fog. It began to drizzle. Spring had just arrived. As they left they could see writing on the wall. The words 'Gambling debts to be settled by blood' were scrawled in red paint on the wall of the house.

Meanwhile, I became panicky and started crying. I banged on the door of the ancestral home but my pleas fell on deaf ears. Inside, my uncle, Mr. Tai, had given strict instructions that I was not to be admitted into the house under any circumstances. I cried until my tears ran dry and my eyes swelled. No one paid me any attention.

This went on until one of the older servants, Ah Bit, took pity on me. She stealthily placed food and water by my side and pulled me under the eaves so that I would be less exposed to the elements. Then, when I fell asleep, she covered me with a blanket. She could see that I was sick.

For the next two days, I lay there dirty, pale and frail as members of the family entered and left the house. I shivered uncontrollably and my poor condition did not escape the attention of my aunt. Mrs. Tai was by nature a kind person but, as a dutiful wife, she could not disobey her husband's rigorous orders.

"Madam, there is this little girl at the door," said Ah Bit. "She looks no older than four or five. She is obviously abandoned by her family. She looks pitiful. She refuses the food and water I bring her. This morning I noticed she was shaking and shivering. She is probably running a fever. Her body looks so frail and weak. Unless we do something, the girl is going to die. To have the child die at our doorstep brings bad luck to your household. Madam, may I have your permission to let her come inside the house? She can stay with us in the servants' quarters. We can train her to do light housework until her mother comes back to reclaim her."

Mrs. Tai pretended ignorance. "You will do nothing of the sort. Mind your own business," she said. "I am sure her mother is returning soon."

That night Mrs. Tai discussed the child with her husband. He did not wish to capitulate to what he perceived was the cruel plot of his sister. Yet, if he did nothing and the child died, it would be on his conscience.

They did not want someone dead on their own doorstep – and, worse, the child was none other than his own niece and a sister of their daughter. Mrs. Tai pleaded with her husband to allow the child to be moved inside and be treated and looked after – even if it meant her living with their servants.

"Let her stay out there a bit longer," said Mr. Tai. "My sister could change her mind and return. I cannot image any mother to be so cruel and leave her own child to die here – not even that witch of a sister."

"Can't you see? She is playing poker with you. She knows that sooner or later you will relent," said his wife. "She is a gambler, isn't she? She knows she has the upper hand. Although her own child's life is at stake, her gambler's instinct tells her that she must win this time. She has judged the situation, may I say, correctly. She knows you well. I am sure she thinks she cannot lose this hand. I hear she left for Shanghai with the family the same day that she abandoned the child on our doorstep."

Mr. Tai knew his wife was right. "You deal with it the way you see fit, but remember we cannot accept her into our family as we did with her sister. It may be a way out if we let the servants bring her up but be patient. Let us give it a bit more time. I am still hopeful that my sister will return. I cannot imagine… Tell me, which mother under the sky could be so heartless that she can take a gamble on the life of her own flesh and blood? What if the child died?"

"A Tai girl – your very own sister," replied his wife.

Early next morning, Ah Bit went outside to see how I was doing. I was curled up in a foetal position. Ah Bit bent down and touched my forehead. It was scorching hot. I was barely conscious. My breathing was faint and I was delirious. A chill went down Ah Bit's spine. She could no longer be passive. She must act immediately before it was too late.

"Madam, the girl is still there," she told Mrs. Tai. "She is so weak I think she is dying. She has a high fever. If we leave her there for another day, I am sure she will die. Please be compassionate. Please save her. We don't want a death on our conscience, especially someone so young, do we?" As Ah Bit spoke, she went down on her knees and begged her mistress.

The fate of that poor little girl reminded her of her own. She was sold to the Tai family when she was hardly twelve years old. She never saw her parents again. She had no idea where they were. She had worked all her life as a servant. Now that Ah Bit was in her forties, she had all but given up hope of meeting the right man, getting married and starting a family of her own. But the maternal instinct in her never died. She yearned to have a child of her own. God in that sense had sent me to fulfil her long-cherished dream.

Mrs. Tai was visibly moved by Ah Bit's plea and, acting within the discretion her husband had given her, she relented. "Bring the child inside," she said. "Bring her into the servants' quarters."

I had slipped into a coma by the time Ah Bit carried me inside. My pulse was so weak that it seemed non-existent. My body was cold. Ah Bit placed me in her own bed. She used warm water to clean me and covered me with blankets. She fed me liquid food as I was too frail to take solids. Thanks to Mrs. Tai, a doctor was summoned.

With treatment, I slowly recovered. I regained consciousness and gradually my strength returned. Downstairs, the servants gathered to celebrate. They were happy that a young life had been saved. Ah Bit, in particular, was thrilled.

From that day onward, Ah Bit took me under her wing. She became a foster mother to me and taught me the ropes of the trade as a servant. It was her job to boil and provide hot water for the entire household. She also did cleaning around the house. I was given chores that were suitable for my age and had to get up at 4 a.m. every morning. I gathered firewood for the stoves, swept the floor and cleared leaves and debris from the courtyards and gardens. I also boiled and filled up hot-water bottles for the family in winter.

My sister meanwhile was raised like a princess. Being the eldest, she was adored by her siblings in the family while I did menial work. As I grew older, I had to comb and set her long hair every morning. Nothing could keep a fire under wraps for long and tongues began to wag downstairs among the servants that I was in fact the sister of Big Missy. This caused unease upstairs.

One day, Mrs. Tai summoned all the servants together. "I hear that some of you have been spreading rumours about Ting Chi. These rumours are malicious. They hurt us as a family. Let me make it clear once and for all. Ting Chi is my first-born. I gave birth to her, so I should know. How dare you think she is not my own child? If I ever catch any one of you spreading these lies I shall immediately dismiss you and send you packing out of the house myself. Do you all understand?"

"Yes, Madam," the servants chanted in unison.

From that day onwards, I had to change my name. It was forbidden to call me Ting Hai because that name bore the character 'Ting' that was the middle character in the name of my sister and indeed in the names of all the other Tai family children. Instead, Mrs. Tai gave the order that I simply be called 'Siaw Ko' – meaning 'Little Cry Child'. The servants gave me the nickname. It was a direct reference to how I was found.

My position in the household was precarious. I was a thorn in the side of the whole Tai family except, perhaps, Mrs. Tai. Mr. Tai in particular resented the thought that his sister had outwitted him. She never returned to reclaim the child. The child was thrust down his throat. He was stuck with a child that he did not want.

He felt cheated and, worse, 'raped' – and that offended his manhood deeply. That very thought troubled and incensed him. Not surprisingly he did not take well to my presence in the house even if I did live with the servants. He would have nothing to do with me – in his eyes I was a symbol of his sister. He was constantly scheming how he could return me to her. But he did not know where she was. All he knew was that the family had moved to Shanghai.

This attitude of the master of the house made my position in the household untenable. To make matters worse, Ting Chi, my sister, took an intense dislike to me. This feeling of prejudice against me spread to the servants' quarters where squabbling and backstabbing often took place.

Some of them had their own axes to grind. Many resented the superior position enjoyed by Ah Bit. Being one of the longest-serving staff, Ah Bit could talk to Mrs. Tai, which did not go down well with the other servants. My vulnerable position made Ah Bit, my protector, an easy target for attacks from her rivals.

Although she constantly taught me how to stay out of trouble, there were limitations on how much she could protect me. After all, she was merely a servant and she was getting on in years.

Fortunately, Mrs. Tai by nature was a kind and caring person. She often showed kindness to me knowing I was her own niece. She gave me food and the old and unwanted clothes of her children. She talked to me often. She frequently enquired how I was, whether I was being treated fairly by the servants, warm in winter and had enough to eat – and questions of the like. She genuinely cared about my well-being.

Ting Chi, however, treated me badly. She, together with her 'siblings', often kicked and beat me, given the slightest excuse.

"Sister, this is for you," I said meekly as I handed Ting Chi the hot-water bottle early one morning.

"For the last time, I am telling you, I am not your sister and don't you ever call me that again," she said. She then threw a tantrum. She slapped me across the face, causing me to drop and break the thermal water bottle. As I bent down to pick up the pieces from the floor a servant quickly arrived on the scene.

"Sorry, very sorry, Missy… this good-for-nothing servant is being rude to you again. I shall teach her a good lesson," said the servant. To appease the young mistress, the servant pinched me by the ear and twisted my head around towards Ting Chi so that I could look straight at her and apologize.

"Take this *ya toa* – slave girl – outside. And let her kneel there as punishment," Ting Chi ordered.

I was taken to the courtyard and made to kneel on the stone-covered ground. It was early spring and the air was chilly. No one dared approach me. Ting Chi was still raging mad. As night fell, Ah Bit stealthily brought warm clothes for me to wear.

"Child… my dear child… why is God so unkind to you?" she said. "What have you done to deserve this? My eyes are dry from crying. My heart bleeds for you… my dear, dear child." Ah Bit ran her fingers through my hair after helping me put on the warm clothes.

"Bit Chai, my dear, dear Bit Chai…" I cried as I embraced 'Sister Bit'.

From the balcony upstairs, Mrs. Tai witnessed the scene. She felt a wrench of sadness in her chest. She knew it was not my fault that I was being punished and gave the order that I was to return to my quarters. Meanwhile however I had caught a cold. A fever developed, which led to pneumonia. I was very sick and Mrs. Tai summoned a doctor. I was unconscious for two days. When I awoke, I saw Ah Bit slumped asleep on the chair at my bedside. She had kept an all-night vigil on me.

"Mother… Mother… my dearest mother," I cried as I touched her. It woke Ah Bit.

We embraced and cried in each other's arms. From that day onward, Ah Bit was no longer 'Bit Chai' to me. She became my mother and I her child.

We remained close until the day Ah Bit died.

≈≈≈≈≈

Since early morning the household had been buzzing with activity. Servants were scrubbing and cleaning the floor. Gardeners were busy trimming and removing unruly weeds that had grown in between the slabs of tiling on the rooftop and in the courtyards. Manservants were removing, unwrapping and dusting the decorative items, large and small.

The house was given a thorough cleaning from top to bottom. The red lanterns were brought out and raised, two huge ones on each side of the main columns at the entrance and smaller ones around the courtyards beneath the balconies. Matching red drapes were hung around the threshold of the entrance door and all other doors. Only red flowers, in pots and vases, were used for the occasion. Red was an auspicious colour befitting such a happy occasion. The house was decorated for the most prominent of all festive occasions. The theatre stage in the grand courtyard was set in gold and red for the right ambience. Workers were busy setting the theme on the stage for the performance of the opera. At one side, seats for the musicians were carefully arranged. Amid the hustle and bustle, much gaiety was in the air. Laughter filled each corner of the house as servants chatted to each other as they worked.

Mrs. Tai was busy giving orders to the housekeeper who in turn told the other servants what to do. Everyone was working. All seemed so happy. It was time to celebrate. The occasion was the fortieth birthday of the master. That evening a big party was planned.

I was then ten. As the youngest member of the household staff, I was assigned to perform small duties such as filling up teacups, bringing hot towels, mopping and sweeping the floor and running small errands as and when required. It was a busy day for me as it was for everyone else.

At six o'clock that evening, the guests began arriving. They were welcomed into the house by the ushers and, one by one, were presented to the host in the main hall. The guests, many local luminaries, were dressed in colourful costumes. Laughter filled the courtyard and the adjacent halls. Banquet tables were set up in the grand courtyard and performers including acrobats, comedians and singers entertained the guests. The highlight of the night was a performance to be staged by the elite Shanghai Opera Troupe. The opera singers had come from Shanghai especially for the occasion.

While I was busy filling teacups, weaving my way in and out of the crowd like a little mouse, an uncle suddenly recognized me. He got up from his seat and pulled me over to one side.

"Aren't you Ting Hai? Why are you working as a servant?" asked Great-Uncle Ding.

I was taken by surprise yet I remembered him well. When I saw him, I became choked with emotion. I had finally met a family member. All the years of grievances came bursting out like lava from a volcano. I just cried as I hugged him.

Slowly I told Great-Uncle Ding my story. He could not believe what he heard. He hugged and consoled me. Then he pulled me with one arm and charged towards his nephew, who was startled as he saw us together. He could figure out what was coming.

"You are my nephew. I am your father's brother," said Great-Uncle Ding. "Do you remember this girl? She is your niece, my dead brother's granddaughter and my own great-niece. We are all members of the same family. How can you be so cruel to your own niece? You should be looking after her, but instead you mistreat her. Look at her tortured state. You make her work as a child servant. Do you not have a conscience? How can you be so cruel? You show no compassion to your own niece. Heaven shall punish you for what you have done to this girl. I know today is your birthday. I should say things to you that are auspicious. But what you have done is unforgivable. You have incurred the wrath of heaven. You will be cursed forever. I am disgusted by what you have done. I am not helping you celebrate your birthday. Your wonderful life is a farce and has no meaning if you don't know what decency is. Your father and all our ancestors in heaven are weeping. I am leaving. Don't bother to see me out."

After his outburst, Great-Uncle Ding turned on his heel and walked out of the house. I was left stunned.

Mr. Tai was shocked by this demonstration of anger from the uncle he respected most. As the brother of his deceased father and the last surviving brother of the Tai family, Great-Uncle Ding was the head of the family. He was held in the greatest esteem not only by his family but also in the community. His outburst not only spoiled the party for Mr. Tai's birthday but also brought shame to his otherwise spotless reputation, all for a girl whose presence in his household Mr. Tai had all but forgotten. He was speechless. He was trying to calculate the damage the outburst could have done to his standing in society, as the words had been broadcast before so many of his guests that night – most of them local dignitaries. Rumours were bound to spread. Worse was the fact that he had lost the confidence of the head of the Tai family, a man whose integrity and deeds he greatly admired and from whom he often sought counsel.

"Take no notice. Please enjoy yourselves and have a good time," said Mr. Tai. He shouted aloud so that all could hear him. "This is my birthday. Be merry."

The incident was the only scar that marked a party which was otherwise perfect.

≈≈≈≈≈

On my sixteenth birthday, Ah Bit wanted to buy me a pair of shoes as the old pair had worn out. It was a Sunday but, as Ah Bit and I were about to leave the house, Ah Mok, the housekeeper, asked if she could stay to help remove a stained patch of damp underneath the balcony just behind the eaves of the grand courtyard.

Ah Bit told me to go ahead and that she would meet me in the emporium at the corner of the main street as soon as the chore was done. The shop was an easily recognizable landmark. Both of us had been there many times before.

Just outside the house, several rickshaw pullers waited for business. It was always the same bunch of pullers. It was as if they had marked the territory out as their turf. No other pullers were allowed to ply their trade there or there were fights.

I would normally walk to the main street, some two miles away. Since it was my birthday that day, I decided to splash out and give myself a rare treat. I beckoned the rickshaw that was first in the waiting line. The young puller happily answered my call. I had seen him many times before. I knew he harboured an interest in me. On the way to the main street he could not stop talking. I ignored him most of the time. However, when we arrived, I was in a good mood and gave him ten cents, asking him to give me five cents' change.

Arriving at the emporium, my mood was further lifted by the array of merchandise that was attractively displayed at the window. As I entered it did not matter that no one came to serve me. I was like a child in a candy store. Everything looked so attractive that I wished I could buy it all.

As I browsed through the shop I was attracted to a mirror there. It was small but pretty and dainty. Red trimmings made of silk encased it. I thought it was delightful and wanted to buy it as a gift for Ah Bit.

"How much is this?" I asked the shopkeeper.

"Forty-five cents."

"Can I have it for forty cents?"

"I can let you have it for forty-two cents and that is the lowest I can offer."

I dug into my pocket for my hand-knitted wallet with one hand while holding the mirror with the other. The wallet was not there. I had difficulty in switching the mirror to my other hand while reaching into the other pocket. In the process, the mirror slipped out of my hand and broke on the ground.

"Oh, no!" I screamed as I cursed myself. I knew it was a bad omen. Something bad was going to happen although I did not know what it was.

Back at the house, Ah Bit was climbing up a long bamboo ladder that was set against the balcony wall. Ah Mok was holding the ladder at the bottom while Ah Bit tried to reach for the mouldy patch. As it was located at the underside of the balcony, she had to stretch one arm around the edge of the eaves. The stained part was located in an awkward spot. It was just beyond Ah Bit's reach.

"I cannot reach it. Give me a stick or something," she said.

A long ruler was handed to her. She tied a knot around the head of the ruler with the mopping cloth.

"Stretch forward a bit more to your right," suggested Ah Mok.

To reach the spot, Ah Bit had to grip the side of the ladder with her left hand. In doing so, half of her body hung precariously and she struggled to remove the patch of damp.

"Stretch a bit more and you will be there… Okay, now scrub," said Ah Mok.

Ah Bit could not see the underside of the balcony as her vision was blocked by the eaves in between. As she lunged forward to remove the stain, she suddenly lost her balance. She fell from the ladder, landing head first. As she lay on the ground, she was twitching, moaning and groaning, her head bleeding badly.

"Tell Madam. Quickly, go and fetch Madam," Ah Mok shouted for help as he bent to check her. She was still conscious.

A servant quickly ascended the staircase to fetch Mrs. Tai but it was unnecessary. Attracted by the commotion, Mrs. Tai had emerged from her chamber and, from the balcony of the courtyard, could see what had happened.

"Go and get Dr. Pong," she shouted before she rushed downstairs to check on Ah Bit's condition. She knew it was serious.

The doctor did not arrive until at least two hours later, by which time Ah Bit had slipped into a coma.

Despite treatment, her condition did not improve in the days that followed. She had suffered concussion and there was internal haemorrhaging in her brain. As Ah Bit lay in bed, it was plain to see that she was dying from her injuries.

I was heartbroken. The only person who cared for and loved me – a person I called Mother – was dying before my very eyes. The pain was unbearable yet I could do nothing except hold her hand. I kept a constant vigil by her bedside.

Then one morning Ah Bit miraculously woke up. "I want to see Siaw Ko. Please get me Siaw Ko," she said feebly.

I hurried to her bedside.

"Siaw Ko, my daughter, please lift me up and take me to the Coal Room," she requested.

"Mother, you are in no condition to get up," I replied.

"I must go to the Coal Room. Please take me there. I insist. I am okay. I know I can get there. Just help me get up and assist me as I walk there," she insisted.

We arrived in the Coal Room.

"Siaw Ko, remove the firewood on the right," said Ah Bit. She pointed to the stack of wood that was piled up shoulder-high in one corner. "Buried in the ground under the spot marked by the brown tile there is a tin box. I want you to get it for me. There is a spade there. Use it to dig."

Soon after I had started digging, the spade hit something metal. A rusted box was unearthed. I handed it to my mother.

"I want you to open the box, Siaw Ko," she said.

I did as I was told. Inside the box was a rolled-up bundle of money and some gold ornaments. These were Ah Bit's savings from a lifetime of working for the Tai family.

"I want you to have it," said Ah Bit as she handed over the box and placed it in my hand.

I was speechless. Tears rolled down my cheeks.

The next day Ah Bit died.

I gave her a decent burial with the money she had given me. Then I left the House of Tai. I set off to find my family in Shanghai. I had not seen them since I was four.

I was able to trace the last abode of the family to a 'stone cove' *lung tong* house in Hing Yip Road in downtown Shanghai.

I walked through the entrance into an intricate network of narrow streets. It was late afternoon. Neighbours sat outside on stools chatting to each other as they prepared dinner: cleaning vegetables, chopping meat into small pieces, removing beans from shells, seasoning and getting the food ready for cooking. As I entered the *lung tong*, the neighbours eyed me curiously. I smiled back at them and asked directions to 5A Hing Yip Road.

I soon found the house and knocked. No one answered. I knocked again. Still there was no answer. I pushed the unlocked door which screeched as it opened. I entered a small courtyard and in the centre there was a well. Apart from a few stools, it was empty but tidy. I walked through and into a kitchen. From the number of stoves, I could see that three families shared the house. As I entered the kitchen a boy approached me.

"Who are you looking for?" he asked politely.

"Do the Wangs live here?" I enquired.

"Which Wang family?" the boy asked. "We have two families here by the surname of Wang. Is it Wang An Chai or Wang Shing Lee you are looking for?"

It was an emotional moment. I knew the name of my father was An Chai. I looked at the boy closely. I could tell from his features – the same nose, mouth, eyebrows, ears, skin colour, right down to the facial mannerisms – that the boy standing in front of me was my long-lost younger brother, Ting Kuan.

"Are you Ting Kuan?" I asked.

"Who are you? How do you know my name?" he asked.

"I am your sister. I am Ting Hai," I said as I bent down to hug him.

"I don't have a sister. I am the only child in the family. You must be mistaken. Can it be the other Wang family you are looking for?"

"How else would I know your name, Ting Kuan?" I said. "I am your elder sister. You are my brother. Where are our parents? Are you home alone?"

"Yes, they are both out but they should be back any time now. Would you like to come inside and wait for them?"

I followed the boy into a room that had a door and two windows opening onto the courtyard. The room was quite long and had curtains that were drawn across the two ends of the room. Two beds were hidden behind the curtains. The middle space was used as a living area. It was sparsely furnished – just a square table and a few wooden chairs. With the afternoon sun that cast a pale shadow in the courtyard, the room looked warm and had a charm of its own. A chill went down my spine. Finally, I was home.

My brother was curious about the sister no one had ever told him about. He was too young to remember when the family had left for Shanghai over ten years ago. He asked me many questions and the two of us talked happily, long-lost siblings who had just discovered each other for the first time.

As night fell, my parents returned. They were overwhelmed by emotion to see me, a mixed feeling of joy, sadness and guilt. But overall the reunion was joyous.

"Are you here alone? Where is your sister, Ting Chi? Is she in Shanghai too?" Mother asked.

"No, I am here alone. Ting Chi is in Zhou Shan. She is not my sister."

"What on earth are you talking about?" said Mother. "Ting Chi and you are sisters. The two of you grew up together. By the way, why on earth are you wearing the white cotton in your hair as if you are mourning the passing of your mother? Take it off.

It is a bad omen. I am still alive. I am not dead. Who are you mourning for?"

"I mourn for my mother. She died recently," I said.

"What nonsense! I am your mother. I am not dead. Take it off."

"I will not. I have to wear this for three years. I mourn the passing of Ah Bit. She was my mother," I said.

"Who is Ah Bit, this so-called mother of yours?" my mother asked. "What are you talking about?"

"It is a long story," I replied.

I helped Mother to prepare dinner and then talked till the early hours of the morning. Outside, the collectors of nightsoil were chanting melodiously, "Fragrance of the night, fragrance of the night – make ready for fragrance – fragrance of the night… fragrance…"

At first, despite many questions and promptings from my parents, I was in no mood to divulge the details of how I was mistreated in my uncle's household and especially how I had suffered at the hands of my very own sister. Both of them assumed that I had lived as a daughter of the Tai family although they felt uneasy about my general appearance.

My skin, hands and clothes gave away the secret that, contrary to what my parents had expected, I had not been living the kind of life that they thought I had. This did not sit easily with the perception that I had had it good as a Tai girl. No daughter of the mighty Tai family would be dressed the way I was. It was obvious that I had been doing menial work all my life.

I eventually told my parents everything that had happened and they listened in disbelief – choked with emotion brought on by a strong sense of guilt. Never in their wildest dreams had they expected the awful ordeal I had been through.

My mother was heartbroken. She was ashamed of herself. She had won the gamble against her brother – but at a terrible price.

She had used me, her daughter, as chips in the gamble and in the process had ruined my life. I was the sacrificial lamb for her own demonic addiction to gambling.

Guilt overcame her. All she could do was embrace me and cry. As dawn broke, she lay awake in bed stroking my hair, thinking that I was asleep. I could hear her sobbing silently.

To be honest, I actually resented being stroked by my own mother, a person for whom I had no feeling. Indeed, I despised her. As I fell asleep I dreamed of Ah Bit who was smiling down on me from heaven.

No sooner had I returned than my own mother began scheming against me again.

"It has been two months since Ting Hai returned," my mother said to my father. "Although she has tried, she has not been able to find work. She is a drain on our resources again. Besides, Shanghai is in chaos. The Japanese are stirring up trouble. Sooner or later, they will march into the city. After Manchuria, Shanghai will be next. Now she is over sixteen years of age, it is about time that we marry her off. We simply cannot afford to keep her here forever. Can you pair her up with someone you know, preferably someone rich, at least better off than we are? Or I shall go and get Ah Sum, the marriage broker, who lives down the road."

"I have just the right person in my workplace," said my father. "He is a clerk in the export department. He must be in his early twenties. He seems like a decent young man. He is hard-working and dedicated to his work. He is reliable, the sort of person who would make a fine husband for Ting Hai. I know he has no girlfriend. I think you should get Ah Sum to test the water first with his parents and see what they think. If they are agreeable then we can talk to Ting Hai. I know his parents are quite rich and he is their only son."

Later that same year, both parents met and a marriage was arranged. We had never met before and we remained strangers until the wedding night when the red veil was lifted in the bridal chamber.

Thus, yet again, my parents had sealed my fate. I had no say in a matter that was of the utmost importance in my life. I was married off to a man I did not know and had no feelings for. But together we had three children, one boy and two girls. It was funny how things worked out. I began to love him. I guess he loved me too. We were a happy family. For the first time in my life I experienced happiness.

But those blissful days did not last long.

My husband was quiet, soft-spoken and, by nature, timid. He was introverted, never the sort who would fully speak his mind or make waves in life. He kept to himself. He lived in his own world and was a thorough pessimist. He took a negative view of almost all things around him.

It was during the Sino-Japanese War that he died. That part of Shanghai was by then under the occupation of the Japanese. The bus that he took daily to go to work had to cross the river where soldiers guarded the bridge. Passengers had to alight from the bus each time at the bridgehead and take turns to bow to the Japanese guard.

One night, my husband returned home and was upset when he saw our home had been partially destroyed by Japanese bombing. The next morning he took the same bus to work. He got out of the bus at the bridge with the other passengers but he resented what they had done and did not bow to the soldier. He was immediately detained, beaten up and punished. He had to kneel by the side of the sentry. It was in the middle of winter. The ground was covered by snow. It was bitterly cold. Twenty-four hours later, when his British boss arrived to bail him out, he was found still lying in the snow, semi-conscious and barely alive. He died on the way to the hospital.

As a widow, I had to bring up my three children alone. My husband left me with little savings. I did not want to go back to my parents and live with them as I knew I would not be welcome there. But my parents-in-law were good to me. They took us under their wing and provided for us until I went back to work in the factory again. They continued to look after the children until they died, one after another, within the same year.

The Communist Party was also good to us. We were given free shelter, medical care and education for the children. With our background we were considered to be 'blue-blood' proletariat members.

≈≈≈≈≈

Such was the life of my aunt, Ting Hai.

As I waited with my sister at the Kowloon-Canton Railway Station for Mother to return, I was intrigued by everything I saw, especially the clock tower. I counted seven vertical windows on the side facing the harbour. The clock was located between the fourth and the fifth, two levels down from the steepled dome. A covered walkway with a series of red-brick arches and ivory-white columns linked the clock tower to a bus terminal. I counted them one by one: there were ten columns and nine arches. The bus station consisted of two parallel bus lanes, each with a covered waiting area at the side. The rest of the train station was red-brick, no more than two storeys tall, with numerous columns. It reminded me of the old buildings on Shanghai's riverfront – the Bund. I had also counted four platforms when we got off the train and walked through the concourse to get to the clock tower.

Mother returned with a basket filled with bread. While we were busy eating, she went back to the store and, from there, managed to call my father. Overjoyed, he raced to the station to fetch his family that he thought had not survived the journey to Hong Kong.

My first impression of Hong Kong was how backward it was, in terms of both the place and its people. The dialect they spoke – Cantonese – sounded like *ngon, ngon, ngon* to me, strange and totally incomprehensible. For all I cared, I may as well have landed on Mars. But there was no denying one thing: the food was good, even for the poor. I could never get enough of the wonton dumpling and the noodle which was springy and seemingly never-ending. Noodles cost thirty cents with the wonton, and ten cents without, at a *dai pai dong* (street hawker stall). I had to cut the noodle, with each mouthful, in between the lower lip and upper incisors.

The local customs were loud and boisterous. It was a new world.

# PART 2

# HONG KONG

Hong Kong in the 1950s was like the Wild West of China, teeming with activity; it was a time of seismic changes.

The end of the Second World War did not herald the start of peace in China. On the contrary, the situation took a turn for the worse as the civil war for the control of China was reignited between the two opposing camps, the Communists and the Nationalists. It raged on until 1949 when the defeated army of the Nationalists took refuge on the island of Taiwan and Mao Tze-tung triumphantly declared the founding of the People's Republic of China at Tiananmen Square in Beijing. However, there were still pockets of resistance along the coastal regions which protected the Nationalist army's route of retreat to Taiwan.

The war disrupted many lives and caused people to flee to the safe haven of Hong Kong, under British rule since 1841. But the big influx did not take place until the early 1950s when, fearful of Communism, refugees began to pour into the Colony in large numbers, coming by land, sea and air.

In the decade that followed the Communist takeover of China in 1949, the population of Hong Kong increased six-fold, from a mere half a million to three million. The new arrivals were rich farmers, capitalists and common people, but among them were criminals taking advantage of the chaos that prevailed at the time.

Triad societies shot up like mushrooms overnight and they thrived in the new environment, gaining power and becoming influential. In this new order, the Hong Kong government faced many problems with a large population impoverished by years of war and no resources of its own. The infrastructure was bursting at the seams. Housing was in acute shortage and the government could do little to ease the situation. The new arrivals built illegal huts on land and hillsides around the old airport at Kai Tak. From a high point, one could see an endless sea of shanty towns on a vast swathe of land that stretched all the way from the airport to the slopes of Lion Rock, so named because of the peak's resemblance to a lion in repose.

The new order created massive social and other problems for the government. There was a huge army of unemployed, many of whom had all but given up hope of finding jobs or returning to China even though many, particularly the rich from Shanghai, still considered the Colony a transit point, a springboard to the USA, their ultimate destination.

For many, the Colony was regarded as a living hell in which they languished while resorting to all the means at their disposal just to stay alive. It was a hotbed of crime. Food was scarce, prompting many of the refugee families to survive on whatever they could lay their hands on. The unhygienic conditions in which the refugees lived were breeding grounds for diseases which were widespread in the so-called 'nest of rats and snakes'.

Every fresh wave of new arrivals brought new problems. Hong Kong became even more ungovernable. Yet, to the British, the Colony on the edge of China was a valuable trade centre which they were determined to keep as a capitalist outpost. This policy was part of Western strategic thinking at the time, a global initiative to keep the advance of Communism at bay.

London ordered the reinforcement of the local garrison amid contingency plans for emergency evacuation of its subjects to Australia if the strategy of containment did not work. Fortunately, the value of Hong Kong was also appreciated by the new Communist government.

The People's Liberation Army was ordered to advance no further than the Sino-British border.

Thus, Hong Kong was saved.

≈≈≈≈≈

On 10th October 1956, riots broke out during the celebration of the revolution that had brought down the Qing Dynasty in China in 1911. Disgruntled refugees took to the streets in their thousands after an officer of the British Crown ordered the removal of certain Nationalist flags. It sparked anger among the refugees.

The various political movements instigated by Mao had turned China topsy-turvy and created havoc for its people. Anti-Communist feeling in Hong Kong was made worse by the living conditions that prevailed at the time. Sentiments reached boiling point.

Riots in the streets at first were patriotic, mostly anti-Communist, before they turned ugly, soon developing into a means for the refugees to air their grievances against the Hong Kong government for its inability to solve the many social and economic problems of the day. Angry mobs came pouring out from the shanty towns in Kowloon, ransacking and looting shops and properties. At first the police did not intervene, thinking that the disturbance would die out quickly, but by the next day it evolved into a fully-fledged riot.

Anything that was considered Communist became a target of attack. Nathan Road became a battle zone. A mob broke into a social centre where they killed a number of people. Factories in Tsuen Wan owned by Communist supporters came under siege and were seized by the mob. Known Communists and their sympathizers were kidnapped and some were brutally killed.

The riots gave street kids the opportunity to see 'life', so to speak, an exhilarating experience that aided the growing-up process. The atmosphere was almost carnival-like. The kids joined the riots, marching, shouting slogans, throwing stones and breaking things along the way.

Kwok Sun and I were just a couple of unruly kids who considered the streets our playground. If something as exciting as riots broke out we thought it our business to find out what was happening there. We took part in the riot because we found it exciting – it enabled us to see the world. During the day of the riot we played truant. We put on school uniform, had our breakfast, said goodbye to our mothers and pretended it was a normal school day when in fact we were joining the riot and could not wait to be there and be a part of the adult world. It sent adrenaline through the system to be able to chant, while stomping the ground in formation, slogans like: "Down, down, down colonisation."

The truth was that neither Kwok Sun nor I knew what the riots were about, let alone the meaning of the many slogans that were chanted by the rioters. It was just plain fun to follow the adults and be part of the street carnival.

On one such occasion, the police cordoned off one section of Nathan Road. A line of policemen in riot gear carrying shields and batons stopped the mob from advancing further. In order to consolidate their defence, the rioters in the front line locked arms to resist being driven back.

The contingent of police was under the command of a single British officer mounted on horseback. After due warning and the crowd refusing to disperse, the police took action – but those in the front row could not disengage themselves because their arms were interlocked. They became sitting ducks as the tall officer dismounted calmly.

He grabbed a man by his hair and lifted his head upward and, after removing the man's thick-rimmed black spectacles, he slowly and methodically folded and placed them into his own front pocket before landing a thunderous blow on the man's head with his baton. As blood came gushing out, the officer lifted the man's head again. Still conscious, he struggled to free himself from the locked arms but in vain. He was helpless, completely at the mercy of the officer as he tried desperately to turn his face away.

Anticipating that another blow could kill him, the crowd of onlookers became agitated. Much to the surprise of everyone, the officer did not attack him again. Instead, he calmly placed the spectacles back onto the man's blood-covered face. The spectators cheered and applauded in relief. But before the roar of approval ended, the officer resumed his one-man hostility against other demonstrators.

One by one, he clobbered the heads of the other front-line demonstrators until all their faces were covered by blood. Heads dropped limply but their bodies were still held together by the human chain until, one by one, they fell to the ground as the connection gave way under their collective weight. The officer then remounted his horse as if nothing had happened.

That cold and callous act petrified my friend Kwok Sun and me. It was too bloody and horrible for us to watch. We left the scene hurriedly, absolutely terrified by what we had seen and vowing never to return.

Night had fallen. The pavements of Shamshuipo were sheltered by overhanging balconies of buildings typical of the time. For as far as the naked eye could see, the pavements were covered by a continuous stretch of makeshift tents, made of any materials the refugees could find to build temporary homes for themselves: sheets of tin, cardboard, paper or just dirty linen. It was also lined with rows of stoves and kitchen utensils.

"Look, this is their dinner," I said to Kwok Sun as I pointed at rats on a tin plate. "They are about to cook and eat them. Can you imagine?"

There were four of these rats, skinned, cleaned and ready to be cooked. The oil in the wok was simmering hot. One by one the rats were picked up by the tail and dipped into the wok, making a sizzling sound in the process. Meanwhile, the rest of the family including two young children sat gleefully on the floor waiting for dinner to be served.

Kwok Sun and I watched in amazement. We could not help but think how lucky we were. My father had a job as an accountant in the cold storage factory and his father was the owner of dens in the Kowloon Walled City where gambling, prostitution and opium-smoking took place.

≈≈≈≈≈

The fascination of the riots proved too great to resist. The next day, Kwok Sun and I went back to the scene. A large crowd of troublemakers had gathered in Nathan Road, waving fists, carrying banners and chanting slogans as they marched down the street.

"Look, look at the car," Kwok Sun suddenly shouted in excitement. "The driver must be crazy. Of all places, he had to come here now. It's show time."

I turned and saw a car suddenly appear from a side street, swerving quickly onto the main road before it came screeching to a stop. The driver had obviously discovered he was in the wrong place at the wrong time. But it was too late. He had driven straight into the crowd and, like a lone sheep straying into a pack of lions, was soon surrounded by the rioters.

Sensing the danger, the driver tried desperately to do a U-turn. The front and back of the car were both blocked by crowds of people shouting, kicking, pushing and hitting it with whatever they had to hand.

The driver hooted the horn incessantly in panic, the sound of which only whipped the rioters into a state of near-frenzy. The passenger in the back – a middle-aged, blonde European woman – was terrified. This gave the rioters an excuse to vent all their years of frustration and anger against colonial rule and the 'white masters'. This woman to them was a symbol of colonialism and all the bad things associated with it, a valve through which they could air the grievances that had been nursed in silence for years since coming to Hong Kong as refugees.

The petrified passenger screamed as she was dragged from the car and a rioter poured gasoline over her. Amid her wailing, screaming and kicking while she was lying on the ground, a match was struck and she was set alight, to the horror of the onlookers.

She was burned alive.

The police later investigated and, from eyewitness accounts, they were able to identify and trace the culprits. They were arrested at their homes and taken back to the station for questioning. After a fair trial, no fewer than four of them were convicted of murder and sent to the gallows.

It was a gruesome sight. I could not understand how the mob could have perpetrated such a cruel act on another human being. The horrific incident created a lasting scar on my young mind.

# THE WALLED CITY

Kwok Sun and I were classmates at a school in Mun Sang at the foot of a hill close to where we both lived. I actually lived in Grampian Road where the school was located. Kwok Sun was indigenous to Hong Kong: his family had been here for at least five generations and his home was inside the Walled City which abutted the school. His family home, a two-storey walled house with its own garden, stood out prominently within and was unique in the sense that it was independent. There was no other house like it in the enclave where all the buildings were linked together in an intricate network of narrow streets.

The Walled City was originally a military outpost going back to the Soong Dynasty, mainly protecting the salt trade. Under the Treaty of Nanking, Hong Kong was ceded to Britain and later, in 1898, the New Territories, located north of Boundary Street, were leased to the British for ninety-nine years.

The later Treaty specifically excluded the Walled City, giving China the continued right to keep officials there as long as they did not interfere with the Colonial Administration of Hong Kong.

This exemption created an anomaly – an enclave within Hong Kong that was considered taboo to the Hong Kong government, thus giving rise to the state of lawlessness that prevailed within its confines. It was a haven for criminals who openly plied their trades with impunity, with brothels and gambling and opium dens.

Later, the Walled City also became a lair for unlicensed doctors and dentists who were mainly new arrivals from China. Not being licensed, they were forbidden to practise elsewhere in the Colony. Thus, the City was a place where 'anything went', ruled by organized crime syndicates known as Triads of which the 14K and Sun Yee On were the most prominent.

There were only a few entrances to the Walled City and there the Triad members kept a watchful eye on all who entered. *Gweilos*, as the locals call foreigners, were absolutely forbidden to enter. When a local asked the guard why his *Gweilo* friend could not get inside, the standard answer was always: "We cannot guarantee his safety."

"Let me show you the Walled City," said Kwok Sun one day. "It is such an exciting place after dark. You will like it." We were both in our early teens at the time.

"My parents always warned me never to set foot there or I would be severely punished," I replied. "Isn't it the most sinful place on earth? There are gangsters, bad women and drug addicts, and it is dirty and smelly."

"Come on. That is exactly why it is so exciting. You have to see it to believe it. I can also show you where I live. You don't have to tell anyone that you have been there. I shall not talk either. I can tell you all about the Walled City. You will never find a better guide than me. I was born there and have lived there all my life. I know every twist and turn, and who lives where and what they do for a living. I know all the secrets. Come on, let's go."

It was too exciting a proposition for me to say "No". Besides, who was going to find out that I had been there? My parents certainly would never know. I had just finished dinner and normally it would be hard for me to get permission to go down to the street to play, but that night my parents had to go out and there was no good reason to keep me in the crammed apartment. I wanted to explore and I could not think of any place more exciting than the Walled City.

It was August. The summers in Hong Kong are hot. Men wore a vest or were bare-chested while women wore a blouse and shorts made in a black material that was popular at the time. During the day the heat was stifling, the air thick and stale. It cooled down at night.

On the way to the Walled City we stopped at Loon Shing Theatre. The streets in and around Lion Rock Road were teeming with activity. It was around the time that the first film screening had just finished and others were waiting to get in for the next show. There were hawkers everywhere peddling fishballs, curried squid, preserved fruits, soft drinks, ice cream and other snacks. Operators covered the pavement with sheets of paper with drawings that depicted fish, shrimps and crabs in different squares. Working in cahoots with the operators, the gang members would place bets on the squares. They were there to lure gamblers to place their bets and play a game of dice.

When all the bets had been placed, and at the critical moment before the dice were cast from a rice bowl, an accomplice at a signal given by the operator would shout aloud: "*Chow kwai, chow kwai, kin chat, kin chat* (run, run, police coming)." The operator would lift the piece of paper by its four corners and bolt. Thus, in one scoop, he would take all the cash that had been placed as bets.

The same trick was successfully pulled off outside the same cinema constantly. Fearful of reprisals, everyone just kept tight-lipped, including the victims, because they all knew these men had triad backgrounds. Customers just kept coming. The first bets were always made by one or more of those who worked as accomplices to the operator and, while they placed bets, they also encouraged others to follow suit.

A customer, including an accomplice, could also remove someone else's bet, say, from the sign of the shrimp to the sign of the chicken. If he did, he assumed the role of the banker. The winnings or losses would be settled directly between the remover and the original punter. If the remover won, he would collect from the banker and if he lost and the original punter won, it would somehow be settled directly between those two parties.

"I think it is chicken this time. Yes, I am sure it will be chicken. Let us move that man's bet. We move it from shrimp to chicken?" I said excitedly. "Quick, quick, Kwok Sun, I am sure it is going to be chicken next round. We will win. Come on, I know it is okay. Just trust me."

"I don't have the money to pay if we lose. Do you?" asked Kwok Sun.

"No, I don't either," I whispered in his ear. "But if we lose, we can just dart off. I don't think they can run faster than us. Come on, it's okay. Don't be chicken."

Kwok Sun then squatted down, lifted the coin and moved it to the chicken sign. The original gambler just looked at us two kids, but did not object or say anything.

As the dice were rolled, I felt a chilling sensation creeping down my spine. I was ready to run. The consequences would be disastrous if the dice showed no chicken heads. We would surely be beaten black and blue. Just as I was about to sprint, Kwok Sun shouted in excitement, "We won. We won." The two of us embraced each other and jumped in excitement. The dice showed three chickens.

We had won $1.50 from the original bet of 50 cents and it wasn't even our own money. An indescribable joy showed on our faces.

"Pay us. Why don't you pay us? We won $1.50, didn't we?" In puzzlement, Kwok Sun, trying to act older than his age, shouted at the operator, "Why don't you fucking pay us?"

"Yes, why don't you fucking pay us?" I too pointed my finger at the operator and tried to act tough.

He looked the other way and ignored us. As bets for the next round of play were placed, we looked up and saw this guy appearing from behind the operator, arms folded with enhanced biceps each the size of a cat.

"Let's go. Let's go," I said gently as I elbowed Kwok Sun.

"Yes, let's go." He nodded.

We started running. Looking back, we saw that no one was following. I sighed in relief. Then we walked spiritedly, bouncing up and down, larking and teasing each other.

"Of the thirty-six stratagems, the best one is to run," I said as I placed my arm around my best friend. "Yes, the best riddle is to run... Ha! Ha! Ha! Life is so exciting!"

A man sat on a tall chair at the entrance to the Walled City. He greeted Kwok Sun as we entered. As we walked down the steps, I noticed some overhead wires that were carried on two poles erected on each side of the street.

"What are they for?" I asked. "Don't you have electricity?"

"No, we don't. Our electricity comes from buildings across the road," replied Kwok Sun. "Nor do we have running water. Our water comes from wells. Nor do we have flush toilets. Our nightsoil is collected. The government can't touch us and they don't do anything for us. The Walled City is built on sunken land. It is literally a hole in the ground. My ancestors dug a huge hole on which they built the city. Then they used the earth to make bricks to build the wall that once stood and surrounded the city. It is built at the foot of a hill on a gentle slope."

At the end of the steps and after a short walk, we came to an open space, a sort of piazza. It was dimly lit and looked rather eerie. We turned into a brightly lit lane no wider than a man with his two arms fully stretched out. A maze of tightly packed, tiny shops lined the two sides. On entry, one was overcome by a stench, a foul smell that is difficult to describe. It could have been a combination of its location, the air that was trapped there, its buildings, old and dilapidated, and its lack of a drainage system, made worse by the poor hygiene conditions.

"Hey, kids, you shouldn't be here," said a woman in a colourful *qipao* with slits so high up her legs one could see the colour of the underwear she was wearing. "This place is for the grown-ups. You are too young even to be spring chickens. Come back in a few years' time when you grow older and I shall give you a red packet for your virginity."

The other women on both sides of the lane burst into laughter at the remark. There must have been at least twenty of these women of different ages lining up against the walls.

"No, no, you come to me first. I shall give you a double red packet if you give me eternal youth," one woman said, half in jest. "Check out my breasts. They are big and firm. And look... who has this crevice? It's long and deep, the best in Loon Shing (Walled City). I shall send you straight up to Seventh Heaven. She is no good for you. Look how old she is."

"Ignore them. Don't look at them," whispered Kwok Sun. "These are prostitutes."

"What are prostitutes?" I asked.

"They sell sex."

"What is sex?"

"You know, a worm going into the black forest," replied Kwok Sun. "I have explained that to you before. Don't you remember?"

"Oh, you mean our dick... doing the big thing." I laughed.

Numerous signs hung in a haphazard manner everywhere, competing against each other for attention: 'Guaranteed Cure for Far Lau, Mango, Pak Chut...' – names for different venereal diseases; and 'Fairy Oil for Chong Yeung, Pak Kui...' – ointment used to rub on one's penis to restore manhood.

At the end of this busy lane, we came to a quiet open space. It was dark but not so dark that we could not see what was going on. On the roof of the buildings below, the mice were having a picnic. There were hundreds of them, larking and chasing each other, frolicking and playing or chewing the debris that had piled up, and the noise they were making was almost deafening. They showed no sign of being fearful of people as we passed.

Then we turned into another dimly lit lane. Men, presumably coolies, could be seen walking slowly, heads down, along the lane. Some of them appeared to be unsteady, listing from side to side, as they walked. They looked somewhat delirious as if they were drunk. One man dressed in black carried a long hammer, the tool of his trade, on his shoulder. As his silhouette passed us, I thought he looked solemn and serious. The atmosphere of the lane was in sharp contrast to the gaiety and laughter of the girls we had just left behind.

"Who are these people?" I asked. "And what are they doing in this dark place?"

"They are junkies," Kwok Sun said. "They smoke opium."

"Where do they smoke?"

"I'll show you."

We came to a door. It was locked. Slivers of light showed through the cracks. The heat was suffocating. The air was still. There was no wind. If there had been any, it would not have reached this part of the city.

"Knock, knock," Kwok Sun said playfully as he knocked on the door.

The wooden door opened slowly, making a screeching noise in the process. A pungent smell met my nose. An old man with a white goatee beard appeared. He was surprised to see two kids standing before him and paused. Then he recognized Kwok Sun.

"Oh, Master Sun, it is you," he said. "What are you doing here at this time of the night? Do you want to see your father? Come in. I shall tell him that you are here. Just wait here."

He was obviously a gentle and kind man who knew Kwok Sun well. He turned and spoke to a man who was standing behind him. "Go and tell Dai Low that his son is here."

The room was not large, a few hundred square feet. It was divided into two parts by a doorway threshold. A couple of rolled-up rattan blinds hung on the underside of the door frame.

The outer portion of the room was used as a reception-cum-restroom while the inner portion had long narrow beds that were lined up in a row, arranged against the walls. On each there was a straw mattress, a wooden headrest and what appeared to be a long smoking pipe placed on a specially designed stool.

The room was dimly lit and smoke-filled. Through the haziness I could see patrons, mostly men, some so skinny I could see their ribcages, lying sideways. All of them seemed to be bare-chested, lying in foetal position, heads resting on the wooden pillows smoking and puffing in a slow, gentle and lethargic manner, eyes closed as if they were in a trance, completely submerged in a state of total gratification.

It was an atmosphere of peace, quiet and tranquillity. They were in heaven. No one spoke, not even the *amah* – a servant with a long plait

– who brought towels and served tea to them. Business was brisk. I was amazed and watched in awe at the comings and goings in this new world.

"*Hung Ka Charn* (instant death to your whole family). You never fucking died before? Fuck you!" A fat man no more than forty years old with tattoos on his chest and arms appeared at the top of the staircase shouting expletives and abuse. "Why do you bring kids into this joint? You know what this is? This is a fucking black house. Where is your fucking sense? You know the rules. You have been here for longer than I can fucking remember."

The man came storming down the staircase, charged forward and grabbed the old man by the collar of his shirt, the same man who had opened the door for us, and slapped him across the face.

"But… but… Master, this is your son. It is Kwok Sun, Sun-chai, your son… your son," said the old man. He was badly shaken.

"*Sze-chai* (dead son), you go home. Leave right away. I shall deal with you when I am home," the man said as he pushed Kwok Sun out of the house. I was horrified.

We left quickly. I never saw a man as fierce as Kwok Sun's father. No wonder he was the overlord of the Walled City.

# GROWING PAINS

After school, Kwok Sun and I often played on the hill behind Mun Sang together with other boys who gathered there every afternoon. From the top of the hill, we could see the whole of Kai Tak airport and its surroundings. Nothing was more exciting than seeing how the planes landed while we dreamt of being pilots one day.

The planes' approaches were difficult and the margin of error for the pilots must have been narrow. As each came down through the surrounding hills dividing the peninsula of Kowloon, it had to fly at an angle and home in on a chequer-board on top of a knoll and then bank sharply before it could head towards the runway.

The angle of the bank was sharp, at least forty-seven degrees. From the perspective above, while descending and factoring in crosswinds, the streets and buildings below seemed to rise up rapidly. It was hairy enough if the pilot had a clear line of sight to the runway while making the turn but the weather could change to cloudy, rainy or just foggy. It thrilled us to bits as we sat there and watched planes land and take off from this location.

The hillside was covered with graves and urns that were used to house exhumed human remains. According to the local custom, the bodies of the dead were buried for a while before the skeletal remains were exhumed, washed, cleaned and placed in urns. These urns were then placed on hillsides in the countryside. The urns were constantly disturbed by us boys looking for snail shells. The best and toughest of these shells, white in colour and known as '*tit kam kong*', could only be found in and among the skeletal remains, often embedded in the bottom of a half-buried urn.

To find them, the urns had to be dug out and overturned and, in the process, the contents would spill out, leaving the ancestral remains exposed or strewn all over the slope, much to the consternation of their descendants. Often we were beaten and chased off the hill by the irate families but we kept going back because the lure to find a prized shell was just too great to resist.

Owning one was an ultimate symbol of superiority. Our game involved pressing the head of one shell against another and the loser would be the shell that gave way under the force.

Once, using a catapult, I managed to shoot down a pigeon. It was fat and large.

"What shall we do with this bird?" I asked. "Why don't we make preserved meat out of the pigeon? Do you know how it is made… you know, like preserved duck and sausage? Are they cooked or are they simply left out in the sun to dry before they sell them at the shops?"

"I have a pretty good idea how preserved meat is made," said Kwok Sun. "You look at all things preserved that are hung at the meat shop: chicken, duck, sausage, pork – you name it. They all look raw and black. I am certain it is not cooked. All we have to do is pluck the feathers, remove the intestines, clean it with water and season it by soaking it in a bowl of soybean sauce overnight. The sauce will give it that black-looking colour like we see at the shop. Then we leave it under the sun for a day or two. The sun will cook it and it will be ready for eating. Come on, it is so exciting. Let's make our preserved pigeon. We can do it. I know we can."

We left the carcass of the pigeon hanging from a pole on the roof of a building and waited for the sun to do the 'roasting' for us, going back to check on its progress whenever we found the time over the next two days. The pigeon was looking darker by the day and, although it did not exactly look like the meat we saw at the shop, it looked close enough in colour and texture.

"It should be ready to eat by tomorrow," said Kwok Sun. "We shall each bring a bottle of Coca Cola and enjoy our lunch, our own preserved pigeon. Oh, how wonderful… I can't wait until we come back tomorrow."

We were both so excited by the prospect of eating our own preserved pigeon that neither Kwok Sun nor I could sleep that night.

"Yuk, the meat tastes like rubber. I can hardly chew it," I said. "It is not like the pigeon we get at the restaurant."

"Of course, this is the first time we have tried to preserve a pigeon and we will get better once we get the hang of it," offered Kwok Sun. "Don't complain. Just eat and enjoy it. Besides, we have saved the money given to us for lunch. Try getting one bite of the pigeon and mix it with a sip of Coca Cola. They blend in well. You will enjoy it."

Even before we finished eating, I noticed something unusual in Kwok Sun's face. It was turning blue and white and he began to sweat profusely. His hands were shaking and he was shivering. Then his face became red and swollen. Rashes began to appear. It was quite apparent that he was allergic to something he had eaten. He threw up. Then his heart began to palpitate. It pumped harder and harder. He was on the verge of collapsing as I made a sprint for the staircase. I ran down to find help for my best friend and I soon found myself pleading with a passer-by in the street.

Kwok Sun was barely conscious when he was carried to a waiting ambulance. On the way to Kowloon Hospital on Argyle Street, I too began to develop the same symptoms – a swollen face, itchy skin and racing heartbeat. I became delirious and incoherent.

We were both hospitalized and not released for two days. The doctor told us it was more than just food poisoning. It was a chemical reaction. Our systems had reacted to what was in the pigeon we ate and we were both extremely lucky to be alive: whatever caused the inflammation had spread to our throats, causing them to swell. If we had arrived fifteen minutes later, the swelling would have blocked our windpipes and we could have suffocated.

Some time later, I noticed tiny worms in my stool and one day I dropped a tapeworm the size of an earthworm.

We soon recovered from the ordeal and went on the rampage again.

≈ ≈ ≈ ≈ ≈

We were Peeping Toms and one rooftop was a particular favourite of ours because from there we could look into another building block – no more than twenty feet away – which was tenanted by army families. In the heat of summer, the wives of British soldiers often walked around either scantily dressed or with no clothes on at all in their apartments with the curtains drawn back. The rooftop was where we ate 'eyes ice cream' when the summer heat became unbearable.

I think only the Chinese can turn an innocuous game such as kite flying into an art; not art in the visual sense but the art of fighting and an instrument for gambling. They say gambling is in the blood of the people.

"What is this?" Kwok Sun asked as he bent down and picked up what appeared to be some kind of powder from the floor when we were up on the rooftop one day. He pinched it hard between his thumb and index finger.

"Shit…" Kwok Sun shouted as he quickly dusted it off his fingers. "It cuts," he screamed.

I took a look. His two fingers were cut and he was bleeding from the wounds. I bent down and examined the powder.

"It's glass powder," I said. "It's abrasive."

"They use the powder to murder people," said Kwok Sun. "You know, if you mix it with food and it goes into the stomach the glass grinds and makes holes in the stomach. Then it kills."

"No – nonsense – they use it for the kite string," I said. "I have seen how the adults make the string lethal. They use two spools to run the string through a tin can in which there are two tiny holes – just large enough for the string to pass through. And the can is filled with liquid paste that is a mixture of glass powder and glue. The processed string is wound from one spool to another. As it moves across the spools it dries up under the sun."

"What do they do with it?" asked Kwok Sun.

"The kite fighting season begins in autumn when the sky is high and the air crisp and breezy. The kite flyers move up to the roof. They are surrounded by spectators who are there to cheer them and often to place bets."

"But how do these kites fight?" Kwok Sun asked again.

"The kites are made of bamboo and paper. When carried by the wind, these kites can be steered. The glass-coated string is what turns the kites into fighters. The kites swerve and swoop as they move across the sky chasing each other. At times a kite goes up from underneath like a rapidly rising sun or somersaulting down like a sinking comet to engage in combat against the other kite. When engaged, the lines in the spools are let loose and delivered into the sky as quickly as possible so that they run and cut each other until the one gives way. Everyone gets a rush of adrenalin as the battle for survival is fought out above. Finally, the string breaks and the loser kite drifts off into the distance while the winner rises victoriously up in the evening sky. The spectators jump with excitement as they watch the aerial combat. Money then changes hands between the banker and the punters."

"Wow! It sounds like those dogfights of fighter planes," said Kwok Sun. "Can we do it?"

"We don't have the money. The string, spool and kite cost a lot. Where do we get the money? But wait, I have an idea. We can hijack the kites."

"How?"

"It's easy. We go up to the right roof. Get in front of them. We tie a piece of small stone to one end of a string and wait until the lines of the kites that are engaged in combat drop onto us. We toss the stone upward until the lines are entangled. Then we pull our line down and bingo! We hijack the kite. It is that simple."

"Wow... you are so clever, Robert." Kwok Sun's eyes brightened as he heaped praise on me. "Why don't we do just that? It sounds so exciting."

"But be prepared," I said. "The kite flyer is not going to be pleased. He can beat the hell out of us – you know, they are not kids like us. They are grown-ups."

"We can run faster than them though, can't we?"

We waited in ambush. The sky was full of kites; many were engaged in the aerial combat. We did not have to wait long. Soon we saw two kites fighting for survival. The crossed lines were clearly visible from above as the kites disappeared into the distant sky and the lines dropped precariously close to our roof. Kwok Sun was the first to toss the stone. I followed suit. It was easy – we managed to bring both lines down. Onlookers on the neighbouring roof raised a hue and cry followed by raised arms and clenched fists amid an outburst of expletives.

"Quick, let's wind the string into the spools before they get us," I shouted to Kwok Sun.

"Wow… it is such a bountiful day," shouted Kwok Sun joyfully. "There are miles and miles of lines. We can fly our own kites and dominate the sky. We will be kings—"

Even before his sentence was finished and as we were busy winding, we heard the loud noise of footsteps coming from the staircase. Two burly men appeared.

"You grab the skinny one and I'll get the other," one shouted.

Before we could run, we were seized from behind. We were smacked and punched.

"Lay off us, you bastard," I screamed as I struggled. "You know who his father is? He is Dai Low, king of the Walled City. If you hurt us, his *machai* (followers) are going to get even with you… Let go, you fucking bastard."

"I don't care if his father is the king of Hong Kong," shouted the man. "How dare you fucking steal our kites? Go and fucking kneel on the glass powder."

While we knelt on the bed of glass powder the two men busied themselves with bringing the kites down – with our own spools.

When the exercise was completed one of them picked the two of us up by the ears. "I don't want to see either of you on this roof ever," he shouted. "If I ever see you here again I will show you no mercy next time. I will twist off the ear from your face. Do you understand me?"

Kwok Sun and I made sure the two men had left before we dared get up again. We tried to lend each other support as we hobbled home. Our faces were bruised black and blue from the beating and our knees were cut and bleeding.

"Where have you been, Robert?" Father shouted at me. "You are late for dinner. Ah… were you fighting again? How many times have I told you not to pick fights in the street? You never listen, do you?"

Father was angry. As he spoke, he held me by the ear and hit me.

"Stop… stop," screamed Mother as she shielded me from more onslaughts. "Can't you see he has been beaten enough and his knees are bleeding?" Then she boiled an egg and used it to remove the swelling on my face. She also used alcohol spirit to treat the cuts and wounds on my face and knees. That night I could hardly sleep. The pain was excruciating.

≈≈≈≈≈

"Robert, this is your English paper," said Brother Wilfred of the school on Perth Street – La Salle College. "You have done well. There is only one mistake: it is 'both friends', not 'both friend', do you understand?"

"Brother Wilfred, I checked with my father," I replied. "He told me it is 'both friend' without the 's'."

"Go to the Potato Room," shouted Brother Wilfred angrily. "I will show you how we deal with argumentative boys."

The Potato Room – so-called because it was where potatoes, the staple food for the Catholic brothers that ran the school, were kept – was located outside the school grounds at the entrance to Perth Street where the brothers had their living quarters. The room had been converted from a garage which had no windows and just one door. At one end there was a rack on which canes were kept – there must have been a dozen of these canes, all different sizes, from thin to thick.

"Pick a cane," Brother Wilfred ordered as he stormed into the room. He was old, fat and sported a long white goatee beard to compensate for his bald head. In his long white gown he looked more like a Jewish rabbi than a brother of the Catholic order. "Roll down your trousers and pants and bend over the bench."

I picked the thinnest cane, not knowing that thinner canes were the most lethal.

He then horsewhipped me. I screamed in pain as the strokes rained down. I lost count after about twelve. My buttocks were bleeding.

"Go back to the classroom and stand on the platform," he commanded. "Do not move until I tell you to."

I hobbled back to the classroom and there I was humiliated again.

"Write about 'My visit to the Potato Room' – I want it first thing tomorrow," he ordered.

The reign of terror continued. I was his particular favourite, constantly subjected to his beatings. Brother Wilfred was like that violent schoolteacher, Mr. Squeers, in the Charles Dickens novel *The Life and Adventures of Nicholas Nickleby*.

The flesh on the part of my buttocks where the strokes came down began to crack; the wounds became inflamed and infected.

Sitting on the wooden bench in the classroom, the pain was unbearable. I had to position myself so that the wounds could sink and fit into the gaps in between the slats of the chair to survive the ordeal of a long day in the classroom.

Brother Wilfred kept a meticulous record of all the beatings: who, when, why and how. The journal recorded the details of the canes used and how many strokes were administered.

One day I was sent again to the Potato Room. Much to my surprise, I was met by a smiling and caring Brother Wilfred. He ushered me into his private room. The room was dark, the curtains drawn. The walls were covered by books.

"Come, Robert, don't be scared," he said. "Sit on my lap."

I did as I was told, all the while shaking and shivering and, at thirteen years old, I had no clue as to what was in store for me.

"Now these are good chocolates." He opened an empty Quink ink bottle and handed me a chocolate. I could see a least a dozen of these ink bottles – all stuffed with chocolates – neatly arranged on the pedestal.

I went through the same routine every time I was sent to the Potato Room. I cannot say that Brother Wilfred was a paedophile because, personally, I was never molested but I think he enjoyed using the cane on boys and probably derived some pleasure, sexual or otherwise, from punishing the boys and comforting them afterwards.

Another of the brothers at the school was a professional boxer before he became a Catholic brother. He came from Ireland. He was strongly built, bald, robust and hardy with a short neck – the sort that one would recognise as either a rugby player or boxer.

He wanted to build a boxing team to represent the school in the Hong Kong Inter-School Amateur Boxing Championships. The participating schools were mostly from the English Schools Foundation. Most local schools were too conservative and shunned the competition because parents did not favour boxing as a sport. Indeed, Brother Felix, the principal of the school, was half-hearted in the blessing he gave to the boxing training.

A group of boys trained twice a week after school hours in the school hall. There was an older boy who went by the name of Bruce Lee. He was a loner. He did not mix much and he seldom spoke. There was something extraordinary about him that marked him out from the others… it might have been his piercing eyes, his theatrical mannerisms, his intensity or his sheer cockiness. He rubbed his nose and would sneer at everyone around him, the trainer included. It could have been his background: born in the USA and into a showbiz family. He grew up in a movie environment. He considered himself a star, having taken part in local films playing the role of a child. He carried himself as if he was superior to others. He certainly spoke better English than the other boys. He was nerdy, temperamental and aloof – a hyperactive and confused teenager. He was not popular and lived in his own world of martial arts. And he was angry.

He was fanatical about fighting skills. It seemed as if his whole world was about fighting and being even better than the best. His piercing and intense eyes warned others he was not a person to be messed with. He was always on the prowl looking for trouble and wanting to prove his mettle. He was very unpleasant. Everyone was afraid of him. When he ran out of targets, he would carry a knife to school and use it to slash the tyres of the bicycles that were parked next to the basketball field. He had a reputation as a troublemaker and was involved in so many fights that he was summoned to see the principal frequently and earned himself many disciplinary warnings.

I idolized Bruce as a boxer and sucked up to him, calling him 'Big Brother' as he was older than me. I went out of my way to befriend him. He called me 'Kid' – a name I accepted as a way of kowtowing to a fighter I admired. And he liked it.

Boxing was our common interest and we both shared a passionate desire to excel in the sport. I had much to learn from Bruce's attitude and skills as a fighter. He was fearless: it was as if he went into every fight either to 'kill or be killed' – the hallmark of a good fighter.

That year, in 1958, I was chosen to represent the school in the B-Team (junior category). The competition was held at St. George's School, located across the road from an army barrack that housed the British garrison. By this time, Bruce Lee had been expelled from La Salle College for getting into so much trouble, and entered St. Francis Xavier School where he continued to focus primarily on his passion, fighting. He was at this inter-schools competition representing St. Francis Xavier Seniors.

"Congratulations, Big Brother," I greeted a victorious Bruce Lee as he descended from the ring. He was sweating profusely.

"Give me one more round and I would have knocked the hell out of that Limey," he boasted. "Three rounds are too short. It is no fun. They should do it like the professionals – twelve rounds. Then it is exciting."

"But you don't box like we are taught. We are trained to jab the opponent with the left and right and, when there is an opening, to throw punches one after another. That is boxing. But, Big Brother, you punch with both fists upfront simultaneously. What kind of boxing is that? It is not the kind that Brother Eugene teaches us."

"To hell with Brother Eugene. I punch *Wing Chun* style. It is a lot more effective than boxing. I will teach you *Wing Chun* one day. You can learn to be a better fighter from me than from Brother Eugene."

"Robert, it is your turn to get into the ring." Brother Eugene patted me on the head. "Remember to keep your chin low and close to the shoulder, protect it well and don't throw punches aimlessly. Be patient. Dance your way out of trouble and wait until you see an opportunity. Then bong… bong… you punch. Do you understand?"

"Yes, Brother Eugene," I said obediently.

I won my bout against the English boy from King George V School and won the Junior Medal for La Salle. Bruce Lee won the Senior Medal for St. Francis Xavier School.

Brother Eugene was visibly pleased. So was Bruce. To him, competition was everything… what life was all about. He had to win it all.

"Robert, let me teach you *Wing Chun*," Bruce said to me at the end of the competition when we were in the changing room together. "In *Wing Chun*, the most basic and fundamental technique to learn is the vertical punch. It's thrown with the elbows kept down and placed in front of the body. Now you look at this demonstration," he continued as he 'saddled on the horseback' – the posture that got his two feet firmly planted on the ground.

He then threw out a blast of straight punches in quick succession.

"Big Brother, where do you get the power if you don't use the body weight?" I asked.

"Don't ask stupid questions," Bruce replied agitatedly. "Just watch me. You rush forward with your full body weight and then you hammer the opponent. Can you see the power? Now do you understand?"

I nodded, in awe of the breezy sound as he let loose a barrage of forward punches followed by the whole body thrusting forward.

"Just learn the basic skills, kid," he said. "I shall teach you more next time."

He was often challenged to fights even before he left the school. The challenges came from newcomers who were eager to gain instant fame and recognition by prevailing over him. Bruce met these challenges head-on and with pleasure each time.

≈≈≈≈≈

There was this boy. His name was David and he just hated Bruce. It was as if he had an axe to grind against him. The hatred was entirely mutual.

The two of them never felt easy in each other's presence and, over time, whatever grievances the two had against each other festered in silence until they became bitter and explosive.

These two arch-enemies met again one day. For some time now the two had exchanged hostile looks, taking the measure of each other. They stared at each other provocatively; neither was prepared to give way. David was bigger than Bruce, taller and more muscular. That morning on the assembly lawn – where students lined up daily for inspection by the principal before being led into the classrooms – the two confronted each other. David started taunting Bruce. Bruce answered his taunts and soon the two were embroiled in a fist-fight. David was a good fighter. He was fast and was trying hard to punch Bruce on the head, all the time going for his chin.

But Bruce just danced methodically around him, moving so well that David could not touch him. Then Bruce saw a weakness open up in the defence. He moved up and landed a series of short Wing Chun punches onto David's face, knocking out a couple of his front teeth before grabbing the half-dazed opponent by the collar and ramming his knee into his chest. The fight was over in minutes. The onlookers who were on the lawn gasped in astonishment as Bruce emerged victorious.

But it did not make him any more popular. Everyone was intimidated by him. No one wanted to have anything to do with him. He was trouble. Bruce did not have many friends but that did not seem to bother him.

Later he was expelled as he was difficult to control and his school work was poor. He continued to enter boxing competitions and eventually won the championship.

La Salle cancelled boxing as a sport and withdrew from the inter-school event. Boxing was giving the school a bad image. There were too many fights both within and outside the school. Soon afterwards Bruce Lee returned to the USA and the best days of his life began.

The last time I saw Bruce was in 1972. He was standing on the concourse of the Star Ferry beside a large billboard that advertised Way of the Dragon – obviously enjoying being recognised by the passers-by. He was there to publicise this new film.

"Hi, Big Brother, you are now big in the movie world!" I greeted him adoringly as I passed on my way to work.

"Hi, Kid." He greeted me softly with a cold and nonchalant look. "Don't talk. Just stand next to me," he whispered and pointed to a spot next to him.

He showed no desire to take the conversation any further. I knew he was big and famous. For the next few minutes, I basked in his glory as passers-by gasped in astonishment when they recognised the larger-than-life Bruce Lee standing by the side of his own billboard image: "Look – it's Bruce Lee."

Bruce was basking in his own success. I had my fifteen minutes of fame standing next to him, occasionally being photographed by tourists, even if I did think we looked like a couple of idiots as the morning crowd surged forward to catch the next ferry to work in Central, the business hub.

Bruce Lee died tragically in 1973 at the age of thirty-two. He died at the home of a Taiwanese actress by the name of Betty Ting Pei. Local folklore had it that he died in her bed while they were making love. Hence, it is said even today: *Sheung sze wan Ting Pui* – 'if a man wants to die, he should go to Ting Pei'. The truth was that Bruce died from a swelling of the brain that could have been caused by an allergic reaction to something he took: it may have been marijuana – traces of the substance were found during the autopsy – or the analgesic that Ting Pei gave him for the headache he complained about. There were also rumours that he was once involved in a fight in Indonesia. He won the fight, but the kicks he received from his opponent resulted in internal injuries for Bruce.

Officially Hong Kong's coroners recorded 'Death by Misadventure'. There was no conclusive evidence on the cause of death.

# THE LOST GENERATION

"Good morning, Uncle John and Aunt Mary." I bowed deeply as I greeted the good-looking couple seated at the back of the bus. The bus was packed with rush-hour commuters and I had to struggle through the crowd to reach the two of them and pay my respects.

"Whose family is this boy?" the man asked in heavily-accented Mandarin, the sort one could easily recognize as being from the north, Beijing or Manchuria, because of the drawl like an Irish twang. His wife whispered into his ear something I could not hear. He twisted his lips, sneered and looked the other way, choosing to ignore me.

The bus ride was tortuously long. Finally, the couple got off. I bowed, this time even deeper, to say goodbye. The couple ignored me.

"This morning I saw the Fans on a bus… you know, Uncle John and Aunt Mary," I said to my mother. "I walked up to greet them. They just ignored me. They behaved as if they did not know me. Are you not on good terms with them?"

"We did get along well. All those years when we lived under the same roof we never quarrelled, not so much as one harsh word," Mother said. "Uncle John is quiet. Aunt Mary is affable. Although they kept very much to themselves, we always got along well. You mustn't blame them. That family went through a hard time. But they are now on their feet again. In fact, I hear that they are doing very well indeed. They just moved into a big house on Kadoorie Hill. I wish them luck. They deserve better after the ordeal they've been through. It's sad, really sad."

Kadoorie Hill is one of the most exclusive residential areas in the Kowloon Peninsula. The entire hill is owned by one family – the Kadoories, a wealthy Jewish family of Iraqi origin. The family also owns the Peninsula Hotel. 'The Pen', as it is affectionately known, is an iconic landmark in Hong Kong.

Of course, houses are hard to come by in land-scarce Hong Kong. To be able to live in a house, let alone one in such an exclusive location, is the ultimate symbol of success, a way to tell the world at large that you have 'arrived'. I just could not believe that the Fans and their son Charles could have got so high up the ladder in such a short time. It seemed like yesterday when we all lived in the same flat together. They must have struck gold.

"Tell me what happened," I said. "How could they become rich so quickly? Why can't we be like them?"

"Ha! Ha! Ha! To start with, you don't have a mother like Aunt Mary. Remember the time you told me that you were woken in the middle of the night by the telephone and when you got up to answer you saw Uncle John leaving the apartment? Shortly afterwards, Aunt Mary entered through the back door and sneaked through the kitchen with a man, a stranger. Both of them had their shoes in their hands as they tiptoed into the bedroom."

I remembered the incident well. I used to share a bunk bed with their son, Charles, a boy about my age, in the tiny room that was the servant's quarters. That night, the phone rang. I got up to answer it but the ringing had stopped by the time I reached it. I took the opportunity to go to the toilet. Then it rang a second time, again briefly, as if it was a prearranged signal. When I picked up the receiver, the line went dead. As I went to the toilet in the dark, except for the lights from the street below, my attention was caught by a hissing sound, like a gust of wind. I turned and saw a silhouette moving quickly to the door. As the door closed gently, I went to the balcony and through the window I could see Uncle John leaving the building in haste. Then I saw Aunt Mary arriving with the man just a few minutes later.

"It is a true tragedy." Mother took a deep breath and sighed. "I can't imagine how they fell from so high to so low. You know the Fans are dignified people. When they came to Hong Kong they brought what valuables they could, gold, jewellery and dollars, but it was not long before they had squandered it all. Then they hit hard times, falling behind in rent and struggling just to feed themselves. You know Uncle John has never worked in his entire life. Indeed, work was considered beneath him. A man of his high birth typically spent his days indulging in calligraphy, poetry, antiques, fighting crickets, tea ceremonies and the like. It was a privileged and dignified kind of existence made possible only by inherited wealth. Thus, he is too proud a person to go out to find work. As things turned from bad to worse, the family became even more despondent. Aunt Mary, that poor woman, 'went into the sea' to work as a ballroom girl and, you know, in that line of business, men expect you to be 'nice' to them."

Hong Kong in the fifties was full of the lost generation: farmers who had lost their land; aristocrats who had lost their status; rich who had lost their fortunes; ordinary people who had lost their jobs; and businessmen who had lost their businesses. They were all in Hong Kong trying to piece together fragments of their lives like the lost generations before them in Shanghai: the White Russians after the Bolshevik revolution, and the Jews escaping the Nazis before the Second World War.

"Unlike the Chang family who were supported by a rich relative that lived in Taiwan, the Fans were self-reliant," Mother continued. "You know they are descendants of royalty from the Qing Dynasty – his grandfather was a half-brother of the Guangxu Emperor. They were used to a way of life that was a combination of history, wealth and upbringing, always surrounded by an army of servants to cater to their every whim.

"The family must have realised how hopeless the situation was. Aunt Mary sacrificed her dignity for the sake of the family just like your great-grandmother did when she sold her body to become a surrogate mother in Zhou Shan. She went to work at the ballroom knowing full well that she was expected to sell her body to anyone who could afford her price – like any common prostitute. It must have been painful for her husband as they were a really loving couple with a marriage that was made in heaven – he was decent, scholarly and handsome, she was beautiful, graceful and elegant. Not only were they both well educated but also they gave off an air of aristocracy which could only be explained by their background.

Not even in their wildest dreams did they expect the family fortunes could change so drastically – from so high to so low and so soon after arriving here. When a person is hit so badly, he will do anything for survival. Pride is the least of his concerns. That is exactly what happened to the Fans."

There was no denying that Aunt Mary was a beautiful woman, elegant and refined, not to mention the fact that she was also well endowed. There was something extraordinary about this woman. She radiated an aura that no man could resist when she chose to turn on the charm. I remember how well she carried herself and how beautiful she looked in that *qipao*, almost always the same dress, every evening when she left for work.

"As soon as she started work, I noticed changes in their lifestyle," said Mother. "They suddenly had a lot more money to spend. The back rent was paid in full and they started buying things, like a new refrigerator, furniture and new clothes. Then they told me they were moving out of the flat."

The two sub-tenants, the Changs and the Fans, knew each other from the old days. Both had been members of the ruling class in China. Mr. Chang was the younger brother of Generalissimo Chang Hsueh Liang whose father was a powerful warlord in Manchuria. The father was assassinated by the Japanese in a train incident. Thus the son bore a big grudge against the Japanese.

When civil war broke out between the Nationalists and the Communists, Chang Hsueh Liang – the 'young general' – served under Chiang Kai Shek as a regional commander. It was he who urged the two sides to stop fighting each other and instead join forces against the invading Japanese. When Chiang Kai Shek visited Xian, it was the young general who had him incarcerated and forced him to agree to a pact with the Communists in what is known in history as the 'Xian Incident'. After the Sino-Japanese war ended, civil war resumed between the two sides until the Nationalists retreated to Formosa (now Taiwan). Chiang never forgot the betrayal in Xian and he took the young general with him to the island where he was placed under house arrest until he died.

The Changs got along well with my parents. They often assured them that one day they would triumphantly return to China. When they did, they would welcome my parents into their huge ancestral house in Manchuria and reward them with unimaginable riches. All along they laboured under the illusion that the Nationalists would soon defeat the Communists and retake China once again. Hong Kong to them, as to so many of the lost generation who languished there, was merely a place of temporary refuge while they waited for the time when they could return to China and the old way of life.

"But this is not the end of the story," Mother continued. "One day, a few years later, we bumped into the family, or rather the extended family, in the street. Charles had grown taller. He took after his father, of the same build and features, and what a good-looking boy he turned out to be. Mary was carrying a baby girl in her arms obviously not fathered by Uncle John as the girl had fair skin and blue eyes. Standing next to Mary was this Englishman and, from the way they behaved, it was obvious they were lovers, holding hands and demonstrating affection for each other even in public and in the presence of her husband. The Fans were quite taken aback when they saw us. It was an awkward encounter and we had to look the other way. We did not greet each other."

Later, from the bits and pieces that I picked up from adult conversations at the dinner table, I was able to piece together an intriguing story of love, passion, money and power.

At the place where she worked, the Oriental Ballroom, Mary was involved with a man called Hak Chai who was a notorious triad figure also known as 'The Tiger of Mongkok'. The district was the most lucrative of all areas for the triads because it had, within a small area, hundreds of drug dealers, brothels, illegal bookies, money lenders, ballrooms, restaurants and bars and shops, some legal, some illegal and some operating within the grey areas of the law.

Some were triad-run, others easy targets for the triads to extract 'protection' money, and the police mostly turned a blind eye.

Those were the days when corruption was endemic, permeating all strata of society, and collaboration between the police and triads reached an art form, with the former using the latter to keep the peace and act as their eyes and ears. If the police wanted someone who might have committed a crime, all they had to do was turn to the triads and, before long, the person would be found and handed over.

At times, if the real culprit could not be found, a dummy would be 'manufactured'. The suspect would confess to a crime he did not commit – all part of a deal made with the police. He was in all likelihood a known offender anyway, and being in and out of prison was his way of life. By toeing the police line, he knew the credit he earned would be paid back next time he returned to crime. This arrangement somehow made Hong Kong one of the safest cities in the world. The underworld was by and large controlled by the triads. Criminals would not make a move without the knowledge and often the consent of triad bosses. By this arrangement, the triads controlled the criminals and the police, in turn, controlled the triads.

One of the ballroom's regular customers was a man called Chien. He frequented the ballroom at least twice a week, almost always after work, either entertaining his customers or on his own. He was a factory owner from Chiu Chow, the part of coastal China where men are known to be gutsy in business, not shy of taking risks, and fiery in character. When provoked they can become fearless and dangerous. Not only was he successful and rich, generous to a fault, but he was also gregarious and outgoing, always willing to help others when they got into trouble.

He was well liked by the girls and staff, being typical of those they called 'dutiful sons of the volcano'; the ballroom was full of hot girls and one's admiration of the 'volcano under the skirt' could consume him and bring about his self-destruction.

On the very first day that Mary started work, the manager took the trouble to telephone Chien and tell him that a new girl had just 'descended into the sea'. He would tip off a good customer like Chien whenever a new girl of quality arrived so that he could be given the first bite of the cherry, so to speak.

From the very first encounter, Chien was besotted with Aunt Mary and, from that day onward, he could never get enough of her, returning every evening to 'buy hours' in order to be with her.

But each 'ticket' hour was good only for a session that lasted twenty minutes, just enough time for two dances and some in-between conversation before she went back into circulation, 'floating' to another table. The merry-go-round made Chien feel as if he was chasing rainbows, losing her constantly to the other men and often for the whole night if they took her out for a 'night snack' – late dinner or to have sex, depending on the degree of familiarity between them. In the nature of things, sex could only come about when a customer had clocked up enough hours and brought the girl sufficient gifts – 'offerings made by the dutiful son of the volcano' – to move her heart and make her finally agree.

If the relationship developed one stage further, the customer would 'set up a golden chamber to house the beauty'. When that happened, the girl would become a concubine, as these 'worshippers of the volcano' were mostly married men. But some lucky ones might also end up marrying the customers.

She could also be ditched after use, in which case the girl, if she was still young, would normally go back to work at the ballroom again. Otherwise, she would end up as a common prostitute at Western Market serving the tradesmen and coolies who congregated there.

Chien was at the Oriental Ballroom one night. He was uneasy, jumpy and nervous. He just could not take his mind off Mary. As usual he placed his order for her to the *mama-san* – manager of the hostesses – who came to welcome him in the foyer even before he was ushered to his usual table. When told that Mary was not available because she had been 'bought out' by another customer, his heart sank. He left the ballroom empty-handed and disappointed. He was in no mood to get any other girl. It was not his lucky day. He decided to go home. On his way out he heard the faint sound of a girl sobbing in a private room. He was surprised to see Mary crouched in one corner of the room with Hak Chai standing over her.

"Why are you crying?" he asked her. "What has this man done to you? You have blood on your face. Did he hit you?"

"Go away," Hak Chai said. "It's none of your business. This is a private room. Can't you see? Just move on."

"I will not go away until I find out why she is crying and who hit her," insisted Chien.

"Why the fuck do you want to be a *ka leung* (a meddler in other people's business)? It is none of your fucking business!" Hak Chai raised his voice. He was getting impatient.

"That woman's business is also my business. We are friends. Do you understand?"

"Stop, Chien," Mary said as she wiped the tears from her face with a handkerchief. "Please leave us alone. I shall join you later. Now, go away."

"Hey, bastard, did you hear her?" Hak Chai provocatively poked his fingers into Chien's chest. "Leave or I shall break your fucking neck. Do you know who you are dealing with?"

"I don't care if you are the emperor of China," Chien shouted as he raised his fist. "You leave her alone or else I will—"

Before he could finish the sentence, Hak Chai landed several punches, sending Chien to the floor, bleeding from the corner of his mouth. Hak Chai then turned. Instinctively Chien got up, grabbed a chair and smashed it onto the head of Hak Chai from behind. The blow knocked him unconscious and as he fell to the ground, blood gushed out from a head wound.

"Chien, look what have you done," Mary shouted in panic. "Leave immediately. Do you know who this man is? He is Hak Chai, the Tiger of Mongkok. Leave quickly."

In the ensuing commotion, the manager arrived. On seeing Hak Chai lying in a pool of blood, he was horrified. He pulled Chien over to one side.

"Mr. Chien, you had better leave immediately, before his men arrive," said the panic-stricken manager, visibly shaking. "Leave it to me to clear up this mess. If you don't leave, his men will kill you. Please go immediately. Go into hiding until the matter is resolved. I am only telling you this because you are such a good customer. I would be placing my own life in jeopardy if his men knew it was I who asked you to leave. You may not know this but he and Mary are close."

"How close?" asked Chien with a tinge of jealousy.

The manager crossed his fingers to indicate they were sleeping together. "Mary needed Hak Chai for protection."

It was well after midnight when Chien arrived at the flat of his friend Song Chai in MacDonnell Road. Song Chai and Chien had been friends since childhood. The two of them knew each other from back home. As teenagers in Chiu Chow, they often roamed the countryside together, dreaming about going to Hong Kong as a way of escaping the harsh reality of life under communism in China. On the other side of Mirs Bay, also known as Tai Pang Wan, lies Hong Kong.

On one calm and moonless summer night, the two teenagers stole a car tyre, removed and inflated the inner tube and, using it as a buoy, slipped into the warm waters of the bay. After swimming for about two hours, they reached the other shore. Then they changed into the dry clothes they had carried with them in watertight polythene bags. After trekking through the bushes in darkness for another hour or so, they reached a road – Clearwater Bay Road – and from there they managed to board a bus, paying the fare with the Hong Kong dollars they carried with them. En route to the city, the bus had to stop at a roadblock manned by the police. A policeman looked casually into the bus and gave the driver clearance to move on. It was during the morning rush hour and he probably thought all the passengers were on their way to work. Under the 'touch-base' policy of that time, illegal immigrants were given amnesty once they reached the urban area.

In Hong Kong, the two friends went their separate ways. Both of them became successful: Chien became a factory owner and Song Chai joined the police. He was promoted to Station Sergeant. Later, he left the force and became an intermediary between the police and the triads. The two friends had remained close.

Song Chai opened the door in his pyjamas, rubbing his eyes and trying to work out who would call so late in the night.

"I am in a fix," said Chien. "Please help me."

"It is you, Chien. Why so late in the night? Did you have a fight with someone? Do come in. Calm down and tell me what happened," Song Chai said.

Then, "Get us some tea," he shouted to his wife and servant who were standing behind him. "Can't you see I have a guest?"

"I just hit someone with a chair," said Chien. "He hit me first."

"That is no big deal." Song Chai reached for the telephone. "You have come to the right place. I shall have it fixed in no time. Where did it happen? Were the police alerted?"

"Wait a minute. The guy I hit is called Hak Chai. I was told to leave the ballroom immediately."

"What? You hit Hak Chai, the Tiger of Mongkok?" Song Chai asked in disbelief. "Do you know who he is? Hak Chai is a 426, a Red Pole, in Sun Yee On Triad. He has at least a hundred men under his command. One word from him and you are dead, ready to be picked up as a street corpse."

"I didn't know who he was. We quarrelled over this girl Mary at the ballroom. He hit me and, in the heat of the moment, anger got the better of me and I retaliated by hitting him with a chair from behind."

"His men must be looking for you now all over town. They are probably at your home already. You are wise to come here. Let me call my contact at the police so that they can send detectives immediately to your home to protect your family. You are crazy. How can you get yourself into this mess?"

Song Chai made a call to Mongkok Police Station. He was an important figure there, a bridge between the police and the triads. He was the one who sent his army to collect dues from the vice establishments run by the triads. The money that was collected was handed over each day to the Detective Station Sergeant at Mongkok. The total takings were reported to Superintendent Garrett James daily who, after verification, ensured that the cash was placed inside sealed envelopes and distributed to all officers above a certain rank – the size of the share being determined by one's seniority at the station.

Superintendent James, being the most senior, got the lion's share. Others got their portion in an envelope which was placed in the drawer of their desks each day. No one was supposed to ask questions. Corruption was endemic and syndicated. It was like a bus: one either got on it or could run alongside it. Anyone who tried to stop it risked being knocked down.

The superintendent was the overlord, the arbiter and the ultimate power, presiding over his own force in the precinct as well as the triads who operated within it. Thus, he was a powerful man, feared by his subordinates and triad officers alike. He could make or break men. He was not a person to be messed with.

"The detectives are going over to your home now. You are lucky to have a friend like me, very lucky." Song Chai shook his head. "Your wife and kids are safe. It is getting late. Why don't you spend the night here? Tomorrow, I shall find out exactly what happened to Hak Chai and see if I can mediate between the two of you. It is not going to be easy."

The bad news came the next day. Song Chai telephoned his home where Chien was still staying. "Chien, I have bad news for you," he said. "Hak Chai is out to get you despite my intervention. He has taken out a 'society contract' to have you bumped off. His cronies are in the streets looking for you. As far as he is concerned, you are already dead. Stay put.

Don't go anywhere until I get back. I am worried, really worried about you."

"Please help me, Song Chai. I am your friend. How much money do you need to fix it? Just let me know and I shall pay. Please do what is necessary."

That night, when Song Chai returned home, he was extremely agitated. He wanted to help but he was at his wits' end. He had exhausted all known avenues. No one seemed able to persuade Hak Chai to change his mind. He was set on getting his revenge.

"I spoke to Detective Sergeant Lui at Mongkok Station today," said Song Chai. "He reckons the only person who can help you is his boss; you know, the Englishman – what is his name? – Superintendent James. But he demands $50,000 as his fee."

"What? $50,000?" said Chien. "You could buy an apartment with that sort of money."

"I am merely passing on the message. It's up to you to decide whether you want his help. The way I see it, you have no choice. The only way to stop a 'society contract' on your life is to go before the Council of Elders in the triad and plead for a 'society protection edict' which only the Council can issue. You need someone influential, either from the black or the white camp or, better still, one who straddles both.

"But as Hak Chai is so high up in the hierarchy of the black camp, I don't think anyone would want to incur his wrath by speaking out on your behalf. The only person who carries enough weight is someone who controls the cash flow. The more I think about it, the more I am convinced. It's got to be that *Gweilo* (foreign devil). No one else can do it."

"Okay, I'll give you the money tomorrow. You go and do what's necessary to get me out of this mess."

A few days later, Song Chai returned.

"I have handed the money over to the sergeant," said Song Chai. "He spoke to the *Gweilo*. The *Gweilo* wants to meet you. He specifically wants to meet that girl, you know, the beautiful woman who makes Hak Chai and you crazy. She must be one hell of a woman. He wants to know what kind of mettle she is made of that can drive the two of you so head over heels in love with her."

It was at the dinner which Song Chai gave that Mary met Garrett James for the first time. After that fateful meeting, she became his de facto 'wife' and bore him a daughter despite the fact she was already married to someone else. Mary and her two husbands lived together at the superintendent's house on Kadoorie Hill.

The Council of Elders was convened and a society protection order was issued. Hak Chai was stopped in his effort to exact revenge but not until Chien threw a lavish party in which he openly kowtowed and apologized to Hak Chai as redemption. The party was attended by leading representatives from both the white and black camps and there Chien handed over a cheque for another twenty thousand dollars, this time for the benefit of 'The Children and Widows Fund'. It was graciously received amidst thunderous applause by the 'Oarsman', the doyen of the triad world. Thus the matter was laid to rest.

# PUPPY LOVE

"Turn off the tap upstairs, turn off the tap upstairs," the woman shouted from her window.

The scene was common when, in 1964, Hong Kong experienced the worst drought in living memory. I was a teenager at that time. The rainfall was fifty-one inches less than the average of eighty-seven inches that year. The reservoirs were so depleted that water rationing was introduced.

It started with a few hours a day; then it became every other day. Then it was every two days and finally the use of water was reduced to four hours every four days. The situation was exacerbated by the fact that it happened in the summer when the heat coupled with the humidity makes everyday life almost unbearable.

When the taps were turned on, there was a mad rush to get as much water as possible. Land-scarce Hong Kong is full of high-rises. Water found its way first up to the tank on the rooftop before it was pumped to the lower floors. Often, by the time buckets on the upper floors were filled, no water would be available for the floors below. Then, on the strike of the clock, the supply would be cut off and not turned on again for four days.

The inequality of supply was a constant cause of friction. Quarrels and fights were everyday occurrences as people struggled to get their share. As the drought continued, people from the lower floors would rush to the rooftop to get water directly from the tank rather than relying on the mercy of the upper floors to turn the tap off.

"Come, let me help you," I said to a pretty girl in the queue. "What's your name?"

"Jean," she replied shyly. "I live on the sixth floor, and you?"

"Hi, Jean, I'm Robert," I said as I stretched out to shake her hand. "I live on the fifteenth. Come, let me help you carry the pail. It's too heavy for you."

"Thank you." She gave me an endearing look. "You are kind."

"Not at all," I said as my heartbeat quickened. "It is my pleasure. You sound as if you are from Ningbo. I am also from Ningbo."

"Yes, I can tell." She smiled. "You also have my accent."

I carried the pail of water and together we descended the many flights of stairs until we got to the sixth floor – using the lift was taboo. At the door, I was not sure whether it was proper for me to enter her apartment so I placed the bucket on the floor.

"Thank you," she said as she opened the iron-grille door. "You can leave the water here. I'll carry it inside."

I looked in. It was a small apartment, clean and tidy but furnished sparsely; just a few chairs and a dining table which gave me the impression that her family were new arrivals. I could also tell from her accent. It was much thicker than mine.

"Okay, I shall see you next time," I said. "Four days from now."

"Sure," she replied with a smile.

I was in good spirits. There was a spring in my step as I returned home. I sat there motionlessly. "Wow, I'm in love," I muttered to myself. "Love is a wonderful feeling. I think she loves me too. Wow."

Then I remembered the water I was supposed to fetch. I jumped off the seat and headed straight back up to the roof.

All through that summer, Jean and I saw each other. I always helped her to fill up her bucket and carry the water to her home.

"Let me give you a hand," she said one day as she reached for the handle of the bucket filled to the brim with water.

"No, no, just let me," I said. "It is not heavy. I can handle it."

Our hands inadvertently touched. A strange tingling sensation crept up my spine, a kind I had never experienced before. I lowered the bucket to the floor, took her hand and instinctively our lips met. It was the first time for both of us. Then we kissed and kissed. We could not get enough of each other until we heard the noise of footsteps coming down the staircase. We quickly stepped apart and moved to opposite corners of the landing as if nothing was happening.

"Have you heard of the band, the Fabulous Echoes?" I asked. "They are really good. They perform nightly at the Bayside Nightclub, you know, just across the road at the top of Astor Hotel. Are you free next Saturday? If you are, I shall take you there."

"I have to ask my mother's permission," she replied. "She probably won't let me go out at night."

"Why don't you just tell her you are going to dinner with a classmate or something? And tell her you will get home early. Please... you will really enjoy the band. Their song *A Little Bit of Soap* has just reached number one spot in 'Top of the Chart' this week. Please... please."

"Okay, I'll try."

I could hardly sleep that week. I was thrilled to bits – my first date and with a girl as pretty as Jean. I could not help thinking how lucky I was.

≈≈≈≈≈

All week long I was thinking about my first date: checking on the cost of the nightclub; getting the money to pay for it; thinking about what I was going to wear; and how best to avoid more pimples on my face and deal with the existing ones. When the day finally arrived, I combed and re-combed my hair – plain, with gel, washed off, plain, and finally with gel again and blown into a 'balcony' like Elvis Presley. My shirt and trousers were starched, ironed and re-ironed. Then I borrowed a tie from my father and took his watch when he was not looking.

At 8 p.m. we met up in the foyer of the apartment building and from there we crossed the road and reached the Astor Hotel. We walked through the lobby and entered the lift. The lift operator, dressed in white from top to bottom, did not even look at us before whisking us to the nightclub on the top floor of the building.

There we were met by a waiter who checked the booking and ushered us to a table by the window. We could not believe our good fortune. It commanded a splendid view of the city, illuminated by lights that stretched all the way through the Kowloon peninsula to Victoria Harbour and the island of Hong Kong. We could see where we lived – Alhambra Building across the road. It was nothing short of exhilarating for a young couple who had never seen anything so magnificent.

I ordered Coca Cola for the two of us and settled down to an intimate evening completely intoxicated by each other's presence. The resident band – the Fabulous Echoes – played our favourite song:

"A little bit of soap will wash away the lipstick on your lips…"

We hurriedly descended onto the dance floor and danced to the latest craze, 'The Shake'. We twisted and shook all night and, when the music slowed down, we danced cheek to cheek. It was truly a marvellous evening – we were in heaven together. We were wishing the evening would never end.

"Your bill, sir," the waiter interrupted us as we were deep in conversation.

I looked at the bill and almost fell off my chair. I went into a cold sweat. I had gone to a lot of trouble to get the HK$14 for the nightclub.

"You've made a mistake," I said nervously. "It should be $14, not $15.40. You advertise at $7 per person. We did not order any extras beside the two glasses of Coca Cola."

I was twitching and biting my fingers, thinking to myself: 'Oh no, not in front of Jean. It's a great loss of face. What am I going to do? I only have the exact amount with me.'

"There is a 10% service charge," said the waiter politely.

I was so embarrassed that I started to get palpitations.

'What can I do?' I thought to myself. "Sorry… I am really sorry, but do you by any chance have $1.40 with you?" I asked Jean.

Her face turned red. It made her look even more beautiful in the candlelight.

"I-I-I don't." Her head dropped, too shy and embarrassed to look at me.

I began to sweat profusely. I was so shaken I did not know what to do next.

"I'm sorry," I apologised to the waiter. "I don't have enough with me, but I live just across the road. I'll give you $14 now and then I can go home and get the difference."

"I'll have to ask the manager," the waiter said. "Please wait."

The manager came. "We cannot let both of you leave," he said. "One of you can go. The other has to stay until the bill is settled in full. You can use our telephone to call home if you want."

I could feel everyone's eyes on me as I was ushered to the telephone. I called home but could not reach my parents. No one else could help me. I returned to the table. I was at my wits' end, embarrassed beyond words.

"Jean, I can't get the money. Both of my parents are out. Can you help?"

"Let me call home," she said. "See if my parents are home."

She twisted and wriggled her way shyly towards the telephone. She was blushing and it was very apparent she was highly embarrassed. She must have felt like a fool as everyone was staring at her and some of the other girls were giggling and whispering to each other. She made the call and returned.

"Well… are they home?"

"My mother is coming over with the money," she said with a disapproving look, the kind that borders on contempt.

It seemed like hours before a woman appeared. She was a big woman with a huge bosom. She looked stern and it was easy to tell that she was upset.

"Tell your little boyfriend never to take you to a swanky nightclub if he doesn't have the money," she said with a strong Ningbo accent. "How dare you date without my permission? I shall teach you a lesson when we get home."

She pulled Jean up from the table but not before she had tossed $1.40 at me like I was a beggar. All the while she did not even look at me. It was plain to see that she despised me. I could see Jean was very distressed and she began to cry. I had humiliated her.

I cursed myself. I was greatly shamed. My dream of Jean evaporated that night. I thought I loved her – the first love of my life.

I was not allowed to see her again after that incident. I was distressed, downtrodden and downright miserable. I was also lovesick and waited in the entrance lobby of the building hoping to catch a glimpse of her. But she was never without a family member. Once I managed to slip a message into her hand: Can I see you? I shall wait for you every day at 4 p.m. in the lobby store until you reply.

Days passed. There was no answer. Then one day my mother passed me a sealed envelope addressed to me that she had collected from our mailbox. I opened it eagerly. It contained a simple note: My mother forbids me to see you. Please do not try telephoning me. J.

This came as no surprise because I did call her a few times. It was always her mother who answered. As soon as she found out it was me, she would slam the receiver down.

I knew the mother had rejected me because I was not considered good enough for her daughter – my coming from what she perceived to be a poor family. Mothers aim high for their daughters and Jean's mother was no exception. Besides, Jean was pretty and deserved something better than a commoner. The family had just arrived from Ningbo after enduring years of hardship under Communist rule. Her two daughters were her only assets in this new land and she was optimistic that one day both of them would be paired off with sons from rich families.

As a desperate act of redemption, I passed my book of 'Pak Tze' (Eight Characters) to Jean when one day I caught her off guard buying provisions on her own in the lobby store.

"What is this?" a surprised Jean asked. "Have you been waiting for me all day again?"

"I just want you to read my 'Pak Tze'."

"What is 'Pak Tze'?"

"Ask your mother. She will tell you. Each and every one of us is born with a set of 'Pak Tze'. It is a sort of life map. Whether a person is rich or poor and how he lives, his life is predetermined by the date and hour of his birth. I want you to know that my 'Pak Tze' reveals that throughout my life I shall be 'close to the rich and famous and shall achieve fame in my own right'. They say in old China: 'wealth and fame is determined by heaven above'. The old proverb has been tested time and time again throughout history. It is true. Please can you show your mother my book of 'Pak Tze'?"

"Why should I do that for you? She won't care. Take it back. Don't show off. Just go away."

"My 'Pak Tze' also says that I shall marry a girl born in the year of the Rooster. You were born a Rooster," I said in desperation.

That meeting was the straw that broke the camel's back. My stupid last-ditch effort to salvage the relationship backfired badly. It gave her even more reasons to stop seeing me – the love-struck nut.

I continued to hang on to the last vestige of hope although it was apparent that it was all but gone. I continued to wait for her at all the places where I thought I might see her. My efforts were not entirely fruitless.

I was in the lift going down from the fifteenth floor. Every time it stopped on the sixth floor my heart jumped in anticipation that I would see her when the door opened. My heart sank when I did not and I had been going up and down that same lift at least three times that afternoon.

A woman entered on the fifteenth. I recognized her as a neighbour. She must have been in her late twenties, young and sexy. She wore heavy make-up. That afternoon she was dressed in a colourful *qipao* and high heels. The building was full of women who made a living working as dancing girls in the ballrooms nearby.

As she entered I looked at her adoringly, too shy to speak, and she looked at me from the corner of her eye. The lift door closed and did not stop until the sixth floor, the button which I had pressed before she entered.

She looked at me and gestured in surprise. "A ghost must have pressed the lift button," she said as she pressed the button to close the door.

"Yes," I replied. "Do you believe in ghosts?"

She then playfully switched off the lift light.

"Wow… a ghost!" she shouted.

Then she turned the light on again. We both laughed.

"Where are you going?" I enquired.

"I am going to '*kung yu*'. And you?" she asked mischievously.

My heart almost jumped out. Phonetically, '*kung yu*' in the local dialect can mean 'park' or 'hourly hotel'. She could not be going to a park the way she was dressed, not to mention in the heat and humidity of the afternoon.

'I don't believe it,' I thought. 'She wants to go to bed with me!'

"Can I come with you?" I asked as a rush of adrenalin went through my blood.

"As you wish." She smiled.

We got on the bus and alighted two stops later.

"What about this one?" I said as I pointed at the billboard that read 'Midnight Kung Yu' – Hotel Midnight – hanging from the first floor of a high-rise residential building.

She nodded in approval.

"How much does a room cost?' I asked the innkeeper nervously.

"Long or short?" the keeper asked.

"What do you mean?" I tried to act older than my age.

"The long for a day is $12. Short for two hours is $6," he replied.

I dipped into my pocket. I only had $3 with me – the money mother gave me for a haircut that day. I looked at her nervously.

"Short and I get a $2 rebate." She handed a $10 note to the keeper.

"Why do you get a rebate?" I asked.

She just looked inscrutable and smiled as she collected the key and the change.

She led the way along the narrow corridor and opened the room door with the key. As I entered, my heart felt as though it was going to jump out of my chest. I was excited beyond words. But I was at a loss as to what to do next. I did not know which one of us should make the next move. Soon I realised my concern was unnecessary.

"Go and take a shower, quickly," she commanded. "I am already late for work."

When I came out of the bathroom she was lying in bed completely naked except for a towel. She was smoking a cigarette. When she saw me she quickly ground the cigarette out in the ashtray and, using her index finger, beckoned me to join her. Even before I had time to remove my towel she had torn it away. Then she began to fondle and kiss me like a sex-starved maniac. I reacted with all the passion that was unleashed by doing 'the thing' for the first time.

When it was all over, I was in a daze. It was the most sensational experience; the feeling was magical. I just could not believe my luck that day. Then fear overtook me.

"Can I get syphilis or gonorrhoea?" I asked her as she dressed. "Is it true that these diseases can kill? I have read about them in newspapers and, amongst friends, we often discuss the horrible symptoms such as boils the size of a mango. Can you tell me?"

"It's too late now." She smiled. "You just have to find out yourself."

'Shit, I think I will get the disease,' I thought. 'I'm going to die.'

She took a shower, put on her underwear and slipped into her *qipao*.

"You stay," she commanded as she opened the door. "The room is still good for two hours." Then she dashed off – almost as if she had to catch the last train.

I sat motionless on the floor in one corner of the room. I had mixed feelings. On the one hand, there was a sense of complete gratification and I was restful. Yet, on the other, I was scared, really scared, of the consequences of sex with a loose woman.

I did not see her again for many months until I bumped into her in the lift, just the two of us.

"This is for you," she said as she dipped into her handbag and took out a red packet. "I have kept this for a while hoping that I would see you again."

"What is this for?"

"Your virginity – spring chicken makes me young." She laughed loudly.

I remembered how the prostitute had teased Kwok Sun and me when we passed the prostitutes' alley at the Walled City that night.

The red packet contained two ten-dollar notes.

# Rich Friends

"Mrs. Wang, there are a bunch of boys at the door asking for Robert," a co-tenant at the shared apartment in Nathan Road shouted from the door.

At the door I almost fainted.

"How did you manage to find me here?" I asked nervously.

There were at least ten of them who came that afternoon. I could not invite them inside because there was no space. The flat, no more than 1300 square feet, was first divided into two units. The inside unit was occupied by four families. My mother was the head tenant of the outside unit that was sub-divided into three rooms. My grandmother, sister and brother occupied one room that was enclosed from a balcony and my parents the other. The middle room was rented to a young couple. We had just one toilet and kitchen to share.

My family took the best room – a room at the front that had a balcony attached to it. As the head tenant, my mother underwrote the rent and charged the sub-tenants higher rents; so much so that, in return, we paid no rent for the space that our family occupied. It could be a severe drain on the resources of the family if the rooms were not fully let but, in practice, this seldom happened because there was such an acute shortage of supply at the time. Any accommodation was quickly taken up once it was released onto the market.

"We just wondered why you don't turn up any more," said Richard Zee. "Kwok Sun gave me your address. We tried to call you but the line was always busy."

"Yes, I know," I said. "The line is used by other tenants. I shall come tomorrow."

I closed the door behind me as I pushed the party towards the staircase landing. It was too small to accommodate all of them. I did not want them to see more of the inside of the flat.

I knew they were all there because they were curious about my background and, perhaps, to embarrass me. Behind my back, they had often joked at my expense. My nickname was 'Tag-Along'. I was seventeen years old at the time. For too long they had all treated me to drinks but I had never once reciprocated. It was no sweat for these rich kids to buy a round of drinks for ten boys but for me it was a different story. I simply could not afford it.

I was a mystery to them because the boys were all known to each other. They could probably guess that I was not from a similar background. It must have taken them by surprise that I lived in such squalid conditions, so many people crammed into one small space.

Richard Zee's parents were divorced. I knew him through Kwok Sun. He lived in a swanky new building in Tsim Sha Tsui, Hong Kong's premier tourist area. Richard's father was a *comprador* with Wheelock Marden, a British *hong* (conglomerate). He was always busy at work and seldom returned until late at night. Their apartment became a social club for boys and girls, mostly from wealthy families. Every afternoon the boys played poker while the girls gathered to chit-chat with Richard's sister who went to Maryknoll Convent, one of the best girls' schools in town. I was exposed to a circle of so-called friends with whom I had nothing in common and to which I certainly did not belong.

It was novel and fun at first but soon events caught up with me. Not being one of them, I was often made the subject of their ridicule. It was particularly hard for me to bear when I was teased in the presence of the girls – their way of earning credits in those girls' eyes.

"Hey, Robert, I'll bet you. I give you hundred to one if you can get any of the girls out on a date," one would say, to the laughter of the others.

Eventually I stopped going to the 'club'. Every time I was there I felt out of place, mostly ignored and, at times, joked at unnecessarily by the others. I did not belong there although Richard Zee and I remained good friends.

The people in the 'club' were almost all children of immigrants from Shanghai, of Ningbo origin. At heart these people, from the parents down to the children, all wanted to be Americans – just like every Indian in those days wanted to be an Englishman.

In the autumn of that year, they were all going abroad to study and the USA was the common destination. A President Line ship was the preferred mode of travel. Family members and friends would gather at the Ocean Terminal Pier to bid them goodbye. The sentimental nature of the occasion never failed to choke me with emotion. As the anchor was winched and the ship set sail, a sense of sadness mingled with loneliness would take a hold of me, not because yet another so-called friend was leaving but more because of self-pity. I could not help but blame my father for being so inadequate.

"Why are they all so lucky?" I asked Mother. "Why can't I be like them?"

Mother smiled. She did not reply.

I was lonely as I was the only one in the group who was left behind. Having tasted what it was like to be rich, I did not want to be with my old friends from my own background again. I was miserable. I desperately wanted to go abroad too – away from the mundane life I led but, above all, away from poverty.

I was perplexed until I remembered my 'Pak Tze': 'You'll break the family's coffers to go abroad. People of high birth will come to your assistance.'

"It is written in my stars," I murmured excitedly to myself after reading the passage for the umpteenth time. "I shall apply to go abroad too. I shall speak to my mother tomorrow."

The next day I waited until Mother had finished her chores and was sitting down.

"Mother, do you remember Richard Zee?" I said. "He called upon us a few months ago with a group of his friends and asked to see me. I felt thoroughly humiliated because they saw the way we live."

"Yes, I remember him. I told you not to mix with rich kids. It can make you miserable. Stick to your own class and be happy. What about Richard?"

"Well, almost everyone in the group has left this autumn," I said matter-of-factly. "They have all gone to the USA to continue their studies. If you approve, I would like to take a gap year. As you know, my high school grades are not particularly good. I can work for a year and save up enough to pay for my passage. I want to study abroad too."

"Be practical, Robert," she said. "You cannot compare yourself to those privileged kids. Even if you save up enough for the passage, we can't afford to support you on your father's salary. You know he only earns $900 a month and he has to support the whole family. Dreaming is good but don't lose sight of reality, my son."

"You mustn't snuff out my only hope in life, Mother," I said sorely. "Why is it that every other father can do it, yet mine can't? It's depressing."

The very next day I went to the British Council and, through them, I applied for a place in what was known as a 'Sink School'. Under the British system, a student gets promoted automatically until he sits public examinations. If he does not get good enough grades, he either drops out or he goes to a 'Sink School' to repeat the subjects until his grades improve and he moves to higher studies. These schools are subsidized by the local government and the tuition fees are low.

"Mother, I have been accepted by a school in London to do my matriculation," I told her. "I have saved up enough to pay for my own passage."

"How have you managed to do that?" Mother asked in surprise. "The trip to London is expensive, you know. It's beyond our means."

"From my salary… I get $300 a month and I have managed to save some of it. I have close to $1,000 in my bank account. With a bit of help from you, I should have enough to buy the plane ticket. Once I get to London, I can work to pay for my own expenses."

"But you know that they don't allow students to work in Britain, unlike the USA, don't you?" Mother said. She must have researched the subject.

I nodded. I could not hide my disappointment.

Strangely, that same year and out of the blue, Father was promoted to become the chief accountant in the company he worked for. His salary was increased by $400. That summer, the family moved out of the flat into even smaller accommodation. Grandmother had to go back to Ningbo. Thus, the family 'scraped together every penny' as predicted by my 'Pak Tze' and sent me to Britain that autumn.

What happened there was nothing short of a miracle.

# PART 3

# STUDENT DAYS

My father telexed his cousin, Lydia Tai Brooks, before I flew to London:

> Son Robert arriving London Heathrow 1 September, BOAC Flight 07, would appreciate it if you could put him up for few days before term starts. Love, Ting Kuan.

The plane made four stops en route to London. As it stopped in Calcutta, passengers took the opportunity to use the toilets in the transit lounge. Four attendants, all wearing overalls that said 'No Tipping' on the back, were at our service. Working as a team, they made sure everyone washed their hands and no one was allowed to leave until a gratuity in whatever currency had been given to the man at the door. Business was thriving. The Indians are enterprising.

The plane arrived as scheduled at Heathrow Airport. As I was expecting to be picked up, I waited for Aunt Lydia in the arrival lobby. She was not there. I had no means of contacting her. The instructions I had received were clear – wait until she comes.

Cleaners for the night shift began to mop the floors.

"Young man," a middle-aged cleaner said to me, "who are you waiting for? The last flight arrived hours ago and there won't be any more incoming flights until tomorrow."

He looked kind, the sort that would help others in distress.

"I'm waiting for my aunt to pick me up," I said, looking up at him from the floor where I had bedded down.

"Come, young man. Your aunt must have gone to Victoria Terminal," he said.

"Where is Victoria Terminal and how can I get there?" I asked, beginning to panic. 'That's it,' I thought, 'I must have waited at the wrong place. She is at the other terminal, wherever that is. How else can I explain her no-show?'

"I will soon be knocking off," said the cleaner. "I shall take you there. It is on my way. Just wait here. I will be back."

We reached Victoria Terminal after a bus ride. There was still no sign of Aunt Lydia. The cleaner took the trouble to enquire among the janitors there. No one had seen a Chinese woman fitting my aunt's description. If she had turned up, she would certainly have stayed long enough to be noticed.

"Thank you, you are very kind," I said. "I shall wait here until she shows up."

That evening, the same cleaner was on his way back to the airport for work. He stopped by at the terminal to see if I was alright. He found me curled up in the same spot. After buying me a cup of tea, he left, but moments later he returned. "I have just called the British Council and told them about you," he said. "A representative will be here soon. I have told them exactly where you are. Don't wander around. Stay put. They have arranged for you to go to a halfway house. Take this money. You will need it."

The stranger gave me two pounds. I told him I had money of my own, but he insisted. I could not thank the cleaner enough. He was the first Irishman I had ever met and what a kind person he was.

Much later, in the early hours of the next morning, an Englishman arrived.

"Are you Mr. Wang?" He bent down and touched me, waking me up. Tired, hungry and cold, I had fallen asleep.

"Yes, I am, sir," I replied excitedly. "You must be from the British Council."

"Yes, I'm Mr. Nicholls... John Nicholls," he introduced himself. "How long have you been lying here?"

"A little over a day here plus another day at Heathrow Airport when I arrived."

"You must be exhausted after such a long journey from Hong Kong and with all this waiting. Now, gather together all your belongings and follow me."

"Where are you taking me to?"

"The British Council has booked a room for you in a youth hostel. They will give you a good meal. You can wash yourself and take a good rest. You look as if you're in need of a good sleep. Tomorrow I will pick you up from there and take you to a cheaper hostel where you can stay until school starts."

At a hostel in Lancaster Gate, John showed me to my room. I was overjoyed by the sight of the bed, warm and inviting. The sheets were clean, lily white and immaculately starched, so tightly tucked into the bed that I had to wriggle hard to slip into their folds. And I had the room all to myself, a real treat and a completely new experience. I never slept better that night as I recovered from the ordeal. The next day I moved to the students' quarters at a university in Kent. I stayed there until the new term started.

My aunt never contacted me. The letters my father sent her were unanswered.

I was given directions on how to get from Kent to South London where Kennington College was located. The college stood in a neighbourhood that was full of old warehouses. Indeed, it took up the ground floor of one. Elephant & Castle was not an attractive area. It was bleak and unpleasant, very working class. But still, for me, it was a marked improvement on the Hong Kong I had come from.

At the college, all new students were asked to fill in the admission forms before they were assigned to a class. It soon became apparent that the school catered mostly to overseas students from various parts of the Commonwealth, with the emphasis on Africa. There was also a large contingent of students from different parts of South-East Asia: Malaysia, Thailand, Singapore and Hong Kong. Hong Kong was well represented. There were at least ten of us in the same class. The attraction among us was immediate. We could identify with each other – students from faraway Hong Kong congregating in a small corner of London – and the sense of endearment was overwhelming. The rest was made up of local drop-outs who were there to re-sit the O-Level subjects they had failed to pass the previous year.

"Why don't you join us for lunch?" a student asked one day. "It has been a while since I last saw you bringing your own lunch to school."

"I'm not hungry," I replied. "I am used to taking breakfast and dinner only. I skip lunch."

"But you used to bring your own lunch to school before."

I smiled and walked away. I did not want to tell him the truth: I could not afford lunch on my meagre allowance – a mere twenty-seven pounds sterling each month. I had nothing left after paying for my food and lodging at the hostel. I had to walk an hour, often in bitter cold, to get to the school at Elephant & Castle. In the beginning, I packed extra food from breakfast as lunch, but I stopped one day when the hostel manager warned me that if I stole food again I would be expelled.

I began to lose weight and I looked haggard, underfed and unkempt. My appearance was the least of my concerns. I was in the country to study; my mission was to pass examinations.

## MEETING AUNT DIANA

When I found the message in the pigeonhole in the hostel, I could not believe my eyes. Aunt Diana, the sister of Aunt Lydia, wanted to see me and suggested that I meet her at the Ritz Hotel.

Throughout my childhood, I had known that my father had a rich cousin who had married into one of the richest families in South-East Asia. Aunt Diana was someone special, dear to the hearts of those who knew her. She was elegant, beautiful and intelligent. She had a heart of gold, always willing to help those less fortunate than herself. The way my parents gloated over her made me, as a child, think that she was from a different planet. Her generosity was legendary. Every time she came to Hong Kong she would insist that she came to our home for dinner. Home was the shared apartment with other families crammed into a small space. Before she arrived, we worked hard to have the room scrubbed from top to bottom. We were given new clothes to wear. Mother would cook dishes from Ningbo that reminded Aunt Diana of home. A table would be set up in between two bunk beds at which we would sit, eat and talk.

As there was never enough money in the family, my father had to pawn his Rolex watch to pay for the 'feast'. My sister and I were posted at each end of the street so that, if we saw a familiar face, we could give a pre-arranged signal to alert Father. He would then change course and walk away from the pawnshop pretending he was going somewhere else.

Aunt Diana would always end the dinner by stuffing a packet into Mother's hand. The same ritual was repeated every time she visited.

"This is for you, Sau Chi," said Aunt Diana. "I didn't have time to buy a gift."

"No, Diana, I can't take this," said Mother as she pushed the packet back to her. "You have always been kind to us. I am grateful, from the bottom of my heart."

"You must. It is just a token gesture from me."

The see-saw ritual would continue as Aunt Diana made her way out of the flat, watched by neighbours who were jealous that my father had such a rich and generous cousin.

After she left, the family would return to the room. With great excitement, the money would be removed from the envelope and spread out on the bed. We would start counting.

"Wow... two thousand dollars!" I screamed. The faces of my parents lit up. It was more than double what father earned in a month. My sister and I embraced each other, jumping and dancing for joy.

"Two thousand dollars, we are rich," my sister screamed in disbelief. "Dad, take us to a restaurant."

"Tomorrow, tomorrow... I shall first redeem the watch from the pawnshop," said Father excitedly. "Then I shall take you all to Ruby's."

"Wow, Ruby's for its roast chicken," I shouted excitedly. A branch of Ruby's was located at Causeway Bay. It was best known for its succulent and tasty spring chicken. Being taken there was always a treat, although it rarely happened.

I was so excited I could not sleep that night.

# The Ritz Hotel, London

"Where do you think you're going, young man?" asked the doorman, wearing a top hat and long, green tailcoat, as I tried to enter the Ritz through the side door in Arlington Street.

"I have an appointment with my aunt for tea," I replied.

"I am sorry," he said, "you're not properly attired. You look untidy. Besides, you need a coat and tie for the Palm Court."

I did look as if I had not taken a bath for weeks. The clothes I was wearing were old and worn-out; they had not been washed in a while as I could not afford the cost of taking them to the launderette.

I had been unaware of my appearance until that afternoon. Arriving ahead of time for my tea meeting, I went to Green Park which is adjacent to The Ritz. It was a hot afternoon and the park was crowded. I found a rare space amongst the sea of sunbathers and, like everyone else, took off my clothes. From the corner of my eye, as I lay on the grass and basked under the sun, I noticed other sunbathers around me moving away one after another until a ring of empty lawn isolated me. Then I realized how bad I must smell.

"Please let me in. My aunt is waiting," I pleaded. "She is an important person."

"I don't care if she's the Queen of England. You still need to be properly attired," the doorman insisted. "But I can page her for you. What's her name?"

"Diana Eu," I replied.

A bellboy wrote the name on a small blackboard that had a bell attached to a pole which he rang as he made his way through the lobby and into the tea room. Shortly, Aunt Diana emerged.

"Can you lend the young man a tie?" Aunt Diana asked the doorman. "If you don't have one, please can you go across the road and buy one. There are plenty of men's shops in Jermyn Street, aren't there?"

As Aunt Diana spoke, she slipped a couple of pound notes into the doorman's palm.

"Yes, my lady." The doorman spoke in a tone that was quite different to how he had spoken to me. He whispered to a man in a tailed black coat and striped grey trousers. He disappeared and came back a few minutes later with a tie.

I could not believe my eyes when I entered Palm Court. The room was splendidly decorated, adorned by gold embellishments and matching coloured draperies and tablecloths. Soaked in the golden rays of the afternoon sun, the room glowed and glittered. I stood there in awe. I had never seen a room so beautiful and the people so elegant. They were as curious about me as I was about them.

"Sit down." Aunt Diana was obviously embarrassed by my unruly and dirty appearance. "What should I call you – Bo Bo or Robert?"

"Oh, it's Robert. Bo Bo is the nickname my grandmother gave me." I tried to impress her that I was no longer the boy she knew from the past.

"Okay, Robert. I need to get to the point. I am late for my appointment with the hairdresser."

As the waitress brought a fresh pot of tea in silverware, I noticed many varieties of finely cut sandwiches. There were smoked salmon, cucumber, cheese and egg mayonnaise. These sandwiches had been left untouched on the decks of the silver stand. The guests who had left obviously ate little.

"I've just bought a house in Golders Green for my children to stay in. You are welcome to stay there as well if you want. Perhaps you can also help me by looking after the house when we are not there. My children go home to Singapore for long holidays such as summer, Christmas and Easter."

I could not believe what I was hearing. She was the answer to all my prayers. She was giving me a place to stay. Think of what that would mean: I would not have to pay for my lodging, which would make a huge difference to my life. I would not have to go hungry any more.

"Of course, I would like to. Thank you, Aunt Diana. Thank you." I jumped at her offer. It was too good to refuse.

As we said goodbye, my mind was in a whirl. I could not believe my good fortune. After all the hardships I had been through, in just one stroke I was out of the woods. Then I thought of my 'Pak Tze': 'People of high birth will come to your assistance.'

I could not get over all those good sandwiches that were wasted on the table. I wished I could cart them off to eat for lunch in the days ahead.

"Would you like to take these sandwiches home?" It seemed as if Aunt Diana could read my mind.

"Yes, please," I said excitedly.

I was just trying to figure out how I could carry them when she summoned a waitress.

I sat on the bench of the underground train with three boxes of sandwiches stacked on my lap. I could not help showing off to the passengers that the boxes came from The Ritz; the crest on the boxes proved it.

# GOLDERS GREEN

Aunt Diana's house was semi-detached and Victorian in appearance and size. It was half an hour's walk from the nearest underground station, Golders Green. The road on which the house stood – Finchley Road – was one of the main conduit roads that channelled traffic from Central London to the north of England. It was a busy road.

The sitting and dining rooms on the ground floor were separate. They were entered from a large foyer. The kitchen was at the back and from there one entered the garden that was structured on two levels: flowerbeds at the back and a lawn at the front. The garden was full of pear trees and roses. It was immaculately maintained when I was first introduced to the house.

There were three bedrooms on the first floor and one in the attic that was as large as the entire floor below. I was assigned the middle room on the first floor which I was to share with David, the second son of the family.

The house was stocked with antique furniture that came with the house when Aunt Diana bought it. It was not the most attractive of houses – large, dark and gloomy as was to be expected from a period house. However, I was in awe of its size, never having seen let alone lived in a Victorian house before.

I moved into the house that summer after Aunt Diana had returned home to Singapore. I had the house all to myself for a couple of months. In the first week I took up residence there, I was moving up and down the stairs and wandering from one room to another literally non-stop just to feel the sensation of living there. It was a completely new experience. Never in my wildest dreams did I think that I would be given this treat – having this great big house all to myself.

"Oh…" I screamed in pain.

I had just finished dinner and was doing the dishes when I felt an excruciating pain in my thumb. Whatever it was, I had squeezed it so hard that it became an unrecognisable mess. My thumb began to swell – it grew bigger and bigger until it was the size of a golf ball. I thought I was going to die. I placed the crushed creature on a clean sheet of paper, drew a circle around it and wrote: This bit me. Then I lay down on the sofa waiting for the worst to happen. It did not dawn upon me then that I had been stung by a hornet.

The next morning the swelling had subsided. I was still alive. I went out into the garden at the back. It should have been a beautiful terraced garden with rose beds on the upper level but unfortunately I had not looked after it as I should have done. I was not to be blamed because I had no notion of gardening. It was not part of my culture to know that the lawn had to be mown, the garden weeded and the apple trees pruned.

"Good morning, Robert," said the next-door neighbour. "I see that you are finally out. I suppose you are here to cut the long grass."

"I am waiting for the snow to cover the grass up," I said cheekily. "Good day, sir."

I returned to the kitchen. I never liked the couple next door. They were mean, always complaining that I did not do this and that in keeping with the neighbourhood.

Knock, knock…

"Who's there?" I asked. I was not expecting a visitor. It was a Sunday and Aunt Diana and her children were not due to arrive for a couple of weeks.

"Is that you, Robert?" A female voice came through the letterbox, the steel flap pushed up from the outside so that the visitor could see through. "It's Lydia."

"Who's Lydia?"

"Diana's sister."

My heart leapt. Although I had seen Aunt Lydia a couple of times when I was a child, I could not remember what she looked like. This was the first time I had met her since I had arrived more than a year before. She was the aunt who was supposed to fetch me from the airport. She had not turned up, nor did she contact me afterwards. At the back of my mind I regarded her as a 'wicked aunt' who wanted nothing to do with her poor nephew. But she was sister to Aunt Diana, my provider, to whom I owed everything.

I quickly opened the door. She came inside with her whole family in tow.

"Hi, Robert," said Aunt Lydia in her impeccable English accent. "Meet my husband, John Brooks, and my daughters, Jacqueline and Phillippa."

The children were lovely. I took to them immediately.

"So, this is the house Diana bought," she said as she looked up and down. "Mind if I take a look?"

"Of course not," I replied nervously.

The house was a mess. I had just got up and was making my breakfast. I was thinking of cleaning that day but I had risen late. I did not know how she would react when she saw the condition the house was in. Her reputation preceded her so I was nervous.

After inspecting the house, she came storming down the staircase.

"Robert, this just won't do. The house looks ghastly. When did you clean up last?"

"Last Sunday."

"Come, come... don't lie. It must be longer. The dust is an inch thick."

"Oh, oh... perhaps it was the Sunday before." I blushed.

"How long have you been moved in?"

"About two months."

"How many times have you cleaned up this place since then?"

I did not wish to lie to her. Before I could answer she continued.

"You know, Diana has not put you here so that you can live in a holiday home." She spoke in the voice of a matron, steely sharp. "You must earn your keep. Do you understand?"

"Yes, Aunt Lydia," I replied meekly.

It was a rude awakening. She had put me in my place. I was not there as a guest; I was there as a houseboy, a sort of caretaker. I was expected to do the household work or I would be booted out.

"Diana will be arriving with her children on the fifth of September," she said. "Robert, can you make sure the house is in good order? Diana will take the master bedroom together with her daughter, Helena. The eldest son, Dick, will use the room facing the front. David will share your bedroom. Please make sure the bed sheets are changed and the house is as clean as a whistle. The house needs to be vacuumed and cleaned and the garden must be tended and—"

"Take it easy on the young man, Lydia. Give him a break." Mr. Brooks spoke for the first time. I was shaking with fear.

"Now, we have brought along lunch," she continued. "Can you set the table? Do you know how to use the oven? The ham and potatoes need reheating."

I nodded.

The two girls became impatient. "Dad, I want to go out," Jacqueline yelled.

Their father opened the door to the garden. It was in an unruly mess. The grass was knee-high and the rose garden had all but disappeared in the thick of the bushes.

"Be careful, wait for me," he shouted at the girls as they ran past him.

No sooner had he gone out than he returned.

"Lydia, put the kettle on," he said. "There's a massive wasps' nest in the tree. Make sure the girls stay inside. See if you can find a hat and a work coat. Get me the pair of sunglasses from my jacket. Also, check if there is a toolbox in the house."

Mr Brooks reappeared fully protected from top to bottom. He carried with him the kettle and was about to go back into the garden. The girls and I watched from the kitchen window with excitement.

"Wait, John," Aunt Lydia shouted. "Come back. You had better get Robert to do the job."

"What's wrong?" he asked. "I am all ready. I can do it."

"No, you stay with the kids," she insisted. "Robert, get dressed. Go out and get rid of that damned nest. It's your job, not John's."

I protected myself as best I could. The nest was in the corner of the back fence, next to an old pear tree. It was the largest nest I had ever seen, measuring some two feet in diameter, and it was buzzing with activity. Even before I started, the wasps began to attack me. I emptied the whole kettle of boiling water onto the nest. Then, using a hammer, I smashed it into bits and, with a spade, flattened what was left on the ground. Hundreds of wasps flew around my head. I was pleased none of the stings penetrated — I was well protected, thanks to Mr. Brooks.

My encounter with Aunt Lydia was a wake-up call for me. When Aunt Diana and her children finally arrived in early September, I was prepared. The house had been given a thorough cleaning. The bed sheets were washed, starched and tucked in the same way as the hostel at Lancaster Gate. The lawn was mown. I had even managed to resurrect the rose garden from what was left on the terrace.

Aunt Diana treated me like one of her own. Together with her children, she took me everywhere before term started. I sampled what it was like to live life at the top – shopping, restaurants, museums and sightseeing, activities that were completely alien to a poor boy.

But the 'honeymoon' was short-lived. Soon my nightmare began. The root cause was that I did not belong there. Like we say in Chinese: 'the host provides the chicken and you contribute the soybean sauce.' It was fine if I could afford the sauce. The truth was I could not. When Aunt Diana was there, she paid for everything. But it was a different story when her eldest son, Dick, was in charge. He was a few years younger than me. Although I did not have to pay rent, I had to share food costs. I could ill afford the kind of food they ate: I could not afford the pork trotter let alone the leg of pork. Before the children arrived, I lived on bread alone and, at times, I went without food. When I craved meat, I would set up a makeshift net to trap wild pigeons. There were many in the garden as the house abutted a park.

The next-door neighbour was horrified and disgusted to see me setting traps for pigeons. It was another source of friction between us.

I spent my first Christmas alone. The Eu children went home to Singapore. The weather was inclement, the sort of day when folks would stay home and enjoy the warmth of a real fire and a traditional Christmas dinner with family and friends, a time to sing carols and exchange presents. It was wet, cold and downright miserable. By nightfall it had started to snow heavily. The fog was so thick one could hardly see ten feet away. I was homesick and I craved meat. I thought about roast goose and the pair of resident geese on the pond in Golders Hill Park.

I plucked up courage, put on my coat and a ski balaclava I found in Dick's room, wore an extra hat over the balaclava as another layer of protection, and rolled a college scarf around my neck before setting off for the park.

It was getting dark. The street was deserted. It was snowing so heavily I could hardly see where I was going. I pushed open the park gate. The path had disappeared under the snow. I came to the pond. It was frozen solid. The pair of geese came wiggling towards me, gleefully honking in anticipation of a feed from a good Samaritan who had not forgotten them, even in such bad weather. As the female goose reached me, I struck quickly. I placed a sack over her head, gripped her neck and pulled with all the might I could muster. Both geese began to squawk and hiss so loudly that it sent shivers down my spine. I became panicky. The weight of the female goose was such that I could not lift the sack over the fence. In the ensuing struggle, the sack came off and the pair of geese began to attack me. I turned and ran for my life. It was the loneliest and most joyless Christmas Eve I have ever had. Yet, on reflection, it was also my funniest.

≈≈≈≈≈

The bowling alley across the road from the house in Finchley Road soon became a clubhouse for Dick and his friends. He was by nature gregarious and outgoing. His friends descended upon the house in droves every weekend, arriving in fancy cars – Ferraris, Lamborghinis, Mercedes Benz, TR4s and the like.

I was caught in an unenviable position. There was no way I could keep up with this lavish lifestyle even if I only had to share the food bills. By the middle of every month, my allowance would be so depleted I could hardly afford the tube fare to get to my college. Queen Mary College in the East End is some distance away from Golders Green.

The financial toll was just part of it. The psychological damage was even worse. Everyone knew that I was the poor boy Dick's mother had installed to live free of charge so that I could look after the house. In the eyes of these rich kids, I was merely a servant.

"Fuck you!" Dick screamed at me. "You burnt the chicken."

I blushed and apologized profusely to the diners at the table who were waiting for dinner to be served. Chicken cooked in thick soybean sauce was my speciality, having learned how to cook the dish from my mother. But on this occasion I had left the chicken in the pot longer than I should have done, as I had other chores to attend to.

"Dick, don't be so harsh on your cousin," a girl at the table said with a giggle.

"What cousin?" Dick retorted. "He is just a sort of cousin."

"Now, Robert, go across the road and buy some chicken curry." Another friend whipped out a fiver from his wallet and tossed it at me.

"Yes, yes, I'm sorry," I said. "I'll do it right away."

I bowed in shame, took the note and dashed across the street to a row of restaurants. The Indian curry house was a favourite of Dick and his friends.

I reheated the curry and dished the best parts of the chicken out on plates to the others, leaving only the wings for myself. Then I poured them drinks – red and white wine with sparkling water – before I settled down at one corner of the table away from the others to eat by myself.

Every now and then I was asked to hand them the chutneys, raisins, shredded coconut and other condiments.

I ate in silence. I was not included in the conversation at the table as Dick and his friends ate, drank, joked and danced.

It was sheer torture. The dinner seemed to last forever.

"I'll do the dishes," one of the girls said to Dick.

"No, let Robert do it," he replied.

"I insist," she said.

"Well, suit yourself," Dick shrugged dismissively. "I've told you you don't have to."

I cleared the table and placed the dirty dishes on one side of the sink to help her when she was washing up. I was happy to go up to my room and forget about the unpleasantness of the evening. However the girl had a sudden change of mind and turned and stopped me as I was walking out of the kitchen.

"Robert, you had better do the dishes."

I nodded in agreement.

I could not sleep that night. The radio by my bed was playing *El Condor Pasa (If I Only Could)* by Simon & Garfunkel:

> *I would rather be the hammer than a nail.*
> *Yes, I would.*
> *If I only could I surely would.*
>
> *I'd rather be a forest than a street.*
> *Yes, I would.*
> *If I could I surely would.*
>
> *I'd rather feel the earth beneath my feet.*
> *Yes, I would.*
> *If I only could I surely would.*

Tears came rolling down my cheeks. I said to myself, "I vow that my children will not have to go through what I am going through."

In my room, I could hear the noise from the party continuing downstairs.

≈≈≈≈≈

About two weeks later I was at Aunt Sheila's house for dinner.

"Please can I have another bowl of rice?" I politely asked the servant, Ah Chut – 'number 7' in a family of daughters in an era when girls were considered inferior to boys.

She ignored me.

"Chut Cher." I addressed her in a more respectful manner as 'cher' means 'sister', "Please can I have another bowl of rice?"

She looked at me out of the corner of one eye, tilted her upper lip and, with arms folded, looked up to the ceiling to avoid any further eye contact with me.

The two servants stood to attention at the table. Other diners had a fresh bowl of food handed to them from behind even before the last was finished. The table was covered with at least ten dishes including shark's fin soup, braised abalone, steamed fish, sea cucumber, vegetables and bird's nest. For me it was a feast, but for Aunt Sheila it was a typical dinner. This time it was laid out for her niece and nephews next door – her house was just four houses down the road. She had three children of her own, Cornelia, Brian and Calvin.

When Aunt Sheila moved to London with her children, two of her best servants accompanied her. Ah Chut and Ah Hing belonged to a sect of servants from Canton who were known as 'comb-ups' – their hair was tied into plaits as a symbol of their vow of celibacy. They stayed single in order to be completely assimilated into the family they served; their loyalty was legendary and, in return, they were often treated as members of the family.

I suppose the servants thought I should not be at the same table as the masters. I should have eaten with the servants instead. I did not know my place.

I didn't know whether anyone else at the table had noticed the embarrassment the servant's slight had caused me. If they had, they did not show it. I swallowed the bitter pill and sat quietly at the table. It would be out of order if I were to rise and fill my own bowl in the kitchen.

My financial situation deteriorated until finally it became quite untenable. A year after arriving in London and a few months into staying in my rich aunt's house I could not make ends meet and, by the middle of the month, I was short of money.

"Mr. Wang, you must live within your means," said John Littleton, manager of the Westminster Bank Golders Green branch. "You cannot come to me at the end of each month and ask for permission to have your account overdrawn by five pounds. I told you last month that I was not prepared to let you have this overdraft again. I am telling you now for the last time."

"I am sorry, Mr. Littleton," I pleaded with him, "but I need the overdraft – just five pounds – to tide me over for the month. My remittance arrives punctually."

"No, I'm sorry," Mr. Littleton said firmly, rising and ushering me out of his room.

I was almost in tears wondering how I was going to survive the next few days and face up to Dick's pressure to foot my share of the food bills, not to mention the fact that I needed the overdraft to pay for my travel to lectures in the East End.

There were not many doors left that I could knock on for help. I could not approach Aunt Lydia, knowing how she had treated me and the kind of person she was. I didn't know what to do.

Then I thought of the Hong Kong Students' Liaison Office and found the address from the telephone directory.

"Yes, Mr. Wang, what can I do for you?" Mr. Ferguson, the Head of the Commission asked as he warmly welcomed me into his posh office in Pall Mall.

It was not every day that a student wanted to see the commissioner. He must have assumed that all students from Hong Kong were wealthy.

"You see, Mr. Ferguson, I am a student," I said.

"Yes, I know," he interjected.

"I'm in a fix," I continued. "I don't have enough money to continue with my studies. I am not permitted to work. If I don't get help, I shall have to go home. I really want to complete my studies in this country. Can you help me, Mr. Ferguson?"

"I have to admit this is a most unusual request. In fact, this is the first time I've come across one of this nature. I'm afraid we have no means of providing financial assistance to needy students. You will have to think of somewhere else. Have you thought of applying for a scholarship? Did you do well in your A-Levels?"

"Well, I got straight credits in the four subjects I took and got accepted into the college to read law," I replied. "If my grades do not qualify me for a scholarship, can I take out a student loan which I'll repay when I start work?"

"I am afraid we don't operate student loans here, old chap, but leave it to me. I'll see what I can do. Don't call me. I'll call you once there is news. Good day, Mr. Wang."

"Thank you, Mr. Ferguson. You are most kind. I will really appreciate it if anything can be done in my case. I need help badly."

I bowed as I left his office.

I waited and waited. Mr. Ferguson never called. None of my calls to him got past his secretary.

Despite being in the depths of despair, a glimmer of hope appeared on the horizon.

"Robert, can you come and babysit for us this weekend?" Aunt Lydia called me unexpectedly one day.

"Of course, Aunt Lydia."

"Take a train to Lewisham this Friday. We will pick you up at the station, say at 6.30 p.m."

I packed my books and headed for Lewisham after my last tutorial class.

The Brooks lived in a modern house in the suburbs. It was not large but, being new, the house had all the facilities associated with modern living: central heating, skylights, a fully-equipped kitchen and a sizeable garden. It was cosy, warm and comfortable, a vast improvement on the dark, cold, impersonal and oppressive house at Golders Green. It was a delight to babysit the two girls.

"I would love to babysit for you again," I said as Mr. Brooks dropped me off at the station. "Jacqueline and Phillippa are such wonderful children."

"Of course, if you wish you can come every weekend," he replied.

It was a good trade-off – a perfect arrangement that was win-win for both sides. The Brooks got me to babysit and do household work for them every weekend and, in return, they gave me food and lodging. I had a quiet room in which I could study undisturbed. I no longer had to work as a houseboy during the many parties that were thrown at the Golders Green house at weekends.

"Robert, you are being exploited by Aunt Lydia," Dick said.

I smiled. Dick could never understand how glad I was to be exploited. With the weekend expenses gone, I was able to live within my means again. It was a lot better than going around begging for help from the likes of the bank manager and the commissioner.

'I'm afraid you'll have to clean up the party mess yourself,' I thought.

# THE REPORT

*Dear Aunt Diana,*

*I write to report to you incidents involving John Kwek. As you know, John is a good friend of Dick. He comes to the house often* when Dick is here. He continues to come after Dick is home for the summer. He brings this English girl to the house with or without Dick being present. Dick used to leave a key underneath a brick in the front garden. Since Dick left, I took the liberty of removing it. Once, John Kwek came with this girl and asked me why the key was not there. He was visibly upset. I told him I needed your permission before I could let him use the house. Nevertheless, he forced his way inside and the two of them went straight up to the attic room. Then I discovered he was coming back repeatedly, sometimes in the middle of the night when I was asleep. I did not know how he gained entry until one day I noticed the window latch in the sitting room was unfastened. He can no longer get in at will after I locked it.

Since then he has been threatening me. He says that, as Dick has given him permission, he can come and go at will. He will show me 'the colour' if I try to stop him again. I took his remark to mean he would subject me to a beating.

John is also known as 'Big John'. He stands 6 foot 4 inches tall and weighs over 200 pounds. I can only say I am physically in awe of him.

What should I do? I await your instructions.

Also, Aunt Diana, I would like to let you know I have signed up for Connaught Hall for the new term that begins in October. It is an inter-collegiate hall, located at Tavistock Square, next to University College.

I would like to take this opportunity to express my deep appreciation for what you have done for me in the past. Without your kindness in allowing me to stay, I really doubt I could have lasted this long in this country. I probably would have had to discontinue my studies and go home.

From the bottom of my heart, Aunt Diana, thank you. You are the kindest person I have ever met.

With lots of love,

Robert

I was eager to get out as I really could no longer keep up with the lifestyle of the rich, and also I longed to be free again. On my own, I could do as I wished and live the modest way to which I was accustomed.

I moved into Connaught Hall just before the start of the new academic year. The hall was a hive of activity. Students were arriving from all over the country and many from overseas. There were some who had returned to stay for another year and those, like me, who were there for the first time. Trunks and bags were piled up haphazardly in the lobby. The porters were busy directing the traffic, assigning rooms and giving out directions.

I was in Room 420 sorting out my belongings when the buzzer beeped. I walked down the staircase from the fourth floor.

"You buzzed me?" I asked the porter.

"You are?"

"Mr. Wang of Room 420."

"Ah, Mr. Wang, you have a visitor. He is somewhere… there he is."

John Kwek came upstairs from the basement. He had been to the toilet. His long shadow cast by the afternoon sun that was shining through the main door reminded me of how big he was. He was not called 'Big John' for nothing. My heart sank and I sensed trouble. Why on earth would Big John want to visit me? We were never friends. He was Dick's friend. Then I remembered the letter I had written to Aunt Diana.

"Robert, can we talk?" he asked. He was visibly upset. The thought of being beaten up by this man in front of all these students in the lobby was unpalatable. My ego got the better of me, even though I knew it would have been safer for me to stay there and have a lot of witnesses if he attempted to use force on me. If I was destined to be his punchbag, I might as well take him up to my room. At least no one would be there to see it.

"Sure," I said. "We can go to my room."

No sooner had we got into the room than he grabbed my collar and lifted me up from the floor, almost to his eye level. Big John was nearly a foot taller than me and weighed twice as much. His facial features were contorted. The whites of his eyes were traversed by red veins. He looked vicious and he was angry, very angry.

"You little bastard, you killed my grandmother," he screamed at me.

"Please let me down," I pleaded. "I can explain."

He tossed me into the corner of the room and started kicking me. I could hardly breathe and was gasping for air.

"Please, please, how could I have killed your grandmother? I don't even know her."

"What did you write to Aunt Diana?"

"I made a report to her. I was asked to let her know everything that happened at the house."

"Do you know she went to our house and confronted my mother? There was a heated argument. My grandmother was caught in the middle and she had a heart attack and died there and then."

He howled as his anger returned and he seized me by the back of the collar with one hand.

"Please let me explain." I was in tears.

He hauled me onto one side of the bed and sat down beside me with my collar still in his grip. Our collective body weight proved too much and, with a loud crack, one bed leg gave way.

"Speak, speak before I break your neck."

"I'm a poor boy. Aunt Diana put me there so that I had somewhere to live and she got someone to look after the house for her," I said as I recovered my breath. "I was just a houseboy. I did the household chores; I swept, dusted and cleaned up. I had to report to her everything that happened at the house. If I did not do as I was told, I would have been dismissed. Please forgive me for writing to her. I was just doing my duty. I am sorry… I am really, really sorry about your grandmother. Not even in my wildest dreams did I expect this harm to come to your family. Please, please forgive me."

Big John listened attentively. Slowly he loosened his grip on me. Then he got up and headed for the door. He didn't speak and I never saw him again.

# The French Connection

Winters in England are cold. The winter of 1966 was particularly so. I yearned for spring to arrive. Connaught Hall, however, was centrally heated. It was warm and students moved around in summer clothes. Everyone was friendly and it was like one big holiday camp. My finances improved. My sister Ruby, who was then nineteen and newly graduated from a secretarial school, had started to work and she dutifully handed over her salary every month to the family. With the extra income, my father was able to increase my monthly allowance by an additional ten pounds. It made a huge difference. I no longer had to go hungry and food at the hall was bountiful. I ate well. Prejudice was a thing of the past and I did not have to live in fear any more. I was my own agent, free to do what I liked. I studied well and enjoyed my leisure. I made new friends from different parts of the world as the hall was so cosmopolitan.

As a concession to the large contingent of foreign students there, I was elected to the House Committee and made the bar convener. It was a plum job much sought after by others. That job thrust me to the centre of social life. I gained instant recognition and respect. It was my duty to open the bar every night for an hour from 9.30 p.m. onwards. A queue of thirsty students cheered me on as I arrived. For the first time in my life, I felt I was someone important and it was a wonderful feeling. Life had taken a turn for the better.

I even saved enough to go on holiday for the first time. That winter, I joined a holiday in the Lake District that had been organized by the British Council. It was enjoyable beyond description and I met a girl.

It was New Year's Eve. After the clock strikes midnight, it is traditional that the first person to cross the threshold should be a dark man with bread in one hand, a piece of coal in the other and carrying a broom under one arm. After the first choice, an African student, refused to play the part – he said it was discriminatory – I volunteered to be that dark person.

A white girl opened the door to a chorus of cheers as the New Year was heralded in. I had noticed her before with the same group of holidaymakers when they had assembled at King's Cross Station in London at the start of the holiday, and at the breakfast table. She was there with another girl from France. Although we had nodded to each other, we had never spoken to each other.

"Happy New Year," I spoke the words as I was instructed. "I sweep away the bad and bring in the good. I bring you food and warmth and good tidings for the New Year."

The girl and I embraced and kissed each other on the cheek. Amidst great gaiety, we danced to the music of the pipes. The Lake District sits on the border with Scotland and the castle was more Scottish than English.

We took an instant liking to each other.

"Where are you from?" I asked as we danced.

"I'm from France," she replied in a heavy French accent.

"Which part?"

"You know Versailles, near Paris? And you?"

"I am from Hong Kong. My name is Robert. I study law at London University. How about you?"

"My name is Aceline. I am an au pair in this country."

"What's an au pair?" I asked.

"I came to England to study English. I live with an English family. They give me free food and lodging and I do the domestic work while I learn English. Last year I graduated with a degree in literature from the Sorbonne University in Paris."

Her reply had a ring of familiarity. It dawned on me there and then that we were from a similar background.

"You know, I was also an au pair," I said. "I did household work. I took care of the house. In exchange I got my lodging for free but I had to pay for my own food."

She listened attentively as I related my story about Golders Green. We had a lot in common to talk about and the conversation flowed.

That night we talked and danced until dawn. It was the most memorable New Year's Eve of my life. By the time dawn broke we had grown very close to each other. We ate breakfast together. It consisted of Scottish whisky, meat and porridge. The porridge tasted awful. It was salty, completely alien to my palate, but it was not important. There was sweetness in my heart.

All through the remainder of the holiday we kissed and held hands. We felt good about each other. It was a joyous holiday.

Back in London, life settled into a routine. We saw each other once a week. We walked in Hyde Park, roamed the streets of London and visited museums and art galleries. We were happy together. I could not help but marvel at my new station in life. I was happy beyond words and head over heels in love... my first love. She was too.

"You are a virgin?" I asked her one day.

"Oui, Oubert, mon cheri," she replied.

"Why? You are already twenty."

"Nobody has ever asked me."

I laughed. It sounded so frightfully honest and naively cute – it was just the way she had been brought up, a protected species.

# THE HOLIDAY

In 1967 the Cultural Revolution in China spilled over into the British colony.

Hong Kong was rocked by daily demonstrations and disturbances. The strikes organized by the leftist trade unions spread like wildfire. In no time, all left-wing organizations were involved. The uprising against the British rule in Hong Kong got into full swing. Schools ceased classes; teachers and students were out in the streets in full force; and workers downed tools and took part in daily demonstrations and riots.

All Communist-owned buildings were hung with anti-British slogans. Revolutionary music played from loudspeakers. In the central business district, the Bank of China blared out messages against continued colonial rule from its many public address systems. In reply, the Colonial Government installed bigger speakers in the Hongkong and Shanghai Bank Building which played loud music to drown out the noise from next door.

The Government closed all leftist schools and banned publication of left-wing newspapers. Police swooped on premises where the troublemakers were known to be hiding. In one raid, the police discovered bombs and weapons and a whole factory dedicated to the manufacture of weapons. They also found a hospital complete with an operating theatre.

The situation in China was unstable and fragile. There was genuine fear that People's Liberation Army (PLA) regiments stationed at the border would storm into Hong Kong. Indeed, armed militia from the People's Republic of China fired at Hong Kong police on the border. Some British officers there wanted to return fire. Luckily they were stopped. Otherwise the situation might have escalated out of control.

There was one incident involving a senior British police officer. He had wandered off into no-man's-land at the border as he wanted to talk to a group of peasants there. He was soon surrounded by an angry crowd carrying hoes and other hand tools. He was thrown to the ground and attacked. When he shouted for help, a lone Gurkha soldier went to his rescue with his *kukri* knife drawn. He charged into the mob, chopping and slashing the attackers. He was then seen to pick up the injured officer and run back to the Hong Kong side of the border. That soldier was later awarded a medal for his bravery.

Thousands of bombs, known then as '*bor law*' because of their resemblance to a pineapple, were planted throughout Hong Kong, some real, others hoaxes. Many people were injured and some were killed.

Those who spoke up against the troublemakers were, in some cases, killed. Lam Bun was a popular anti-leftist radio commentator. His broadcasts attracted a large following. He condemned the riots, the leaders and those who took part. He was targeted by a death squad. They dressed up as road workers and a roadblock was set up. When his car was stopped, he was prevented from getting out. The car was set alight and Lam was burned to death.

Speculation was rife that a regiment of PLA soldiers under the command of Lin Piao, Mao's designated successor, was given the order to retake Hong Kong. Rumour had it that the British sent a high-powered secret mission to Beijing to ask Zhou En Lai, the Premier, whether it was indeed the wish of Beijing to take back Hong Kong.

Hong Kong was an extremely jittery city at this time and property prices plummeted. Many of its citizens left for safer shores. They sold what they could and uprooted their families to Vancouver – the favourite destination for most families due to its large enclave of immigrants from Hong Kong. Those who punted against Hong Kong lost; others like Li Ka Shing, Hong Kong's richest man, who bet the other way, amassed fortunes on the back of the fears of others. It was a time when fortunes changed hands on an epic scale.

I watched Lee Kuan Yew, Singapore's Prime Minister, in an interview on the BBC while he was in London for the Commonwealth Prime Ministers' Conference. He left a deep impression on me.

Lee was asked something that obviously he did not want to answer. "Since the Commonwealth leaders last met, the earth has spun around the sun and the moon around the earth…" he said.

When he was asked about Hong Kong, he replied quite bluntly, "Hong Kong is doomed. Singapore is having a mild boom." The sentences almost rhymed. He spoke perfect English.

I could not help myself. I alone stood up in salute and applauded his comments in the hall's TV room. I had found my hero there and then. The man filled me with admiration and, after that, I studiously read every speech he made and every article written about him. As a Chinese, I was proud of him as a compatriot who could not only measure up but, in many ways, could also show he was better than the best of the Brits in those days. He was a leader I could easily identify with.

The next day, Lee's picture was splashed across the front page of the Daily Mail with the caption:

"Lee Kuan Yew, a Prime Minister we would rather have to be our own."

My father apparently also thought Hong Kong was doomed. He gathered every penny he could lay his hands on and borrowed the rest. That summer I received one hundred pounds.

He wrote in a blue aerogramme:

*Dear Son,*

*The situation in Hong Kong goes from bad to worse. There are bombs everywhere. Today a popular broadcaster was assassinated by a death squad. God knows who is next. The situation can easily get out of control. PLA soldiers can cross over the border and retake Hong Kong any time. I have scraped together every penny I can lay my hands on and will send you by telegraphic transfer 100 pounds, enough for you to last for a few months. If indeed Hong Kong goes under then I am afraid you will have to make do with this money and fend for yourself. Go find yourself a part-time job. Hong Kong holds no future for you if the Communists take over. Stay in London, your only hope for a better life. Under no circumstances should you return.*

*We all miss you.*

*Love,*

*Dad*

I was completely overwhelmed, never having had so much money. Instead of saving it for the next few months, I planned a holiday with Aceline.

Packing a tent and our few belongings, we set off for Europe. We crossed the Channel and landed at the French port of Le Havre. From there we hitched our way to Paris. While in Paris we visited the Notre Dame. There is a fountain into which people, mostly tourists, toss coins for good luck. Not every coin finds its way into the fountain basin. Some fall into the pool surrounding it. No one took any notice of the coins, least of all us. We were rich then.

From Paris we got lifts down to Lyon, then Montpellier, west to Toulouse and the south of France. All through France we stayed in pensions and ate in restaurants. In the Bordeaux area, we visited the vineyards. We learned that during the time of Louis XIV, sixty-five vineyards were accredited with Vin De Grand Cru status. Today, only a handful more have been added to the original list.

"I know how the vineyards were graded in those days because my family are descendants of Louis XIV," said Aceline. "On the wrong side of the bed, that is – we are descended from a mistress of the king."

"Are you proud of your heritage?" I asked.

"Fiercely proud. Not many people in France can claim to be descendants of Louis XIV, you know."

Hitching a ride is easy if one knows where to wait. The best spot is any roundabout indicating 'Centre Ville' and 'Toutes Directions'. Cars slow down there and drivers are inclined to stop. Perhaps they were student hitch-hikers once and so they are glad to stop for others as a way of repaying those who stopped for them before. That way a good tradition continues.

Once, somewhere in the south of France, we hitched a long ride, more than eight hours in the same car. By the time it got dark, we were tired and hungry. The driver dropped us off at the first campsite. When we got up the next day, we found we were in the middle of nowhere in an area where the farmers grew peaches.

After a hearty breakfast of peaches, sweet and juicy beyond description and the size of small melons, we started hitching for a ride but no car would stop on the highway.

"Aceline, you'd better act as bait," I suggested. "Lift your skirt a bit higher and show your legs. I'll hide behind that peach tree."

Aceline nodded in agreement. We had pulled the same trick before. It worked every time. Normally, when I emerged from hiding, it was too late for the driver to change his mind and we would be given another ride.

The hot legs worked. A driver took the bait and his car came to a screeching stop. However, it overshot us by at least thirty yards. As Aceline rushed towards the car, the driver must have noticed me following closely on her heels. The disappointed driver put his foot down and took off like a rocket again.

A party of workers arrived late morning to repair the road on the opposite side. Road signs reading 'Danger' and 'Roadworks Ahead' were set up to warn the motorists. By the time the workers left in late afternoon, Aceline and I were still trying to hitch a lift. We were dehydrated, tired and hungry, having remained under the blazing sun all day.

"Robert, why don't you go over to the other side of the road?" Aceline said. "Bring those signs over here."

"What a smart girl!"

We set up our own checkpoint. Cars had to slow down as the drivers negotiated their way through the remaining open lane. We managed to hitch a ride into the next town. I just could not believe how clever Aceline was. It was getting dark by this time and, without her quick thinking, we would have been stuck all night on the highway miles away from civilization.

From France we travelled over the border into Spain. We went through Madrid and Toledo down to Granada and the Alhambra and up the coast, arriving at the Costa Dorada on the east side.

There we settled down at a campsite near the Roman town of Tarragona. It was an upmarket campsite frequented by wealthy holidaymakers from northern Europe: mostly British, Germans, Dutch, Belgians and Scandinavians.

"Look, we're completely dwarfed by the 'skyscrapers' around us," Aceline said, pointing to the huge tents and caravans of our neighbours. "Look at the size of that kitchen."

We could not help but marvel at the gadgets the campers had brought with them. Some of the tents were the size of marquees, with sitting, dining and sleeping areas, and equipped with toilets. They had all their home comforts. Our little tent was pitiful by comparison; folded up, it could fit into a backpack.

"We're in for the long haul," I said. "We can even plant some flowers around the tent. Tomorrow we'll go into town and buy a stove and cooking utensils. Wine is cheaper than water and is available everywhere. At the market they sell cheap fish that have been freshly caught. Seafood cooked in wine – how does that sound to you? It's delicious. Let's settle in for a really good holiday. I'm fed up with all the hitch-hiking we've done to get here."

For the next month or so, we spent our days on the beach and at night we roamed the narrow cobblestone streets of Tarragona, watching young men in black capes playing guitars, with singing, dancing and merrymaking against the backdrop of old buildings, some dating back to Roman times. Tarragona is romantic. We were pleased we had planned the journey so that we were able to spend time there. We were completely immersed in the festive atmosphere of the town's piazza which was filled with revellers every night.

We were also intoxicated by each other's company. We were blissfully in love.

Spain is supposed to be dry and sunny. Much of the land is arid giving rise to the illusion that it never rains. This is not the case.

In the middle of one night, we were awakened by the sound of lightning and torrential rain. Within minutes, water had inundated the campsite. All our belongings were submerged under a couple of inches of water. Then the flood came and washed away everything in its path. We managed to grab a few of our possessions and took shelter in the utility room. The rain lasted for a whole day and created havoc in our otherwise tranquil life. When the rain finally stopped and the sun came out, we counted the cost of the damage. We were shocked to see that our little tent and the rest of our belongings had all but disappeared. There was nothing left at the campsite.

"Count your blessings," said Aceline, seeing the anguished look on my face. "At least we are both still alive."

We managed to retrieve what was left of our tent and belongings almost half a mile down the valley. In the process we also found a 'treasure trove' of other washed-away items from the campsite in the mud and debris; food and daily necessities were cleaned up and used, much to our delight. Few, if any, of the campers seemed to bother about trying to find the stuff they had lost to the storm so it was perfectly alright for us to be on the treasure hunt.

We spent the next two days rebuilding our little 'home', repairing the tent, hanging our belongings up to dry, digging elaborate trenches in and around the campsite and generally taking preventive measures in preparation for the next storm. But it never came. For the remainder of our holiday in Tarragona, it was as hot and sunny as one would expect Spain to be.

By the time we were ready to leave, we had used up most of our money. On our return journey, not only did we have to hitch-hike but we also had to avoid campsite dues by sneaking in and out before and after the office opened and closed. We could no longer afford hot food. We lived on bread and water alone and at times we had to go without food altogether.

By the time we reached Paris we had been without hot food for two weeks.

Then we remembered the wishing fountain and the coins on the floor. We went back to Notre Dame and managed to retrieve six one-franc coins. With great expectations, we took the coins to the nearest self-service canteen. The cheapest item from the counter was seven francs. We mixed the six francs with a shilling coin which was similar in size and appearance. While we queued up, we prayed and hoped that the busy cashier would not notice the shilling coin. She did. We had to return the dish. Our hope for a hot meal was dashed. We left the canteen completely disheartened. We were so close to eating a hot meal that day, but it was not to be.

The hunger was painful and we looked unkempt.

"Aceline, you must have friends in Paris," I said. "Can you borrow some money for us to eat and go back to London? I'm fed up with this existence."

"I don't have anyone in Paris I can turn to. My home is in Versailles which is some distance outside Paris."

"Can we turn to your family for help? Unless we get the money to go back we will end up begging on the streets of Paris."

"Mon cheri, Oubert," she said in her cute French accent. "I never told you this but my family is ultra-conservative. My father is a judge. He almost fell off his chair when I told him about you. He cannot imagine his daughter's boyfriend is a Chinese."

"Huh, racism. I'm used to it."

"Do you know what he did last time I was home? He tried to apply to court for an injunction to stop me from going back to London."

"How can he do that?" I asked her. "You're a grown-up. He does not have the right."

"Believe me. He actually got the injunction."

"What happened?"

"Before the papers were served on me," Aceline said, "I packed my belongings and left home."

"I don't believe it!"

"It's the truth, mon cheri," she retorted. "Now you understand why I am so cut off. I have not contacted my family since I last left home. You haven't heard me mention my family all through this trip even when we are in France, have you?"

Life is full of rude awakenings – I woke up to yet another. I was grateful that she was prepared to make these sacrifices on my account. We held hands as we walked in silence along the Avenue des Champs-Elysées.

≈≈≈≈≈

Daniel and Mark were two brothers from the Philippines who stayed in the same hall. Both of them were good-looking – the sort that attract girls. They were popular with the many au pair girls who worked at the hall canteen. They both had fine features, dark skin and long, soft hair that fell over part of their faces. Both brothers studied at the London School of Economics. I heard through the grapevine that their father was the serving Ambassador of the Philippines in France.

Through the embassy, we managed to find their address – Hameau de Bougainvilleas near Avenue Mozart.

I rang the bell.

"How can I help you, sir?" the French butler asked as he took the measure of us from top to bottom. Our clothes had last been washed when we were in Spain three weeks before. We had hitched through Spain and France and, for the last couple of days, we had lived rough on the streets of Paris.

"Is Daniel home? We were students together in London," I said as I introduced myself.

"Master Daniel is out," the butler replied in English with a strong French accent.

"What about his brother, Mark?"

"They are out together. They are not expected back until late afternoon."

"Please tell either of them that Robert from Connaught Hall came," I said. "We shall return later in the evening."

We were excited. At last help was on the way. We had found the two brothers. They could help us. There was a glimmer of hope.

We went back to the house that evening. The butler answered the bell again. He recognised us immediately and, after ushering us into a reception area, he turned and went to fetch one of the brothers – he must have spoken to them about our earlier call.

Daniel came to greet us. I was not sure if he was at all happy to see us. We were never close. The two brothers were in the elite group in the hall. They seldom mixed with foreign students. All their friends were English, the upper-crust ones. Their crowd was in a class of its own. They were the 'untouchables', all born with silver spoons in their mouths and from a public school background. They only came to London after being rejected by Oxford or Cambridge, the sort that is known in the academic world as 'first-class rejects' meaning that, if they had had just a little more, they would have been accepted by Oxbridge instead of having to languish in London. Even the London School of Economics was considered to be inferior and beneath them.

His piercing dark eyes looked the two of us up and down. Then he broke into laughter.

"What has gotten into you? Look at the condition you are in. You must have slept and lived rough for quite some time. How did you manage to find us?"

"We have been hitch-hiking from France to Spain and back for most of the summer," I replied. "We found you through the Embassy of the Philippines. Oh, let me introduce you. This is Aceline. You've seen her with me at Connaught Hall, haven't you?"

"Oh yes, I remember Aceline," exclaimed Daniel. "She's French, isn't she? You brought her to the dance at the hall and introduced her to me. We spoke to each other in French. How are you, Aceline?"

"I am well," replied Aceline. "Well, not that well…" She wriggled uncomfortably under his stare, turned her head and looked at me, her face blushing. She obviously wanted me to explain our recent plight.

"We haven't eaten a hot meal for the last couple of weeks," I explained with a forced smile.

"Is that so?" said Daniel. "Then you must stay and dine with us, mustn't you? I will be delighted to hear what you have been through. I am sure Mark will too. He'll be back soon with my parents. They have gone shopping."

It was sheer music to our ears: we were being asked to stay for dinner.

Soon Mark and his parents, Mr. and Mrs. Ambassador, returned home. Daniel dashed out of the reception room and exchanged some quiet words with his family members. Then they all came into the room where we were introduced to his parents. We exchanged pleasantries. The parents were not a bit surprised by our appearances. On the contrary, they were warm and hospitable, and treated us like a couple of their sons' friends.

Dinner was served in a formal dining room adorned by extravagant hand-painted wall murals, opulent curtains, ceiling embellishments, crystal glassware, silver cutlery and luxurious antique furnishings. It is difficult to describe how we felt at that moment. We hadn't eaten a hot meal for several weeks and looked scruffy, yet here we were in such a palatial setting. It was a truly memorable meal, one that I would remember and talk about for the rest of my life. We had pumpkin soup followed by an entrée of roast duck with orange sauce and a side salad, and a dessert of home-baked apple pie with cream which we washed down with a Grand Cru red from Bordeaux. Then came the coffee – oh, that aroma – followed by whisky and cognac. We took it all in our stride, including the Cuban cigars. Two butlers stood to attention as the courses were served. We were in heaven. Our joy was overwhelming.

The brothers' parents enjoyed themselves as well. Our adventures intrigued them and were an excellent source of conversation for the table. As we finished dinner, they left the table, discreetly giving us a further opportunity to talk to the brothers. The two brothers were extremely friendly and hospitable.

Finally, the time came for us to leave, albeit reluctantly. As we were about to depart, and while we waited for the butler to bring us our coats, I pulled Daniel to one side.

"Can I borrow ten pounds from you, please?" I asked him.

He was taken completely by surprise. He was probably thinking: 'How dare you? We have already treated you to this sumptuous meal. Yet you are so thankless that you dare to ask for a loan. How can you be so shameless?'

He was visibly upset. I realised that I had perhaps gone too far and my request was quite inappropriate in the circumstances.

"No, I'm sorry. I can't help you there," he said bluntly as he signalled the butler to usher us out.

For the next few days we continued to live off the streets of Paris while desperately trying to get money to go back to London.

"We can beg," said Aceline. "We will each hang a placard around our necks that reads 'Student Needs Money – Return to London'. The place to go is Avenue Montaigne where the rich go shopping."

I took a position outside Plaza Athenée Hotel where the rich tourists stayed while Aceline posted herself outside the Chanel shop across the road.

It totally surprised us that, within the same day, we got enough money to buy tickets to return to London. This included a US$20 donation from a kind-hearted American from Plaza Athenée who empathised with us, remembering he himself had been in a similar plight in his young student days.

≈≈≈≈≈

It was the beginning of a new academic year and Connaught Hall as usual was bustling with activity. Students were returning from the long summer break. I had managed to retain my old room.

"Aceline, we have to share this room until you find employment. You stay in the room and I'll get you food from the canteen. The cleaner always comes after 10 a.m. so if you leave the room with me before that time we will be okay."

A week or two passed and she had no luck with her job-hunting. The situation at the hall became difficult as Aceline had to leave the room stealthily to use the toilet across the corridor and she had already been spotted by the warden a couple of times during his inspection tours.

"We cannot continue like this much longer," I said as we sat on a bench in Tavistock Square Garden. "You can't get a job and I'm up to my neck with my studies. Tongues are wagging that I keep a woman in my room. It's only a matter of time before I'm warned and, if I don't get you out of the hall, I will be asked to leave. I know you have tremendous pressure from your family. We have to make a decision on what to do next. Here is a piece of paper. I want you to think carefully before you write the answer down. I'm giving you half an hour to make up your mind. Do you want to stay or go home? Just write it down."

Aceline wandered off by herself.

Just fifteen minutes later she handed me back the piece of paper on which was written: This is my home. I shall stay.

I was choked with emotion. I admired her loyalty and was glad we were so madly in love with each other. I would have been very disappointed indeed if she had said she wanted to go home.

Another week went by and still there was no job. The situation became even more desperate. We knew we had no other choice. She had to return to France. It was a painful decision.

At Waterloo Station, we said our goodbyes as the train moved from the platform. That day, and the image of her leaning halfway out of the train door window waving goodbye to me, is stamped indelibly in my memory. I ran along the platform after the moving train and then stood at the end waving until her silhouette disappeared into the late autumn fog.

"Come back and marry me next year when I graduate," I shouted.

"Oui, mon cheri," she shouted back. "I will be back at Easter."

The 'Dear John' letter arrived three months later. I was heartbroken. I could not believe she could be so cruel as to betray me in the way she did. All the solemn vows made during the ups and downs of our times together now seemed to have meant nothing, and we had gone through unspeakable hardships together.

I cried myself to sleep every night for over six months. Then I burned all her pictures and discarded anything that reminded me of her.

# Western Rain and Eastern Sunshine

I graduated with a degree in law in 1969 and went home, the first time since I had left Hong Kong more than five years before.

Landing at the old Kai Tak airport was a roller-coaster experience. On the approach, the plane banked sharply before it regained its equilibrium and aligned itself with the runway for the touchdown. From my window seat, I could see people going about their daily lives in the living rooms of high-rise blocks of flats on either side of the flight path.

It was as if time had stood still for all those years I had been away. The sight of all these people in their homes sent a sensation down my spine. I alone knew what I had been through. All that hardship and sadness melted away as the plane landed. I was excited beyond words – home at last.

The family laid on a tumultuous welcome. As I walked across the tarmac, I could hear them shouting my name and waving frantically from the roof of the terminal building. It seemed as if everyone I knew was there: Kwok Sun, Charles, the whole lot of them. It was an emotional reunion. We hugged and tears flowed.

"You have lost weight," Mother said. "You look tired. When was the last time you had a haircut?"

"Oh, long hair is fashionable in London," I replied. "It was a long flight. I was so excited about coming home that I hardly slept all week. I know I look thin but, believe me, I'm as strong and as healthy as an ox."

I did not want to tell her I was still recovering from the trauma over Aceline. Although it was water under the bridge, the hurt lingered.

It was apparent that the fortunes of the family had improved. My family had a flat to themselves except for one bedroom at the back which was rented to a single woman. It was a vast improvement on when I had left.

Ruby, my sister, gave a party and I was asked to go and pick up two of her friends.

The two girls were there at 86 Waterloo Road when I arrived by taxi. I hopped out and held the door for them as they got in. One caught my attention. There was something unusual about this girl whose name was Elaine. She was tall and slender and wore a gold globe ring with a matching bracelet that complemented the colour of her skin – a deep, healthy tan. Her hair was pitch-black, wavy and shoulder-length. She had long arms and slim ankles. She looked stunning in her blue and saffron trouser suit, but she did not really look Chinese. I could not take my eyes off her.

At the party we danced.

"You don't really look Chinese," I said to her. "Your skin is dark and you have round eyes like a Caucasian. You know, we have slit eyes – like this." I pulled the two ends of my eyes to show her.

"I must have taken after my grandmother," Elaine said. "She was half Polynesian. My great-grandfather went to Hawaii and married a native woman. At seventeen, my grandmother was sent back to Canton to find a husband. She married my grandfather."

As the night wore on, we found that we had a lot in common and talked non-stop with each other. Later the party adjourned to a hip bar in the Empress Hotel where we played a hair game. The hair is tied to a ring and each person pulls a hair. If it spins clockwise, the child is a girl and anti-clockwise, a boy. Our hair spun once either way in the same order.

"We are destined to be married to each other," I said, "and together we will have two children, a boy and a girl."

Elaine laughed.

"Which animal sign were you born under?" I asked.

"Rooster."

"Wow, my future wife is supposed to be born a rooster. It is written in my 'Pak Tze'."

"I don't believe in that stuff. What age were you when you had the 'Pak Tze' done?"

"I was seventeen. I once tried to impress another girl who was also born a rooster and told her she would be my wife."

"Did it work?"

"Yes, it did," I said cheekily. "She is now my wife."

"You are a naughty man."

I held her hand. It was long, slim and bony like a chicken's claw yet soft and elastic like rubber.

The night slipped away too quickly. It was in the small hours of the morning when we left the Empress Hotel. I flagged down a taxi to take her home. It would be too expensive if I were to escort her home and then return to mine. Luckily, the hotel was close to my home. I bid her goodnight or rather good morning and made arrangements to see her for lunch the very next day in Central where she worked as a secretary.

≈≈≈≈≈

Elaine called me one day. "My parents would like to invite you to stay with us over the weekend. My father is a doctor. He is the head of the voluntary drug rehabilitation centre at Sek Kwu Chau. Take the 9 a.m. ferry to Cheung Chau on Saturday. We will be at the pier to meet you."

The outlying island of Cheung Chau is one hour by public ferry from Hong Kong Island. I arrived on time but could not see Elaine at the pier.

"You are Robert, aren't you?" An elderly lady approached me. "I am Mrs. Kwan, Elaine's mother. Elaine is at the house preparing lunch. She asked me to come instead. We have half an hour before the next ferry to Sek Kwu Chau. Come, join me for tea."

She spoke excellent English, the sort that could only be spoken by a refined and educated lady well versed in the Western way of life. And, judging from the accent, I could tell she was from Shanghai.

Aunt Ting Hai, alias Siaw Ko (middle row, second from right) and my grandmother; cousin Chun Shin is second from left in back row

My maternal grandparents, Yee Ting and Ah Boo, circa 1920s; Mother is front row, second from left

My family, circa 1953

The "lost generation", my parents fifth from left

Right: member of the La Salle boxing team

Below left: with Aunt Lydia and her children Jacqueline and Phillippa

Below right: hitch-hiking in France with Aceline

With Cheng Yu Tung at Universal Studios, Orlando

With Philip Yeo (chairman of EDB, Singapore), Cheng Yu Tung, Wee Cho Yaw and Chow Chung Kai

The ladies' committee of the Singapore Chamber of Commerce with PM Lee Hsien Loong and Mrs. Lee; Elaine is third from left

With Shaul Eisenberg and Shimon Peres in Israel

With Tan Boon Teik, Attorney General of Singapore, and Woo Tchi Chu, my partner in Singapore

With Cheng Yu Tung, Run Run and Mona Shaw

With the late President Ong Teng Cheong of Singapore

At the grand opening of Suntec City: Cheng Yu Tung, Chow Chung Kai, myself, Anthony Yeh, Senior Minister Lee Kuan Yew and Frank Tsao

Members of Run Run Shaw's entourage in China; T.K. Ann in the middle

Elaine with Mrs. Kvan

Celebrating our 30th anniversary ...

... and Sir Run Run Shaw's 103rd birthday

Above: the wedding of Gillian and Dennis

Below left: Change Luck Chamber at Wudang Temple

Below right: with my grandsons Nathan and David

"Take some *dim sum*," said Mrs. Kwan as she picked up a roast pork bun for me. "How long have you known Elaine?"

"Just over a month."

"Elaine has asked us for permission to go and join you in London," she continued. "Can you tell me why?"

"Well, Mrs. Kwan," I hesitated, "I have to be back in a month to do a course in order to be qualified as a solicitor."

"Yes, I know, but you have not answered my question: why would you like Elaine to be there?"

I really did not know how to answer. After all, we had been together for barely a month. Our relationship was just beginning to take off. I could not lie just to please her. I had to give her an honest answer. And that was a big mistake.

"I-I-I would like to…" I stammered.

"You would like to… what?" she asked again.

"I would like to try it out with Elaine." I finally plucked up the courage and finished the sentence.

She was visibly upset and signalled for the bill. The conversation stopped abruptly. All the way to the island we did not talk again.

At the superintendent's villa up at the top of the island, the mother chose to ignore me throughout the weekend. Instead of giving me the guest room, I was asked to lay out a canvas bed that they provided me with in the sitting room.

I deserved the treatment meted out to me. I had given her a bad first impression. In hindsight, I should perhaps have been more tactful instead of being so blunt and stupid – Elaine was her only daughter and they were close, very close.

Nevertheless, I met Elaine's father, Dr. Kwan, and we got along well. We had much in common and talked a lot that weekend. Sadly it was the first and last time we spent together.

≈≈≈≈≈

Before Elaine left for London that summer, notices to announce our engagement were inserted in the *South China Morning Post* by the parents of both families – a precondition that I was only too glad to accept.

The day I met Elaine again was the happiest day of my life.

That morning I attended an interview with the Law Society for admission to become an articled clerk.

"Young man, tell me: what do you consider to be the most important ingredient of a solicitor?" asked the council member.

"To help the needy and, when necessary, to offer my services for free." I had learned to be tactful and thought the answer would please him.

"No, no, young man." The interviewer shook his head. "Integrity, always remember, it is integrity. Do you understand, young man?"

"Yes, thank you, sir." I was grateful for his advice.

I shared a house in Golders Green with four other overseas students including three from Hong Kong. The landlady was a Dutch lady married to a Chinese. She was prim and proper and stern, and ruled her student tenants with an iron fist. Yet she cared about the welfare and well-being of her subjects and she was always there for us.

"Who is this young girl?" she asked when one day she came to collect the rent. She had seen Elaine.

"Her name is Elaine," I said nervously. "She has just arrived from Hong Kong. She is my fiancée."

"But you aren't married, are you?"

"No, but we soon will be."

"I am afraid I cannot allow an unmarried couple to live together. The two of you can either get married or move out."

The next day Elaine and I went to the Marriage Registry at High Barnet and asked to see the registrar.

"How may I help you, young man?" the registrar asked.

"We want to get married. We are both over eighteen," I said as I showed him our passports.

"Ah, we have a law just to deal with passionate young lovers like you," he said with a smile. "We can't just marry you immediately. You have to give us a minimum of twenty-one days' notice. This 'cooling-off' period is there in case either of you should change your mind… you know, when the passion is over. A shorter duration notice can be arranged if you are prepared to pay a fee."

"How much is that?"

"Twenty-five pounds."

"We can't afford it," I said as I looked at Elaine. She nodded.

So we gave the requisite notice. Twenty-one days later, on Christmas Eve, we were married at the same registry.

We prepared our own wedding 'banquet'. No fewer than thirty guests turned up including Mrs. Goh, the landlady. I cooked my speciality: chicken in soybean sauce. It was a rowdy and joyous occasion.

At the party, Mrs. Goh pulled me to one side. "I hope you haven't done it on my account."

"How do you mean?"

"You know… I told you how boys and girls shouldn't live together."

"Oh, you mean that bit," I said cheekily, under the influence of alcohol. "Of course I did. Why else would I marry someone so soon after meeting her?"

"You are not serious, Robert!" Mrs. Goh exclaimed. "How long have you known each other?"

"Six months to the day. Take off the three months I was in London and she was in Hong Kong, we have been together for just three months."

"You must be kidding. How can you make a decision that affects your life so lightly? Honestly, why did you marry her in such haste?"

"I just told you – it was *you*."

"Oh, Robert, don't give me that guilt stuff. Look me straight in the eye… now, tell me the truth."

I did as I was told and said, "Being away for over five years, every girl in Hong Kong looked so beautiful. I married the first one I met."

"Robert, you are drunk," retorted Mrs. Goh. "I don't like your cavalier attitude. You act so frivolously: end of conversation." But then she asked, "Oh, one more thing… why aren't you wearing a ring?"

"My wife is married," I replied, tongue in cheek. "I am not."

"You bad man," she reprimanded me. "I feel sorry for that girl who has married you today."

What I did not tell her was that we could afford only one ring.

I was the first one to get drunk and had to be carried into the 'bridal chamber' which was a room completely devoid of furniture save for a mattress on the floor.

Another one – and a truly momentous one – of my 'Pak Tze' predictions came true: 'Wife was born in the year of the Rooster and she will render you lifelong assistance.'

# PART 4

# THE PRACTICE

In the winter of 1970, Dr. Kwan, my father-in-law, passed away. Elaine was heartbroken. She returned to Hong Kong for the funeral. I was then serving my articles of clerkship with a London firm. I quit and went home to join her.

"Young man, you are in the right place at the right time," a senior doctor I met through Elaine's family said. "The timing couldn't be better. The streets of Hong Kong are paved with gold. Do you understand the phrase '*fat sham see*'?"

"No, I don't," I replied. "I know '*sham*' is three, '*fat*' means prosperous, but what is '*see*'?"

"How do you pronounce lawyer in Chinese?"

"*Lut see.*"

"Yes, '*lut see*', '*yee see*' and '*chit see*' are all '*sees*'," he said with a smile.

"Oh, you mean lawyers, doctors and architects prosper?" I said excitedly.

"Exactly, all the '*sees*' are in great demand. There are simply not enough of them as Hong Kong emerges from the overspill of the Cultural Revolution. The economy is growing quickly. The businessmen who left during the turbulent times are returning. Those who did not leave are now sitting pretty: the value of the assets they own is going in one direction – up and up. Too much money is being pumped into the economy. It's crazy – everyone is in a mad scramble to jump on the bandwagon."

He was right. Even before my articles of clerkship expired, I received several offers of partnership in Hong Kong.

I accepted an offer to join a small two-partner local firm that had been started by an Englishman, John. I had to pay a modest premium. My father borrowed HK$100,000 against his pension fund.

It was a proud moment when the new nameplate of the firm was installed – my name was on it.

"Robert, we will soon be able to draw $10,000 a month each for the three partners," said Winston Tan, the second partner. "Can you imagine? It's a lot of money. You and I are starters."

Winston had qualified as a solicitor a year before me, although we were students in the same class – the College of Law at Lancaster Gate, London, 1969 – preparing for the Law Society Qualifying Examinations. My admission to be a solicitor was delayed by a year because in those days only British subjects could become solicitors. It took me an extra year to be admitted to the roll because I had to wait for my naturalisation application to come through. Winston was the Managing Partner when I joined the firm. He was also a one-third equity partner.

I had known him since our teens but we were never close. He came from a well-to-do family. I did not. We met up in London again and, through our circumstances, we became close: we were both law students and articled clerks at the same time.

"I can't believe how far we have come," I said. "Remember those days when your father died and your mother sent you £5,000 as your share of the estate and you took the money straight to the casino—"

"Robert, don't rub it in again," Winston interrupted. "Yes, I took the money to the casino in Park Lane. Not only did I lose all of it but I also ran up debts and owed the casino another £5,000. But I worked my butt off, day and night, didn't I? I repaid the debt and told you that I would never ever gamble again. I have kept the promise."

"What about wanting to rob a bank one night at Finchley Central?"

"Come on… it was meant as a joke and you know it. I just picked up a large stone and tossed it against the window of Barclays Bank. The stone bounced back. It didn't break anything. I sobered up. It was silly of me. This is the last time we talk about my past. I don't want news to leak out that I gamble. It does you no good either – remember you are now my partner and we have a thriving business together. By the way, tell me that postal worker story again… you know, the one you told me in London. I am absolutely intrigued by that story."

"What? You mean that legal aid case I handled as an articled clerk?"

"Yes, that's the one."

"It was his job to stamp envelopes showing the date and time the mails came through. He got smart. He wanted to make a couple of pounds on the side. He affixed a postal time on the stamp of an unsealed envelope and put it aside. Then he listened to the radio for the race results. When they were known, he entered the right bet and slipped it into the stamped envelope before it was sealed. The betting people validated the bet according to the postmark. He did it every week and got back a couple of pounds as a way of supplementing the meagre income he earned as a postal worker. Then one Christmas he got greedy because he wanted to buy his kid a bicycle. He put in a large bet and got twenty pounds winnings. It alerted the processing officer who saw something unusual in the betting pattern. An investigation ensued and that was how he was caught."

"It's absolutely fascinating," exclaimed Winston. "What a smart fellow this postman was. The scheme was almost foolproof."

"Well, in the end he was caught, wasn't he?"

"That's beside the point," said Winston. "He could have gotten away with it, couldn't he?"

"Doesn't that tell you something about gambling: nine out of ten times they cheat?"

"That is interesting, really interesting," said Winston with a smug look on his face.

≈≈≈≈≈

Everyone who knew Winston adored the man. He was gregarious, affable, witty, charming and intelligent – a veritable extrovert. His sense of humour endeared him to everyone, particularly women. His jokes were so funny that his audience would burst out laughing and ask for more.

And, like a magician, Winston had all sorts of tricks up his sleeve. One of them was to place a cigarette on the table. He placed a finger in front of it and the cigarette followed the finger and moved. No one knew how he did it until, one day, someone noticed he was blowing the cigarette from behind.

He also played this 'guess my middle finger' game. He had his right hand wrapped around the fingers of his left and would ask you to find the middle finger – no one could, and no one had ever succeeded in finding out how he did it. He was certainly the life and soul at every party.

"Winston is more intelligent than you are," even my mother told me.

And he was an excellent criminal lawyer…

"How did you manage to get that client off the hook?" I asked him once. "He was guilty as hell – the evidence was stacked against him."

"Yes, I know, but the victim got confused. There were two flats, one on the left and the other on the right. The doors faced each other. She thought she was taken to the left one when in fact it was the right one and, in doing so, she got the rooms mixed up. She didn't even know where she had been. The prosecution failed to prove the case beyond reasonable doubt. He was acquitted."

Then a serious incident occurred.

"Mr. Wang, I think you should know," said Alice, the firm's chief accountant. "Last Thursday a client deposited $460,000 with us. It was late afternoon and the bank was closed. I therefore locked the cash in the safe. That same afternoon Mr. Tan asked me to give him the cash. I did as I was told."

"What!" I exclaimed. "He took the cash and kept it until today – six days! Why didn't you tell me before? It is a client's money, isn't it?"

I approached John, the precedent partner. He was an Englishman and was by nature an honest and trusting person. He always looked on the bright side, not the sort of person who would fault others. He was mild, soft-spoken, civil, courteous and modest to a fault and he was a darn good lawyer.

"Robert, we are partners, aren't we?" he said with a grin. "Partners should trust each other. Don't pick every hair that shows its head. I don't read anything wrong into what Winston did. He probably took the money and locked it up in his own safe. Then he forgot about it until today. It was an oversight. No harm is done, so what's the fuss? You shouldn't be so suspicious. Give Winston the benefit of the doubt. Don't rush into my room and act as if you have caught him red-handed in a sinister act. There is nothing sinister in what Winston did."

I related the incident to Tien Oung (T.O.). T.O. had come to me as a client. For some reason, we got along well despite a significant age difference. Soon he became my mentor and, in many ways, like another father. We talked freely about anything under the sky. I consulted him often and he could obviously read me and my raw ambition. Nevertheless, he was willing to accept me as a protégé.

"Wow… be careful, Robert," he said. "It is an important matter. One can't afford to make a mistake. A partner is as important as the person one marries. A mistake can cause irreparable damage, like the proverb says: 'One slip of the foot and one will regret it for a thousand years'."

"I know, but what can I do? I just bought into the partnership. My father had to borrow the money. If I get out now I could lose everything. No, I can't do that. I have to take a chance. The partnership is doing well. As soon as I earn enough to pay back my father and start on my own, I will get out, but not now."

"You are in it with your eyes wide open. I hope nothing will happen in the meantime. Otherwise your decision could place you in great jeopardy one day."

T.O. was old-school. He graduated from Beijing's prestigious Tsinghua University. He was bright and upright, a man of high intellect and principles, with an integrity that was completely beyond reproach. He worked for the Central Bank of China in his youth, rising to a position of such seniority that he was tipped to become the Minister of Finance of the Central Government of China.

He was always well dressed and impeccably groomed – a true gentleman in every sense of the word. And his word was always his bond. Hence he was universally admired by all who knew him. Even his peers often sought his advice. Mrs. Liu, his wife, came from a good family in Zhou Shan. Her intelligence and elegance were matched by her wit and grace – a true lady. They made a handsome and elegant couple together.

T.O. was an entrepreneur. He had a good nose for business and was an astute judge of people and opportunities. Although he invested in companies, he chose not to get involved in their management.

"I prefer to be able to recognize the wood for the trees," he used to say. "When one gets too caught up in every little detail, one will fail to see the bigger picture. As an outsider I get to see the whole game better. If you have doubts, don't employ the person; once employed, you should never doubt him."

He was a major shareholder in two listed companies in Hong Kong: Smart Shirts, that made shirts for export, and Cheong Sum, a property developer. In his spare time he managed a sizeable portfolio of his own including US equities of which Boeing was his favourite. He and his partner, Kung Ka Luen, also dabbled in property redevelopment.

His office was simple, a small room which he shared with his secretary. He and his wife lived simply in the same rented apartment for over thirty years.

"You are a wealthy man," I commented to T.O. "I don't understand why you live such a spartan life."

"Ha, ha, ha, I'm glad you ask. Suppression is the mother of utility."

"How do you mean?"

"When one is thirsty, the first glass of water gives more satisfaction than the tenth, doesn't it?"

"Oh, you mean the law of diminishing returns? But I still don't know why a man of your wealth lives so frugally. One works hard to get rich so that one can be surrounded by all the trappings that wealth can bring – mansions, servants, yachts, luxury cars, mistresses and so forth."

"Slow down, Robert. Money is not everything. Keeping one's sense of values is more important – it is the key to happiness."

T.O. inducted me into his private club. The club had among its members many industrialists from Shanghai – the ones who created the cotton spinning industry in the 1950s that laid the foundation for Hong Kong's economic success.

"Robert, you know Kung Ka Luen, my classmate from Tsinghua University," said T.O. "Ka Luen graduated top of the class. His mind is razor-sharp, like a computer. I won't challenge his 'abacus' – he is always right when it comes to figures. We have bought an old building in Happy Valley that we hope to tear down and rebuild. I have spoken to Ka Luen. He has agreed to let you cut in for a twenty per cent stake."

"What! You can't be serious, can you?" I exclaimed. "I don't have that kind of money to invest. I barely earn enough to support my family. Besides, Elaine is pregnant with our first child. I appreciate the gesture but I can't accept it."

T.O. smiled and gave me an inscrutable look.

Six months later, he gave me a cheque.

"What is this?" I asked in surprise. "Why are you giving me such a large sum of money?"

By then I had all but forgotten our conversation and the project.

"Well, this is your share of the profits, less tax," T.O. replied. "We sold the building."

"What!" I exclaimed in disbelief. It dawned on me that he was referring to the old building he and his partner had bought. "It was a casual conversation. I told you I did not have the money. The conversation ended there. It was the last time we spoke. I can't believe that you are now giving me this cheque. Thank you anyway. I appreciate the gesture but I can't take it."

"I must insist. A deal is a deal. That was our agreement and this is your share of the profits. How am I going to explain to my partner otherwise? I can't tell him that you never agreed, can I? It would complicate matters. You can see the cheque is signed by both of us. Please take it."

I was speechless. I could see his thinking. He knew I was mired in the thick of a bad partnership which I could not get out of – at least for a while – and every day I waited, I was at risk. He wanted to help me to get out, and the sooner the better.

I accepted the cheque and used the money to set up my own firm.

"Dissolution is like a divorce," said Winston. "It is always messy. May I suggest a way for a swift ending – a guillotine? We send a circular to all members of staff and ask them to choose sides. A choice, once made, is binding. Neither side will employ anyone who reneges."

It sounded reasonable so I agreed.

I was surprised but gratified to see most of the staff opted to follow me. However, when the initial jubilation had subsided, I had to come to terms with reality. The new firm – Robert W.H. Wang & Co., Solicitors and Notaries – was bottom heavy and top light. I had to find solicitors of partnership material to justify the large support base. I approached T.O.

"Think of a tripod," he said. "Get the three legs in place. You take care of the Shanghai business. Get someone – an Englishman – to do the British work. Hong Kong is a colony. You can't escape them. They are everywhere – in government, in the judiciary, in banking, in business – you name it and they are there. And get a local to do property work. Developers are mostly locals. The industrialists don't believe in properties. They were burnt once in Shanghai, and once bitten, twice shy. Locals didn't have the same hiccup – sad in a way because we planted the seeds and they now reap the benefits. The tripod can bring you success."

I went to London to recruit. St. James's Club was chosen as the venue for the interviews. At Berry Brothers & Rudd, the old wine merchants in St. James, I asked for directions. No one seemed to have heard of the club until a man impeccably dressed in the best mode of a true English gentleman spoke to me in his upper-class accent.

"Oh, you mean that new 'club'." He spoke in a nasal tone and had a condescending manner – the 'club' was beneath him. "It's located just down the road, next to the Overseas League Club."

Many interviews were lined up for the day. The response to my advertisement had been overwhelming.

"Tell me, why are you interested in applying for this position?" I asked Michael Dalton, the first candidate I interviewed.

"Well, you see… after so many years of socialist government, the abolition of the conveyancing scale, and the encouragement of 'do-it-yourself' divorce and this and that, solicitors in this country have to run faster and faster just to stay in the same place," he replied. "Conveyancing was our bread and butter. The abolition has brought havoc to solicitors' practices. They are badly affected."

In the British context, 'conveyancing' means passing the title of a property from one to another. The charges for this work are laid down in a scale by which all solicitors have to abide. A breach can lead to a solicitor being sanctioned by their professional body, the Law Society.

Conveyancing was more than just bread and butter, as it might be for a run-of-the-mill practice in England. In land-scarce Hong Kong, buildings can go only one way: up and up, like trees in a jungle struggling to reach the sunlight.

Not only was conveyancing the main source of income for most firms but it was also a lucrative area of work; especially in block conveyancing in which the solicitor prepares just one set of documents which then applies to all the units. And there can be hundreds, or even thousands, of such units in the block.

Thus, it is as close to mass production as a service industry can ever get. Indeed, solicitors look upon the work as a 'licence to print money' given the unique geography of Hong Kong – a large population packed into a small area where almost all buildings are high-rise.

I was glad that Hong Kong had not abolished the scale and there was no sign it would any time soon.

I interviewed at least a dozen candidates. In the end, I recruited three of them. One of them, Leslie Simon, had been to Oxford. He bore a strong resemblance to Enoch Powell, a Conservative Party MP – the same intense brown eyes, bushy eyebrows, strong jawline and build, and with an intellect to match. I admired Enoch Powell greatly, not only as a politician but also as a classical scholar, writer and military man even though his famous and controversial 'Rivers of Blood' speech that he made in opposition to immigration into the United Kingdom filled me with revulsion. Leslie later became our Managing Partner and, under him, the firm bloomed and prospered.

The other, David Rimmer, an old Etonian and a Conservative county councillor, had his own practice in London before he joined the firm as a consultant. He later left to start his own practice in Hong Kong.

More importantly, perhaps, I also recruited Michael who was a senior and seasoned solicitor. It was my best decision. Michael brought into the practice his experience and a vast network of connections. Virtually in one stroke the firm built up the British leg of the tripod.

"At this time, Robert, you need to muster some political clout," said T.O. "You have this partner in your firm… what is her name? You know, the pretty one with rosy cheeks. Her name keeps on popping up in the newspapers…"

"Oh, you mean Anna Wu. She loves the limelight."

"Yes, Anna Wu. That girl is smart and intelligent. She talks well. You should encourage her to be more involved in local politics."

"She is a member of the Observers' Group, formed by a group of young intellectuals to monitor the performance of the Colonial Government. I am not sure if the group goes down well with the Government. It is viewed as a sort of troublemaker and its activities are closely monitored. It could send the wrong signal if I push Anna to the forefront."

"But the political picture is changing. The British will give us more democracy in the run-up to 1997. The Observers' Group is just the kind of moderate organization that the government would tap into for talent, and Anna has that quality."

With my encouragement, Anna became active in the political arena, picking up many statutory appointments. She moved into the good books of the Government. She was Chris Patten's last appointee to LEGCO (the Legislative Council, or Parliament). Patten was the last Colonial Governor of Hong Kong. She sponsored the Equal Opportunities Bill that was later passed into law. She headed the Equal Opportunities Commission and later served as a member of EXCO (the Executive Council, or Cabinet).

The firm had hit the right note. It grew from strength to strength. A major breakthrough came when the Hongkong and Shanghai Banking Corporation (HSBC) added the firm to its List of Approved Solicitors which in those days comprised a precious few. Being on the bank's panel not only brought prestige but also attracted large clients. 'If it is good for the bank, it must be good for us,' the client would believe.

By the mid-eighties the firm was one of the top law firms in Hong Kong – *Asia Law Journal* ranked it as the fifth largest.

I was lucky, very lucky, thanks to T.O. My mentor's foresight saved me from ruination. Thank God… when disaster struck my old firm, I was completely out of harm's way.

Everyone knew what happened to Winston and his firm. His love for gambling proved to be his undoing. Shortly after I left, Winston took money from clients by forging signatures and title deeds. He created fictitious mortgages, took the money to Macau and gambled it away. Then he borrowed from syndicates that operated at the casinos and lost more. As he became mired deeper in gambling debt, he took even more money from clients. Then he ran away to Taiwan. One day he was caught through Interpol as he transited at Singapore's Changi Airport on his way back from Indonesia. He was extradited to Hong Kong, pleaded guilty to the charges and was sent down for six years.

Dishonesty of partners is not covered by insurance. His partners had to pay out of their own pockets.

T.O. was wise and prophetic. He was right: one cannot afford to make a mistake when one chooses a partner because such a mistake can result in irreparable damage; an innocent partner is just as liable as the guilty one. The liability is unlimited and it is joint and several amongst the partners.

The saga of Winston continued. After he served his time and came out of prison, he was readily welcomed back into the business empire of his friend, Albert, who had just started a joint venture for soccer betting with Stanley Ho, the casino king of Macau. Winston was made the manager of the new company. The first shop was opened in the basement of Casino de Lisboa. The business was an instant success. It caught the right wave. Soccer betting was becoming increasingly popular and the business went from strength to strength. The turnover of the shop increased exponentially. It made Winston a shining star. While he basked in the sun of the success, his lifestyle changed dramatically. No longer was he that timid underdog after years of being on the run and, later, serving time inside. He returned to the same Winston I always knew – confident, flamboyant and cocky. He had a lifestyle to match his new-found status. To see his recovery pleased me no end, however – after all, we were friends.

"Come and visit me, Robert," said Winston. "I'll show you around Macau. You'll be amazed."

I took a ferry to Macau. Winston arranged a limousine to pick me up from the pier. A uniformed chauffeur drove me to the Casino de Lisboa. Winston was at the door to welcome me. He was obviously a big man there from the way the doormen humbled themselves in his presence. At the casino, the staff bent over backwards to ensure I got the same kind of treatment that was usually reserved for a VIP guest. Everywhere we went we were greeted enthusiastically by the casino staff and even the normally serious-faced security guards bowed deeply to us. It impressed me.

Winston was wearing a beige suit. His hair was dyed blond. Underneath he wore a black shirt and a matching coloured tie. He reminded me of a Yakuza – a Japanese gangster.

"Welcome to Macau," he said. "Welcome to my Macau."

"When was the last time I saw you, Winston? You are well, aren't you? I can see life is treating you well. Your darkest hours have passed. Congratulations!"

"Now let me see," Winston reflected. "I was sent down for six years, given one-third remission for good conduct... I served four years altogether and I have been out for a year and a half now – it must be five and a half years ago then. That is how long it is since we last saw each other."

That afternoon, during lunch at his private club, we reminisced over the past. Both of us had a lot of catching up to do.

"Tell me, Winston, what was it like to be inside?"

"You know, it wasn't that bad. It gave me the opportunity to reflect on my life –coming to grips with where I came from and where I was headed. It also gave me the chance to lose some weight. I lost over twenty pounds. The worst part perhaps was the sexual predators. The prison was full of them. They were all so deprived of the usual thing that they became depraved. Many were downright sadistic perverts."

"How do they solve the sexual need?"

"I should perhaps tell you what they do to the dick first. The perverts are mostly long-timers. Some are lifers. There is no hope for them to return to a normal sex life. What do they do? Well, like everything else, they adapt to prison life. Even the straight become homosexual. Some stalk the other inmates, especially the young, new ones. Inside, the most valuable commodity is the cigarette. It is used as a 'currency' by which all things, service and whatever else is available inside, are measured. The most expensive service that 'money' can buy – yes, it's true, I was there – is a 'surgery' on the penis. And there are only one or two 'surgeons' from among the inmates who are experienced enough to do this operation. He makes an incision on the underside of the penis and through the opening he inserts small round beads into the length of the penis. The operation is supposed to make the prisoner a better performer. He becomes more attractive as a sexual partner. Consequently, he becomes the macho so-and-so that young handsome inmates are attracted to."

"Wow! That is disgusting. You're not bullshitting me again, are you?"

"I swear to God, I'm not," Winston said. "I'm telling you the truth, the whole truth and nothing but the truth."

"I don't believe what you tell me. I have to take what you say with a pinch of salt."

"Suit yourself, Robert, if that is what you think."

"Where do they get the instruments to carry out the operation and where do the beads come from? You're talking about prison conditions. It's hardly an operating theatre, is it?"

"Everything is made from plastic. It comes from the handle of a toothbrush. It can be sharpened as a knife. It can also be ground into beads. The finished products are then boiled for sterilization."

"What if the operation goes wrong or if the wound is infected by germs?"

"The prison has a sick bay and, in a serious case, they can always get outside help – the emergency ward of a government hospital."

"Why did you do it?"

"Do what?"

"You took clients' money and fled to Taiwan," I reminded him.

"It is a long story."

"We have plenty of time. I'm listening."

"I had this sense of a mission. I had to get my revenge against the casino. I just could not accept the fact that the casino was better than me. I thought I could beat them. Believe me, I really did. That was how it all started, or, should I say, restarted. In the beginning I was winning. I made a couple of million. Can you believe it? I was so elated that I actually invited the whole office to go on a Macau holiday. On top of paying for the expenses, I also gave each and every one of them $200 to play on the tables. I thought that would please the staff and make them loyal to me.

"However, victory went to my head. Every time I arrived, the casino rolled out the red carpet and treated me like a king – a limousine waited for me at the pier; there was a complimentary suite in the most exclusive wing reserved only for its best customers; girls, food and booze, you name it… they were all available at the snap of a finger. It was too good to be true. I never had it so good. It was a glorious time.

"Then my luck turned. I couldn't explain it. I was always known to the syndicates that operated on the casino floor. The loan sharks always respected me, calling me 'lawyer this' and 'solicitor that'. And from time to time I helped them when they got into trouble with the law. They knew I did well as a solicitor. The money was always there for me if I wanted it but I resisted. I knew once I got involved I would not be able to get out. They were all triads and they could be mean to defaulters. As I lost more money, I became desperate. I thought of ways to recoup my losses. I needed gambling capital. That was the time when I started dipping into the till. I created fictitious mortgages without the knowledge of the owner clients. I certified that the mortgage was executed against which the bank paid the loan into the clients' accounts which I could operate freely. As my losing streak got worse, I became even more desperate. Then I met a woman at the table. I was completely captivated by her beauty. It was she who finally persuaded me to take loans from the syndicates. My nightmare began."

"It sounds so terribly like my grandmother's story," I said. "She was a pathological gambler. She got into the same trouble and the whole family suffered on her account. In the end, the family was broken up. It was a tragedy. One day I will write a book about it. Carry on, Winston. What happened next?"

"Things came to a head. The loan sharks were on my back. The interest was so high and compounded in such a manner that, every other month, the original loan sum more than doubled. Then the last straw came when the partners found out what I had done and threatened to report me if I did not make restitution. I promised them that I would repay it within three days. The amount was so large – more than $40 million – there was no way I could. It was the end of the line for me. I thought of suicide but did not have the courage to go through with it. The only alternative was to flee.

"I went home, told my wife to pack immediately and head straight for the airport with my two sons. I gave them plane tickets. My good wife was completely taken by surprise. She had absolutely no idea what was going on.

"After my family had left, I managed to buy a passage on a boat to flee Hong Kong. I paid $250,000 for the journey to Taiwan. I thought with the money I had spent to charter the fishing junk, I would be the only passenger. Not so. On board I was surprised to find at least five other passengers. They were all members of the same gang escaping Hong Kong to 'wear grass' – lie low until the heat died down. They were wanted by a rival gang and the police. In a turf war, they had attacked rival gang members with chains and knives, killing at least one of them. It was reported in the newspapers.

"I soon noticed the sluggish speed at which the boat was moving, and the waterline on the side of the boat was a long way below the water. It was clear that the boat was carrying a heavy cargo.

"A few hours into the journey, and even before I had the opportunity to speak to anyone on board, I went up on deck. It was a sunny day. I took off my clothes and sunbathed. Then I noticed something strange about the sun's position. It moved from the port side to the starboard side then back to the port side. I realised that the boat was not moving forward in a straight line but was going in circles. Even before I could get down to confront the captain, I saw a boat approaching us at high speed. It turned out to be a China Coastguard patrol boat. It quickly caught up with us. The patrol boat aligned itself alongside our vessel and one of the crew shouted through a loudspeaker for us to stop and let soldiers board the boat for inspection.

"I was terrified. I didn't think that I had come this far only to be caught and brought back to Hong Kong to face justice.

"A party of soldiers boarded with handguns drawn. We were ordered to line up and show them our identification papers. I produced my forged Swedish passport. We were then asked to empty our pockets and the soldiers frisked our bodies to make sure nothing was left. They then searched the cabins. I could see that they took whatever valuables they could find there – gold and US dollars. They behaved more like pirates than soldiers, ransacking and pillaging. The captain was asked to unlock the cargo hold.

"'*Faat-lot, faat-lot* (bountiful, bountiful),' one soldier muttered to another in a dialect which I could understand. He could not hide his excitement. There were cartons upon cartons of cigarettes stacked from floor to ceiling, filling the hold like tinned sardines.

"'Shut up and pick up the items on the floor. Place everything in the basket,' shouted the officer in charge. "Round up the smugglers and guard them in the cabin. Interrogate them and find out who is the leader. Pay special attention to the man with the moustache who showed the foreign passport. He must be the leader. Take the boat into port."

"The control room was taken over and the captain was ordered to move into port with the patrol boat in tow. The so-called port was nothing more than a small fishing village. It was quite primitive. We were taken into the coastguard station building. It had two floors and was sparsely furnished with steel desks and chairs. Red banners with gold embroidered words depicting rescues and other acts of bravery hung on the wall alongside a portrait of Mao. Except for the sign and motif on the exterior wall, one could hardly tell the building belonged to the coastguard.

"I was ushered into a small room upstairs. It contained even less furniture – just a table and several folding chairs. There I was interrogated by three of the coastguards."

"How did you feel?" I asked. "Were you scared?"

"Hell, was I scared? Of course I was scared but I remained calm. I said to them, 'I don't know what you are talking about.' I kept shaking my head. I pretended I didn't speak Chinese. I spoke only in English: 'I am Swedish. I want to see my ambassador.' No one could understand me."

"So what happened next?" I interjected.

"Then a civilian arrived. He spoke a little English. He acted as the interpreter. 'From where you come?' the young man asked. 'You understand me English?'

"'Sweden.' I broke into a smile as if I was relieved to see him. I spoke in my best English accent which I picked up from those years spent in London as a student.

"'Finally, someone who speaks my language,' I said to him. 'Please tell the captain that I want to see my ambassador. Send me to Beijing. I insist. Do you understand?'

"'He says he is Swedish and wants to see the Swedish Ambassador in Beijing,' the interpreter translated. 'He speaks with a drawl and the accent is not at all Chinese, like the way I speak. I am certain he is Swedish. Otherwise, how can one explain that his voice comes not from the mouth but from the nose? No Chinese speak English like him. He is definitely not a Chinese.'

"The interpreter was asked to leave the room. Then the group started an animated discussion in my presence. They thought I could not understand what they were talking about."

"What were they saying?" I interrupted him again.

"Just listen," retorted Winston impatiently. "Don't keep butting in. 'Today we landed a big fish,' the leader said. 'I calculate each of you can get as many as fifty cartons of cigarettes. Of course, as the leader I get double. If we do as he asks and report this matter to Beijing then we will lose our catch for the day. Tell you what, why don't we just take the cigarettes and set these bastards free? Get Ah Shum back and tell him to ask what the moustache wanted.'

"I told the interpreter we wanted the boat to be replenished – water, food and diesel – and to be pushed back into the open sea. The coastguard agreed. That was how I arrived in Taiwan."

Winston and I talked from lunch until past dinner time. We must have finished four bottles of good Bordeaux wine between us – Haut Brion 1989, rated ten out of ten by Robert Parker.

"The night is still young," said Winston. "Let's paint the town red. But first let me show you the 'sand circuit'."

He took me down to the basement of the casino.

"This is not the racecourse," I said. "This is where you work – Casino de Lisboa."

"Who said we were going to the racecourse? I said 'sand circuit' not 'race circuit'."

A sexy young girl in a short skirt walked past, turned her head, smiled and asked: "Go or no go?" Other girls, equally attractive, followed closely on her heels and asked the same question. The girls kept on walking. None stopped.

"Wow! They're attractive," I said. "Why do they just walk in circles?"

"They are all prostitutes. The rule is that they have to keep walking. They are not allowed to stop or they'll be booted out of the casino for loitering. Almost all of them are from China. There are many white Russians too. But they operate outside the casino and hotel. None of them are allowed inside. These white Russian girls come from Vladivostok or other parts of Russia's Far Eastern coast. They work for gangs and don't pay protection money, whereas the Chinese girls work for themselves. Not only are they willing to pay but they are also generous when it comes to giving sexual favours to guards and gang members alike. Hence they enjoy the privilege of being able to walk the 'sand circuit'. They are also allowed to rent rooms upstairs on the sixth floor. The hotel imposes a quota of not more than sixty rooms to be let to prostitutes each day. There are two 'sand circuit' floors in the basement: the lower floor is reserved for 'high-class' while the upper floor is given to the less attractive prostitutes. Several girls normally share one room. It is where they receive customers and rest. If a room is occupied and a girl wants to rest – one can imagine that after walking the 'sand circuit' continuously she must often be tired – she will just sit out in the corridor until the room is free again."

"Do you get freebies from these girls?"

"I don't need free service. I pay. I get nine in a row and time my orgasm only when I reach the last of them."

I broke into laughter. I took it with a pinch of salt. I knew it was another one of Winston's jokes. He loved to brag.

"What about this one just passing?" said Winston. "Isn't she sexy?"

I was really glad that Winston had recovered from his long ordeal. He was back on his feet. Soccer-betting was getting hot. Even the iconic Jockey Club – Hong Kong's leading charitable institution – was getting into the game. He was doing well.

Then one day at a social gathering I bumped into Ricky, the brother of Albert who twice took Winston under his wing; once when he escaped to Taiwan and the second time when he was released from prison – not to mention that when Winston practised as a solicitor, Albert was one of his biggest clients.

"Do you know what happened to Winston?" Ricky asked.

"I saw him in Macau. He's doing well… oh, what am I talking about? You must know. He works for you."

"When was the last time you saw him?"

"A few months ago, why do you ask?"

"Do you know what has happened to him since?"

"No, I don't. Why, what has happened to him?"

"He fiddled on the computer, placing the bets after the match results were known."

"What, you aren't serious, are you?" I exclaimed. "He stole money again!"

"Yes, he took close to $200 million this time. They caught him, beat the hell out of him and he coughed up some $20 million. He said he would pay it back in full if he was allowed to go free. He pleaded for a couple of days. Then he did a Houdini act – disappeared into thin air. No one knows where he is today."

"Wow… he 'picked lice out of the tiger's head'!" I exclaimed. "He's so audacious. It's like playing Russian roulette on himself."

I remembered what I had told Winston about the postal worker in London who stamped the envelope before the bet was placed as a means of earning a couple of extra pounds every week.

"No, you're wrong, Robert," said Ricky. "Winston did not consider what he did as cheating. He was trying to beat the system. The truth is that he thought he was smarter than all of us. He couldn't understand nor could he accept the fact that he languished behind people like us. It is a classic case of how philandering, power and greed can all destroy a person and his family. A young man in a hurry will never reach his destination." Ricky sighed and continued philosophically. "Each generation's futile pursuit of a better life for themselves may all come crashing down one day."

I could not agree more. I had my grandmother's experience to prove it. I did not know Ricky was capable of such wisdom when his family was so embroiled in the gambling business.

## SHANGHAI PARTIES

Success brought about a change in lifestyle. I was thrust into circulation with the rich and famous of Hong Kong, which in those days was dominated by the industrialists – owners of cotton spinning factories – and almost all of them came from Shanghai.

Those were the days of wine and roses. The Shanghainese parties were unique: wealth and elegance were in abundance and high fashion filled the room, the kind of stuff that legends were made of. The ladies flaunted their diamonds and jewellery, each trying to outdo the other while the men behaved according to their pecking order in society – how successful each was, how much they gave to charities, how senior they were in the government hierarchy, and how high up their companies were in the corporate league.

M.W. Wong was known as the 'King of Textiles'. He headed the group of entrepreneurs who came from Shanghai and, during the 1950s, started the cotton spinning industry that transformed Hong Kong. He owned the largest spinning mill. Its size was measured by the number of spindles. He had the most. His mill stretched from one end of the street to the other. M.W., as he was affectionately known, was from Zhou Shan. In the heyday of textiles, M.W. and his family were as close as one could get to being Hong Kong's own royal family.

He was a handsome man, even in his old age – regal, tall, witty, well spoken and always elegant and magnanimous. But he had a sharp tongue and could at times be brash and overbearing. He would not mince his words if he wanted to dress down someone. Yet, to the people he liked, he was charming and generous.

"Let us drink a toast," said M.W. at a party. "I have more than you in the glass. We empty the glasses together."

"I am sorry," said the girl. "I don't drink."

M.W. was noticeably upset. "Then why are you here?" he barked at her as he walked away in disgust.

Once we shared a table with Sir Philip Haddon-Cave, then the Colony's Financial Secretary. It was at a charity ball to raise funds for the local orphanage, the Po Leung Kuk.

"M.W., can you sponsor the Hong Kong Philharmonic?" asked Lady Haddon-Cave.

M.W. either did not register what was being asked of him or he did not know what 'philharmonic' was. He did not respond.

"Your father is the most insincere man I have ever met," said Lady Haddon-Cave to M.W.'s daughter, who was seated across the table.

M.W. obviously found the remark extremely offensive. He was not going to let her get away with it even though she was the wife of a high colonial official. All night long he plotted his revenge. Then the opportunity arose.

"Oh, Betty, what beautiful jewellery." M.W. suddenly gripped the wrist of Lady Haddon-Cave, lifted it up high and shook it. Her gold-plated bracelet had small bells embedded in it. The bells made a tinkling sound and it seemed as if he was ringing bells.

Everyone at the table burst out laughing.

"Scrap iron and metals," M.W. shouted in a Shanghai dialect. Everyone at the table except Lady Haddon-Cave understood what he had said – they all came from Shanghai – and were taken aback by his sarcastic remark.

A stony silence prevailed as the wives at the table tried to hide the jewellery they wore – diamonds, emeralds and rubies, some the size of quails' eggs.

The 'king' had had his tit-for-tat and he was gleeful.

≈≈≈≈≈

On another occasion, the textile tycoons – mostly of Ningbo origin – got together at the Furama Hotel in the Central Business District to welcome the contestants in the Miss Universe Pageant. The party was thrown by a tycoon who was a well-known playboy. While waiting for the beauties in the contest to arrive, the guests gathered and the conversation centred on who owned the most spindles. The king happily acknowledged the compliments the group paid him. He knew when it came to spindles no one could match him – he had the most. As the conversation continued, a pretender to the throne of the textile kingdom walked past. There was intense rivalry between the men, both vying to be the largest in the trade.

"There is this young man." M.W. raised his voice just as the pretender walked past the group. "He tries to catch up with me. He will need a long life... ha, ha, ha..."

At the table the two ignored each other.

"Mr. Lily Cheung." M.W. suddenly raised his voice and greeted the pretender. "You are well, aren't you?"

The address was insulting and it rubbed salt into a new wound. The pretender was infuriated. He had just emerged from an unhappy chapter of his life. His mistress, Lily Cheung, a well-known cabaret singer, was pregnant with what he thought was his son. It was such a big thing for him that he could not stop talking about his good fortune – that at his age he could produce a son and an heir to his vast business empire. Imagine his disappointment when he discovered that the baby was born with the hair and features of a different race.

≈≈≈≈≈

M.W. gave lavish parties at his Peak home. The house commanded an unobstructed 360-degree view of Victoria Harbour and its surroundings. From its sprawling lawns, the guests gathered to chat and admire the view as the cool breeze primed with the scent of autumn and sea air gently blew. The moon hung in the sky, accompanied by sparkling stars. The ships in the harbour gleamed like fireflies. On both sides of the harbour, the water, lights and the moon met to create an illusion of a cluster of glittering diamonds. Champagne flowed and waiters wove through the crowd serving canapés on silver trays. Laughter filled the air. It was heavenly.

The party would begin on a sombre note but would become rowdy when the drinking started. Glasses were raised and clinked at each other in toasts. It was a way to show respect to the guests and the host and among themselves. Toasts were of two kinds – 'salutes' and 'bitter'. The latter was reserved as punishment meted out to someone who spoke or acted in a manner that was considered to be 'unbecoming'. The drinking rituals in Shanghainese parties put Hong Kong on the map. It made Hong Kong the largest consumption centre per capita of French cognacs and Scotch whiskies.

Yet, throughout the drinking ritual, cheating was prevalent and, in more ways than one, perfected to an art. One trick was to drink without swallowing, take a bite of food and spit them out together. But it could be easily spotted. The other way was to fake drinks: soy sauce, cola and tea were all diluted to make them look like whisky or cognac. Normally out of courtesy, especially to the host, the guests would turn a blind eye, but not so if the toast was made to a person whose position or station was perceived to be superior. It would be considered an act of disrespect and, if caught, the offending party would be asked to drink a 'bitter' toast as punishment.

"Ah, the honourable Mrs. Sung." Mrs. Chao came to pay her respects to the wife of a top government official one evening.

Mrs. Chao was the wife of a well-known industrialist. She was wealthy and she had a tendency to appear to look up to the wives only as long as their husbands were in power. In other words, she was only as close to the wives as their husbands were useful. As soon as their official status ended or was reduced, she would completely ignore them, looking through them as if they were transparent, even if they met at the same party. In truth, it was rare if ever that 'fallen couples' – as they were called – were invited to a Shanghai party.

Mrs. Sung was well aware that she was only being toasted because of her husband's position and she disliked Mrs. Chao intensely although, on the surface, the two appeared to be on friendly terms.

"Let me pay you my respects by drinking this 'salute' toast to you."

"Thank you, Mrs. Chao." Mrs. Sung smiled as she emptied her glass of cognac. "Wait a minute," she hesitated, "let me check the glass. What is this veneer of steam on the inside?"

Mrs. Chao emptied the glass quickly but it was too late. Mrs. Sung snatched the glass and tasted what was left in it.

"It's tea!" she shouted. "Mrs. Chao, you cheated."

Mrs. Chao was greatly embarrassed. With the other guests now all staring at her, she asked the waiter to bring her a bottle of cognac. She then drank and emptied the bottle. No one tried to stop her, not even her husband.

Mrs. Sung certainly did not try. She glowed with satisfaction as Mrs. Chao quickly passed out and collapsed on the floor.

I could not believe my good fortune. I was seated next to Kitty Law, the newly crowned Hong Kong beauty queen. One of the perks of winning the pageant was being able to move in the circles of Hong Kong's high society where she hoped to meet Mr. Right, get married, have children and lead the pampered life of a *tai tai* – a wealthy wife. Unfortunately, not every dream came true. Many became prey for predators – the married men who stalked the Shanghai parties.

Kitty was young, beautiful and, rare for a Chinese woman, actually voluptuous. Her curvy figure would make any man drool. No sooner had I taken my seat than I felt a tap on my shoulder. I looked up and saw the familiar face of a textile tycoon. He was someone to whom I was beholden. He often gave me work.

"Robert, can we swap seats?" he asked.

"Of course," I said as I discreetly moved to his table with my place name card.

Throughout the evening I noticed Kitty and the tycoon were engaged in animated conversation.

"Robert, I'm giving Kitty a lift home," he said later. "I need an alibi. Can you come with me?"

The tycoon muttered something into the ear of his wife. She turned to me and gave me a sour look. Then he returned. I knew he was using me as a front. I was a willing accomplice. I really had little choice.

In his Rolls-Royce, it was apparent he was excited and 'hot'.

"Kitty, you are one in a million," he said as he slipped a stack of notes into her hand. "No, you are more than one in a million. Out of six million people in Hong Kong, you have been chosen as this year's pageant queen. Do you know this is quite an achievement... yes, quite an honour. You ought to be proud of yourself. So should your parents. You are an exceptional girl. When you have come so far, I am sure you don't want to be wasted upon just another young man, someone who has to work nine to five, do you? No... no, that would be a waste of your opportunity cost. Do you understand what it means – opportunity cost? It means your biggest asset is youth and beauty and, if you have a brain, you will come round to my way of thinking.

"Now let me celebrate your crowning success with this little gesture – a token we call a 'meet-each-other courtesy'. Now, don't be shy. Just take it," he said as he slipped another wad of notes into her hand.

I was flabbergasted. This 'courtesy' must have been worth more than HK$400,000 – a wad of crisp new $1,000 notes neatly bundled together measuring more than a few inches thick. He had obviously come prepared… first, test the reaction with a token and, if it was favourable, the big gift.

The blush on her cheeks made Kitty look even more beautiful. She withdrew her hand from under his and pushed the money back to the tycoon who must have been older than her father.

"I cannot accept this," she said.

"No, no, no… that would make me unhappy."

The shuffling backwards and forwards of the wad of money continued until I noticed a signal from the corner of Kitty's eyes.

The movement stopped. "Don't embarrass me in front of this young man. Call me another time," she whispered into his ear, thinking that I was not listening.

Kitty had a good run with the tycoon. He satisfied her material needs and pandered to her every whim. He bought her properties, jewellery and everything a young woman's heart desired until one day the two fell out. No one knew who was tired of whom.

"I'm in Tokyo with Kitty," the chaperon reported. "We are in a fur shop. Kitty wants to buy a Fendi long mink coat. It's US$75,000. Can you approve it?"

"Yes," replied the tycoon. He was caught in the middle of a busy day going from one meeting to another.

"Kitty also wants another designer brand – a blue mercury Russian sable," the chaperon called again. "It costs US$250,000. Can you approve it?"

The tycoon hung up. As far as I know, that was the end of the relationship.

# CITY IN JITTERS

In the early 1980s, Hong Kong was hit by political shocks. Margaret Thatcher, Prime Minister of Britain, went to Beijing to discuss the future of the colony. Deng Hsiao Ping told her that the lease of Hong Kong was non-negotiable and China wanted Hong Kong back. They agreed on the principle of 'One Country, Two Systems' as a formula to maintain Hong Kong's stability and prosperity.

On the way out, Mrs Thatcher slipped, stumbled and fell down the steps. It was a bad omen. Despite assurances given by the Government that investors could set their minds at ease, the citizens were definitely uncomfortable.

As the terms of Hong Kong's future return to China were being formalized, the territory was hit by the jitters. The value of its currency dropped dramatically – at one point to as low as HK$10 for US$1 – as the outflow of capital increased. It became nothing less than a raging torrent. Over-the-counter trades at some banks were suspended altogether. The onslaught caused the overnight money rate to soar to over 200%. Panic was widespread. The citizens swept supermarket shelves clean. In desperation, the government reactivated the idea of reverting to a currency board regime. In 1983 the peg to the US dollar was introduced on the advice of an economist, John Greenwood. The peg level of HK$7.80 to US$1 was settled at a crisis meeting.

But the fear continued. Hong Kong residents continued to scurry around the world looking for safe havens. And disaster did not strike just once. It struck again in 1989 when the Tiananmen Square crackdown shook already fragile confidence to the core. Another wave of emigration, massive and unprecedented this time, started. Queues for emigrant visas were common sights outside the usual Western consulates. The 'brain drain' took a turn for the worse – emigration peaked at 67,000 families in one year.

Meanwhile, Hong Kong's role as a manufacturing centre ended. Factories moved across the border into Guangdong Province and the Pearl River Delta area to take advantage of cheaper labour there. It was remarkable that the transformation was achieved without creating a dent in the growth rate of the economy – the vacuum left behind by the departing factories was simply filled by the growth in the service sector. Unemployment during the period was negligibly small.

Instead of following the flow and moving north, the Hong Kong industrialists who originated from Shanghai chose to close their mills. As they sold the factories, the textile era of Hong Kong drew to a close. A new era arrived with its crop of new emerging 'kings' – the property tycoons. The textile 'kings' were on their way out, their reign over.

"Robert, you are well connected. Can you do me a favour?" asked M.W. one day. "I want to sell all my factory buildings. Do you know of someone who may be interested?"

"I can try to find out for you. Give me the area and the price per square foot."

"It is about one million square feet. I hope to get $900 per square foot – that's about market rate."

Li Ka Shing was the richest man in Hong Kong and the richest Chinese in the world. He was ranked No. 1 in Hong Kong and No. 14 of the World's Richest with a net worth of US$22 billion according to *Forbes*. He was known as 'Superman' for his uncanny ability to always smell a good deal and his Midas touch.

Money came so easily to the man that he once told me: "Robert, there is so much money on the ground that I simply don't have the time to bend down and pick it all up."

After the textile era passed, Superman emerged as the new 'King of Hong Kong'.

Li was among those I called that morning. He showed interest immediately but said he would call me back.

His response was swift. Within half an hour he called back.

"Yes, Robert, I am interested." He was brief and direct. "Albert Chow will follow it up with you."

Richard Ellis, the international firm of surveyors, was asked to physically measure up the area and conduct a survey of the property.

"There is an additional 50,000 square feet that is omitted from the calculation," said M.W. after the parties shook hands on the price. "Please can you let Mr. Li know?"

I did as I was told.

"But the additional floor area is an illegal structure." Li's response was swift. He had done his homework well and had the information at his fingertips. "Please tell Mr. Wong that I shall pay half of the agreed price per square foot."

I dutifully related the message to M.W. and went out for lunch. I was surprised to see him waiting in the reception when I returned. He was there with his daughter, Andrea.

"Father, please tell Robert what we have agreed." Andrea spoke to her father.

"Ah… erm… yes," said M.W. "My daughter tells me we can't ask Mr. Li to pay for the illegal structures. Please tell him that he doesn't have to pay the additional amount."

"Anything else, Father?" prompted Andrea.

"Yes, from now on you should only listen to her," he said. "I am out of the picture. She calls the shots."

I asked Patricia, my secretary, to put a call through to Li Ka Shing.

"No, I insist," said Li. "If Mr. Wong doesn't accept then I shall personally go up to his office with the cheque."

The father and the daughter looked at each other in bewilderment and after some discussion I was asked to hand the phone to M.W. Li was still on the line.

"Mr. Li, you are more than correct and honourable. All I can say is that 'obedience is my highest form of respect' for you," M.W. said.

Shortly after the acquisition Li broke the buildings up into small strata-titled units, did a flip and sold the premises retail to end users, and in the process reaped a handsome profit – hundreds of millions of dollars.

"We sold the premises at market to Mr. Li," said M.W. to me when he learned about the sub-sales. He was not sour. "The name of Li Ka Shing created a premium in the market and he sold higher. Good luck to him."

Later M.W. hosted a lunch at home for Li. It was a memorable occasion when the two 'kings', one from the past and the other from the present, sat together and got along well, chatting amicably throughout the meal in the presence of members of the two families including Li's elder son and M.W.'s granddaughter – both of whom were then unmarried.

≈≈≈≈≈

Come rain or shine, Li Ka Shing played golf every morning at the Royal Hong Kong Golf Club in Deepwater Bay. His house was a stone's throw from the club. He teed off punctually at 7 a.m. One morning I was there to tee off ahead of him.

"Mr. Li, after you." I gave him the signal to pass through. "Your time is more valuable than mine."

"Thank you, Robert," Li said cheerfully as he passed. "I appreciate what you did. You are now a thousand times closer to Cheung Kong."

I knew after the sale of M.W.'s properties I was in his good books but it was gratifying to hear from the man himself that he appreciated my efforts.

Whether it was that morning or some other time, I heard a roar followed by a round of applause. I looked around and saw Li emerging from a concealed tee, walking in his hallmark swaggering style beaming with a broad smile.

"Hole in one – my ninth, Robert," Li said light-heartedly, enjoying the adulation of the other golfers. "Oh, by the way, I have a project for you. Albert Chow will follow up with you."

Li was not the only person to be happy that day. The papers for a substantial property development and all the related conveyancing arrived even before me at the office that morning.

≈≈≈≈≈

Despite the booming economy and the continuing good life in Hong Kong, the worries over 1997 – the year when sovereignty would be given back to China – would not go away. Anyone with the means to do so was looking for a way either to get out of the colony ahead of time and before the Communists arrived, or to obtain the right of abode somewhere in the West. Like most of my friends, I was actively thinking about Canada as a possible immigration destination.

However, Canada is far away. To move there would mean uprooting and severing ties for good – a prospect that was as unpalatable as it would be to remain and do nothing. Almost everyone I knew had either left or made immigration plans in case the transition should go awry. They were the pillars of Hong Kong without whom the economy would falter.

"The world around us is changing," lamented T.O. "It is picking up speed even before 1997 arrives. Look at the rate at which factories are moving north and the economy is being transformed. Soon we will have no more industries. The service sector will take over. How do these changes bode for Hong Kong? I don't know. All I know is that we must all make contingency plans."

"What will you do?" I asked.

"Like everyone else, I will probably go to Vancouver," said T.O. "I am different from you. I can retire there but you are young. Your career hangs like a midday sun. I really don't know how to advise you, except to say that you too must make contingency plans. By the way, from what I read in the papers, it is almost certain that the Conveyancing Scale will be abolished. Have you assessed how abolition will affect your practice?"

"No," I replied, "but I think about it constantly. I am worried sick. But what can I do? You tell me."

"Why not try Singapore?" T.O. said after pausing for a moment. "Singapore is safe. It is an integral part of the West. I admire Lee Kuan Yew. He is a capable man, a leader with vision. Set up a base and from there you can monitor Hong Kong as events unfold before the deadline arrives. With a base there, you can also harmonize and work the two together as one. The two territories are close enough for one to commute. That way you deal with career and immigration needs all at the same time – it is killing two birds with one stone."

I wrote to the Attorney General of Singapore in the early 1980s. I did not receive a reply, not even an acknowledgement.

I spoke to my Aunt Diana, who lived in Singapore. She said she would speak to the Attorney General. Aunt Diana's family was well known in Singapore. Over the years she had been pleased to see the progress I had made in my career.

She called me one day. "I spoke to Tan Boon Teik, the Attorney General. He remembers your letter. He has not replied because he thinks your efforts will be futile – the law does not allow lawyers from Hong Kong to practise, let alone set up a branch here. Nevertheless, I have made an appointment for you to see him next Tuesday... mark it down, Tuesday at 10.30 a.m."

"Thank you, Aunt Diana," I said gratefully, excited by the new opportunity. There was light at the end of the tunnel. Singapore was my best shot. If I had to emigrate, I would face an uncertain future and would have to start all over again.

I arrived punctually and was ushered into a windowless waiting room. The Attorney General was busy that morning. Despite my appointment, he could not find a slot to see me. At lunchtime I was asked to return at 2.30 p.m. At 3 p.m. he finally saw me.

"Mr. Wang, as you can tell, I have had a busy day," he said. "I can only repeat what I told Diana Eu – our law does not allow Hong Kong lawyers to practise here."

"But, sir, I recently read an article that a City (London) firm was given an off-shore licence."

"Ah yes, that one... the local Bar Association was up in arms against me."

I returned home empty-handed and disheartened. It seemed that Singapore was a non-starter.

"I read in the paper that Singapore is promoting Confucian studies," said T.O. "I informed John Tung. He is an ardent follower of Confucianism. He says he will donate S$3 million to support the cause. He agrees to let you handle this donation."

I knew immediately what T.O. was up to. He knew I wanted Singapore badly. In his subtle way, he was giving me another chance even though he knew it was just a shot in the dark.

I knew John Tung well. He was slight in stature and a man of few words yet behind the face lay a deep and extremely intelligent person. He had come from Shanghai in the 1950s and built up an empire in enamelware, popular for household items in Hong Kong at the time. The thermos flasks his factory made were popular and its trademark – I-Feng – was a household name. When enamelware ceased to be popular in Hong Kong, he had the foresight to move his operations to Nigeria and there he prospered – enamelware is popular in African households even in this day and age.

I took the unsolicited offer of the donation to the Attorney General. He declined my offer politely, telling me that it was none of his concern.

My hopes were once more dashed. Then one day, out of the blue, I received a message from the Attorney General's Office that the Deputy Prime Minister – Dr. Goh Keng Swee – wanted to see me. My hopes were rekindled.

"Mr. Wang, I would like to hear from you myself. Why are you so eager to practise in Singapore? What are the concerns of Hong Kong lawyers?"

"I speak for myself, but I know many lawyers share my concerns. I am faced with this dilemma: to leave or to stay. If I stay, I am worried that the transition may not be smooth. If I leave, I face an uncertain future in a foreign country. We are between the devil and the deep blue sea. Yet lawyers will leave in droves if the current jitters continue. An exodus could undermine the legal system. What we need is peace of mind, an assurance that if the transition goes wrong we have somewhere to go. Singapore is culturally compatible and has political stability. It is my choice and, I believe, theirs too."

Dr. Goh listened politely and patiently. He said little. "We do not agree with your assessment of Hong Kong's situation. We believe the transition will be smooth. An unstable Hong Kong would serve no one's interest, least of all Singapore's."

The conversation then switched to the donation. Singapore was about to launch the Institute of Asian Philosophies at the National University of Singapore.

"It would be timely if the donation was made before the Institute is launched," said Dr. Goh as the meeting ended.

John Tung discreetly and modestly excused himself. I took his S$3 million donation to Singapore

≈≈≈≈≈

In Hong Kong, life appeared on the surface to be back to normal. Yet the anxiety continued. It was a testing time. Unless the concerns of its businessmen and professionals were addressed the brain drain could only intensify and this would spell more trouble for Hong Kong.

To counteract this, the British government rolled out the Right of Abode Scheme which conferred British nationality on locals and gave passports to no fewer than 50,000 of its leading citizens, the pillars of Hong Kong society.

I had, by then, all but forgotten about Singapore when I received a message that Dr. Goh wanted me to prepare a paper setting out the concerns of Hong Kong lawyers and make proposals on what Singapore could do to assist them.

No sooner had the paper been delivered than I was informed that the Prime Minister would be in Hong Kong. He had asked to see me.

It was a momentous occasion when I met with the Prime Minister. I was thrilled yet nervous to see Lee Kuan Yew at his modest suite in the Shangri-la Hotel. I took along my partner in the practice, Anna Wu. Anna was young and pretty with cheeks rosy as red apples.

The Prime Minister was direct and succinct. He did not mince his words. "Mr. Wang, I don't know you. You come on the recommendation of the Deputy Prime Minister. I wish to find out as much about you as possible. I am going to ask you questions which you may find offensive. Please bear with me."

"Yes, Prime Minister." I nodded nervously.

"Who is this young woman you've brought along?" he asked.

"She is Anna Wu," I replied shakily. "Anna is my partner. Your office told me that I could bring an associate to this meeting."

For more than an hour, I was put through a most gruelling session of cross-examination, at the end of which the Prime Minister seemed to be satisfied.

"Please go ahead and form a committee to 'propose, vet and recommend' Hong Kong lawyers to us," he said as he quoted from the paper I had prepared for the Deputy Prime Minister. "I am willing to offer them a bolt-hole. I will take a punt on Hong Kong. I have nothing to lose. An unstable Hong Kong is not in our interests."

The Prime Minister later wrote:

> *Their media believed Singapore wanted to cream off its talent, but it was in our interests to have Hong Kong succeed after it returned to Chinese sovereignty. To raid and deplete Hong Kong of talent is a one-off exercise. A thriving Hong Kong will be a continuing source of business and benefits.*

I proceeded to form the Vetting Committee. I was not short of volunteers. Eminent lawyers from both disciplines – barristers and solicitors – chairmen, past and present, of the Bar Association and the Law Society joined. In the years that followed, the Committee received and vetted numerous applications. Over half of the Hong Kong lawyers applied.

Singapore's Legal Profession Act was amended in the process to allow successful applicants to be admitted to practise. They were also given residential rights in Singapore which, at their option, could be taken up at any time within a specified time frame.

I became the first from Hong Kong to be admitted to practise in Singapore.

"Robert, I am happy for you and I admire your tenacity. You moved heaven and earth to reach your goal," said T.O., "but your battle has just begun. Singaporeans are famously *ganshu* (afraid to lose out). Your partner there – what is his name? – I am getting forgetful, a sign of old age… yes, Mr. Woo is not going to let you get away for long unless you can contribute.

"You told me Singapore celebrated its twenty-fifth anniversary and many of the top businessmen from Hong Kong were invited to see for themselves her achievements. Why don't you prepare another paper for the Prime Minister? Say something along the lines that you can organize a scheme for the eminent entrepreneurs of Hong Kong, modelled after the lawyers' scheme. In exchange for their investments, Singapore shall give them residential rights. I am certain such a proposal would be well received. It benefits all three sides: Singapore, Hong Kong and the entrepreneurs.

"You stand to benefit most. In one stroke not only would you consolidate your base of existing clients but also gain a crop of new ones. Once you solve the immigration problems for them, these entrepreneurs will be indebted to you for life. The two-way traffic will enable you to build bridges spanning Singapore and Hong Kong – the advantages go on and on. Oh, I am so excited just talking about it."

I submitted a paper entitled 'Scheme for Eminent Entrepreneurs' to the Prime Minister.

As predicted, the proposal was well received. The Prime Minister gave his blessing. It gave birth to the CSHS (Corporate Special Holding Status Scheme) which in essence allowed an approved entrepreneur to nominate one person for permanent residence in Singapore for each S$1 million he invested. The nominations could come from approved categories that included immediate family members, relatives, senior members of staff and co-investors. Thus the net was cast to cover not only the entrepreneur but also those who mattered most to him: family, relatives, key employees, friends and business associates.

"Robert, I would like to nominate two sisters using my quota for permanent residence," said Li Ka Shing. "They are owners of the stockbrokers' firm that handles seventy per cent of my portfolio. Do you know how big this business is?"

"It must be mind-boggling," I said.

"Yes, they are big brokers," Li continued. "Please make sure you do not bill them. Send the bills direct to me."

"Mr. Li, I will make sure we send you no bills. This is a small matter. You have been most supportive. It's the least we can do for you."

"Alright then, I shall send them to your office and give you the details."

The two sisters came. They were both young and pretty. The older sister was known to me by reputation. She was married into a prominent family.

I sent the papers over to the Singapore office and gave specific instructions that under no circumstances should Li be billed for this simple work.

That morning I was in the conference room with a group of lawyers from San Francisco and we were talking about a possible tie-up of the two firms. One of the lawyers from the firm of Kaplan Russin & Vecchi, whose name was Paul, was there with his wife Nancy Pelosi. Nancy later became the sixtieth Speaker of the House of Representatives.

"Mr. Wang, there is an urgent call for you," announced Patricia, my secretary.

"Can't you see I am busy? Who is calling?"

"I think you will want to take this call. It is Li Ka Shing."

Everyone in the room recognized the name. It was people like Li on our clients list that had attracted the American firm to seek us out for an association. The call could not have come at a more opportune moment as we were just about to conclude the tie-up terms and I knew Nancy Pelosi was an important politician.

"Put the line through to the conference room," I told Patricia.

The secretary gave me a worried look as she left the room.

"Good morning to you, Mr. Li," I said jubilantly.

"Robert, I am really upset with you," shouted an obviously agitated Li. "You have betrayed my trust. Do you know what embarrassment your action has caused me?"

"Oh-oh-oh, Mr. Li," I stammered and blushed nervously in the presence of the Americans. "Wh-what have I done, Mr. Li?"

"You idiot. Why did you send the bill to my office against your previous promise?" He continued to shout.

It suddenly dawned on me that Li was referring to the two sisters.

"I am sorry. I am sorry, Mr. Li. Who sent you the bill?"

"Ask your Singapore office!" Li's anger did not subside. He was even more furious.

"Let me check," I said nervously. "I shall do so right away."

I apologised to the Americans, who sensed something had gone terribly wrong in my dealings with the richest man in Hong Kong, and turned to the secretary to ask her to put a call through to Singapore immediately.

I cursed my partner when I learned that indeed a note of fee was sent to Li's office. It was their *ganshu* mentality at work again – not wishing to lose out in any case even if it meant a small fee that could upset a client as important as Li Ka Shing despite my repeated reminders over the matter.

"Please accept my apologies," I pleaded with Li whose anger had by then subsided. "All I can say is that 'the calculation of earth is different from heaven' (the best laid plans of mice and men tend to go awry). Please forgive me."

"I will accept this explanation," said Li. "The matter is now closed."

# The Tycoons' Club

The Corporate Special Holding Status Scheme attracted top entrepreneurs. They combined to make up a substantial chunk of Hong Kong's market capitalization. Many of them were household names and others, though less known, were nevertheless luminaries in their own right.

The Scheme was extended to Hong Kong families. Combined with Britain's Right of Abode Scheme it played a major role in stabilising Hong Kong when it was at its most vulnerable.

Lee Kuan Yew wrote:

> *Six weeks after Tiananmen, we offered to give 25,000 Hong Kong families Approval In-Principle (AIP) permanent residence, without their having to move to Singapore until the need arose. This AIP would be valid for five years and could be extended for another five. It did not draw talent away from Hong Kong at a time of great uncertainty. Huge queues formed outside our Singapore Commission to get the application forms, and nearly caused a riot.*
>
> *When I met Governor Wilson in Hong Kong in January 1990, I assured him that I had no intention of damaging Hong Kong by the offer of AIPs, that we would lend Hong Kong our skills and credit when they were short, and vice versa, and each would profit from the capital, skills and talent of the other. We had not expected such a tumultuous response. After a year, we had granted a total of 50,000 AIPs, double the intended number. Hong Kong soon recovered from the shock of Tiananmen and was doing well. The people earned good money in Hong Kong, more than they could in Singapore or elsewhere. Indeed, many who had emigrated to Canada, Australia and New Zealand returned to work in Hong Kong, leaving their families behind.*

"It is Hong Kong that you've taken to Singapore!" said Richard, the younger son of Li Ka Shing, who sat next to me on a flight to Singapore. His father and his friends – Lee Shau Kee and Cheng Yu Tung – were seated at the back, playing a card game called 'Dig the Big Brother'.

The Trio are three of Hong Kong's richest. Li Ka Shing is number 1 and Lee Shau Kee is not far behind in the number 2 spot – based on listed wealth. But when unlisted wealth is included, Cheng must be close and may even be the richest individual in Hong Kong and, by extension, the richest Chinese in the world.

Cheng is legendary. His mind is razor-sharp and works like a computer. He is a mathematical genius. He has no ego to speak of and he is also a cautious man. He always gives careful consideration to everything, ensuring that no stone is left unturned in the process. Over the years I have witnessed how others, including the likes of Li Ka Shing and Lee Shau Kee, overtly two of Hong Kong's richest, defer to him when important decisions are made. It seems he is seldom if ever wrong. When he sees an opportunity, he is bold beyond words. He strikes daringly, accurately and mercilessly. It has earned him the nickname 'Sandy Gutsy Tung' – Tung the Brave Heart.

His fortune is vast. It is a known fact that what appears on the surface – his listed flagship, New World Development – as his known wealth is merely the tip of the iceberg, a fraction of his true worth. Chow Tai Fook, his family company which is not listed, is reputed to be worth hundreds of billions. His investment tentacles are far-reaching. They embrace property, hotels, telecommunications, casinos, utilities, construction, insurance, jewellery, container terminals, mines and retailing.

New World Centre, the headquarters building of his business empire, contains a large wall mural that depicts an oversized patriarch dressed in the garb of a money god smiling approvingly at a money tree that bears '*yuan po*' (gold fruits). Smaller figures denote his descendants. They are there to reap the '*yuan po*' from the tree.

There was intense rivalry between Li Ka Shing and Lee Shau Kee. They were often at each other's throats vying to be number one. Yet, when they were not involved in fierce competition, the hatchets were buried. They found ways to work together and be friends. It lends testimony to the fact that, in politics as in business, there are no permanent enemies nor are there permanent friends. What matters is current interest. Amazingly both of them were friends with Cheng even when they were nemeses of each other.

The launch of the Scheme led to the opening of the floodgates. All of a sudden, Singapore saw an influx of entrepreneurs who were eager to invest in the country – there were simply not enough investment opportunities.

"Shall we group some of them together into one company?" I asked Mrs. Syn of the Singapore Economic Development Board. "The company can be a pathfinder and they can find large projects together."

"That's a good idea. What should we call the company?" she asked.

"Your name is Mrs. Syn and Singapore goes for hi-tech so why don't we just call it Suntec?" I quipped.

Thus, in 1985, the first Suntec was born. It managed to attract twenty-one shareholders. Seven of the most prominent directors were to serve as chairman by rotation. It was designed as a way of stimulating competition among these extraordinary business talents.

Li Ka Shing declined the offer to be its first chairman. He would not chair any company he did not control as a matter of principle. Instead, Cheng Yu Tung became the Chairman.

The first Board meeting was held in the conference room of my law firm. It was furnished with a long table. Cheng, the Chairman, was the first to arrive and sat himself at the top of the table. I sat next to him as I had to take the minutes. As other directors arrived, they discreetly moved to the other end of the table as a time-honoured Chinese gesture of modesty.

When Li Ka Shing entered, he took a seat at the head of the table next to the Chairman instead of following the other directors to the far end. One immediately noticed that there was something unusual about Li that marked him out. He had this unmistakable presence – an aura, panache, charisma, whatever one calls it – that lights up any gathering. He was not tall yet his well-proportioned physique made him appear to have a greater stature than he actually had. His rigid regime of daily exercise kept him slender and fit. He was always immaculately dressed in a well-tailored blue suit and on his wrist he wore a steel Seiko watch. He walked with a swagger and his protruding forehead made him easily recognizable.

He was unquestionably the most admired man in Hong Kong. As soon as he took his seat he seemed to take over the meeting effortlessly and seamlessly. He became the centre of attention; others stopped and listened when he spoke.

The conversations centred on the topic that was splashed across the front pages of the newspapers that morning: the Trio of Li Ka Shing, Lee Shau Kee and Cheng Yu Tung – three of Hong Kong's richest – had together launched a bid to take over Hongkong Land, which owned Hong Kong's most prestigious office buildings in the prime business district of Central – the turf that was traditionally in the hands of the Brits. The Keswick family that controlled Hongkong Land had just struck a buy-back deal at an inflated price from the Trio against an undertaking that they would not, either acting together or alone, for an agreed period of time, lay another siege against Hongkong Land. In the 'money-is-everything' culture of Hong Kong, the press hailed the Trio as local heroes and they basked in the glory of success that morning.

"I won't stand on ceremony and call you Sir Run Run," Li shouted so that those directors seated at the opposite end could hear him. He was obviously in a good mood and Sir Run Run Shaw was the most senior and the best known among them. "I shall simply call you the Sixth Uncle. Sixth Uncle, why don't you take over Cheung Kong?"

Cheung Kong was the flagship of Li through which he controlled his stable of companies that accounted for more than fifteen per cent of Hong Kong's market capitalisation.

Sir Run Run was an entertainment and film mogul. He was affectionately known as 'Sixth Uncle'. His Rolls-Royce bore the registration plate '6'. Everyone knew him. He controlled the television station and entertainment outlets and, in a bygone era, he had made films that everyone grew up with. He was equally well known as a philanthropist, having donated billions to charities. The schools he built in China provided education to millions of children. He founded the Shaw Prize, the Nobel Prize of the East. He was much admired and universally loved.

'Sixth Uncle' nodded as if in acquiescence when in fact he had not heard what was said to him because he was seated at the far end of the table.

"Take over Cheung Kong, Sixth Uncle," Li repeated loudly.

"Take over Cheung Kong!" exclaimed Sir Run Run. He displayed a wit as sharp as a razor. "Oh… never… not even in my *sixth* life!"

Li was clearly pleased by the humble remark. He broke into laughter.

≈≈≈≈≈

Suntec was headline news both in Singapore and Hong Kong. Not only was it unusual for such a formidable group of Hong Kong tycoons to form a company together but also it was registered in Singapore. The news added a new dimension of fear to an already jittery Hong Kong.

The editor of the *South China Morning Post* sent me a fax and demanded immediate answers to a list of questions, threatening that if no satisfactory answers were received the paper would publish an article on its front page the next day to say that Hong Kong's richest were abandoning the territory collectively for Singapore.

Hong Kong at the time was a city under siege; as the Chinese proverb has it, 'every grass and tree was perceived to be enemy soldiers'. It was rather like America at the time of the McCarthy witch-hunt against supposed communists, when the US Government was seeing 'reds under the bed'. Any news could aggravate an already fragile situation.

Fortunately my assurance that nothing unusual should be read into the new company was accepted by Hong Kong's leading English-language newspaper.

To the Chairman, Cheng Yu Tung, Suntec was just another investment. He did not need Suntec as a vehicle to advance his career. He was already a household name and had a huge business empire under his control – perhaps too much on his plate to concern himself with the management. All he wanted was to be seen as heading a company that had many tycoons as its shareholders. Furthermore, he spoke little or no English. He was happy to let me be the face of the company. Thus I was thrust into the limelight and became the spokesperson for what was potentially a most powerful company – a company that had some forty per cent of Hong Kong's market capitalisation as its shareholders.

The company attracted not only the media but also business leaders from around the world. Like bees to honey they arrived in swarms, sniffing out opportunities with the group. To them it was nothing short of Corporate Hong Kong itself.

The State of Israel was the first to arrive. Israel Corporation was founded by the government to attract foreign investments into Israel. Its chairman, Shaul Eisenberg, was internationally known as 'Mr. Ten Percent' – his cut of every deal he put together. Eisenberg wanted Suntec to take part in the privatization of government-owned companies in Israel. Elaine and I, together with a couple of partners from my law practice who I invited along because they were Jewish, were flown to Israel to meet with Mr. Eisenberg and some members of the Cabinet.

At Immigration I was specifically asked whether or not I wanted my passport stamped as it was feared that a passport bearing an entry record might prevent me from entering an Arab country in the future. I was told this immigration procedure could be waived. We all opted for the waiver. There was nothing on our passports to show that we had ever entered Israel.

At a dinner hosted by Eisenberg in my honour, I found myself seated next to Shimon Peres who in 1986 was the Foreign Minister. We had an animated discussion about the Six-Day War and the subsequent occupation of Arab land. I asked him how Israel would deal with the occupied territories.

"Our policy must be built on the ground of morality," he replied.

The conversation left me with the impression that Israel would deal with the problem at the right time. But Jerusalem was non-negotiable.

The next day we drove up to Jerusalem from Tel Aviv. We had an ex-army colonel as our guide. As we ascended the hill, it seemed as if Jerusalem was shrouded by a fog that hung halfway down the city wall from the sky. Rays of light that broke through seemed to wash and cast a ring of holiness on the city.

In Jerusalem, we stayed at the penthouse of Mr. Eisenberg in his hotel – the Sheraton. Among the city's many holy sites, we were taken to visit the Church of the Holy Sepulchre, believed to be where Jesus Christ was crucified, buried and resurrected. We entered the church with a group of nuns. I could see that the nuns were so overcome by the atmosphere that one by one they went down on their knees and broke into hymns of praise to the Lord. It gave me goose pimples.

On the way to the Dead Sea, the limousine driven by the guide had to stop at checkpoints manned by young soldiers with machine guns slung across their shoulders. Some of them looked unruly and undisciplined, more like street thugs than soldiers. At one checkpoint, two of the soldiers were particularly out of control. They had been drinking, and burning tyres to amuse themselves. I could see that our colonel was upset. Instead of stopping, he stepped on the accelerator before bringing the car to a sudden stop. The soldiers panicked when they saw the speeding car coming towards them and were equally surprised when the brakes were applied.

The colonel unbuckled his seat belt, opened the door, jumped out and dashed towards the soldiers, all in quick succession. The soldiers instinctively turned their guns in his direction. The colonel was fearless. He shouted in Hebrew – probably to identify himself – then he reached for the barrel of the machine gun of one soldier and pulled it towards him. He smacked the soldier across the face, causing his hat to fall off. The shaken soldiers collected themselves, stood to attention and saluted the colonel in true military style.

We drove for hours on end. The landscape was arid and barren. Not even shrubs grew in such terrain. It was nothing but wilderness – Biblical wilderness. The car suddenly stopped.

"Why do you stop?" I asked.

"Walk towards the boulder there," our guide said with a smile.

After a short walk, Elaine and I found ourselves looking into a steep valley from the edge of a cliff. We could not believe our eyes. The valley was green and lush. A small waterfall cascaded down from one end of the gorge. The scenery was stunning. Can you imagine? We were in the middle of a desert. There was nothing for miles and miles in a terrain where no vegetation grew. Yet just below us was this oasis and that was not all: a monastery in white and blue was perched precariously on the cliff face.

The scenery reminded me of the time we were in Egypt. We stayed at the Old Cataract where scenes from Agatha Christie's *Murder on the Nile* were shot. The view from our room was absolutely breathtaking: historical ruins from ancient Egypt on one side, an oasis on the other and the mausoleum of the Aga Khan (a descendant of Prophet Muhammad) in the middle, and when we looked down below the cliff we saw numerous riverboats sailing the waters of the River Nile.

On the way to the Dead Sea we passed the cave where the Dead Sea Scrolls were unearthed.

Masada is a hill surrounded on all four sides by cliffs rising up hundreds and hundreds of feet. The top of the plateau is flat and is protected by a wall thousands of feet long, with towers, storehouses, living quarters – even a palace – and reservoirs that were refilled by rainwater that came thundering down the valley after rainstorms that occurred once or twice a year. Masada is a natural fortress.

In the cable car that took us to the top we found ourselves in the company of a group of zealots with long beards, dressed in black. Elaine wanted her picture taken with this group of men but they refused – they would not allow women in their company. They had no such qualms when I asked to have a picture taken with them.

In 67 A.D., an extremist splinter group of the Zealots who had tired of running away from the Romans lived in the settlement that was built originally by King Herod as a sanctuary to protect himself from the rebellions of his own people. They were not subservient to the Romans. Thus, in 72 A.D., a Roman legion surrounded and laid siege to Masada. Using forced labour – mostly Jewish slaves – they built a siege ramp against one face of the plateau, moving thousands of tons of stones and earth in the process.

The night before the big battle, the defenders and their families gathered together in the synagogue. "Tomorrow, the Romans will arrive," said Sicarii, the commander of the sect. "All the men will be killed, the women raped and the children sold as slaves. Would it not be better if we choose another course? We shall deprive our enemy of this pleasure. Let us go to heaven together this very night, hand in hand with family and loved ones."

The assembly then drew lots to decide on the 'sinners' who would undertake the gruesome task of killing the rest of the sect members, as it was believed that these 'executioners' would be barred from entering heaven. Then, one by one, they committed mass suicide as the sword fell upon them. Masada has since become a potent symbol of Jewish nationalism.

It was a delightful holiday but otherwise a total waste of time as few businessmen from Hong Kong were interested in investing in Israel.

When Eisenberg visited Hong Kong, I was unable to return his hospitality on the scale he had perhaps expected. None of the tycoons except Sir Run Run was interested in seeing Israel's probable richest man. Sir Run Run gave a dinner at his Shaw Studio villa in honour of our guest and his wife. He invited a few of his close friends, all couples. They included Sir Jack Cater and his wife, Lady Cater. Sir Jack was the Chief Secretary in the colonial government and his wife Penny was conservative, always prim and proper. It was not long after the conversation had started that she discovered the woman she originally thought to be Mrs.

Eisenberg was in fact someone else. She must have shown her displeasure to her host.

Sir Run Run was unhappy that Eisenberg had brought his mistress to the party. "Who is that woman?" Sir Run Run asked me. "Is she his wife?"

"I don't think so," I replied. I had met Mrs. Eisenberg, who was Japanese, in Tel Aviv.

"Let me know if it's to be that kind of a party next time," Sir Run Run chided me. He was annoyed that I had compromised the dignity of Lady Cater by asking him to host the dinner for Eisenberg.

When Dr. Wang Ann of the now-defunct Wang Computers offered to fly me to San Francisco on his private jet, I told him I would only be prepared to accept the invitation if I was paid a fixed fee for each day I was out of office, plus expenses. He agreed. At Hillsborough, on the outskirts of San Francisco, we went through four days of gruelling discussions involving Taiwan's Minister of Finance in a tripartite joint venture to develop electronic products on a scale that would rival what Steve Jobs had done with Apple. I had no idea that Dr. Wang had planned a three-way venture involving Taiwan and Suntec. If consummated, it would have bailed Dr. Wang out of the economic woes that eventually toppled Wang Computers and led to his untimely death. Wang Computers had overstretched itself and, unbeknownst to anyone except a few insiders, was then in dire financial trouble. The matter died a natural death when ill health got the better of Wang.

Algie Cluff, a stalwart of the Conservative Party of Britain, wanted to partner us in his oil business. He also introduced me to Mark Thatcher, whose mother Margaret Thatcher was then the serving Prime Minister.

"Thank you for introducing Li Ka Shing to me," said Mark. "We have since worked together."

"I know," I said. "Li has invested in your Dallas ventures. He tells me that you are a good businessman."

"I am indebted to you. Sorry I have to cancel the dinner tonight because I have to get back to London. I promised a couple of children that I would show them around Number 10 Downing Street tomorrow. We can't let children down, can we?"

Li Ka Shing went on to invest in England and was later knighted by the Queen.

There were many other suitors.

≈≈≈≈≈

It was a busy time for me. Not only was there a lot of work for the practice, but I was also in demand as a financial advisor to entrepreneurs from Hong Kong wanting to invest in Singapore, and vice versa, on their own and not linked to Suntec. The sudden influx of deals enabled me to start a merchant bank as an extension to my legal practice – instead of taking care of the legal documentation, I moved towards putting deals together and in the process created work for both entities.

As they say, every dog has its day. My day had arrived. I basked in the sun of success and my contemporaries were in awe of what I had achieved. It was a happy time. The only sad spot in my life was my mentor's state of health.

"T.O., you look pale," I remarked. "You have lost weight and you look tired. Are you alright?"

"I don't know. I have problems with my prostate. It's worrying. Worst is the fatigue. I don't feel well. By the way, tell me, what have you been up to lately?"

"I took your advice and started a merchant bank. Then I sold fifty per cent of the share capital to UOB, United Overseas Bank. I also sold small stakes – ten per cent to Suntec and another five per cent to its new Chairman, Tan Sri, in his personal capacity. I hope to use the two as buffers against the dominance of UOB. Wee Cho Yaw, the Chairman of UOB, has taken over as chairman of the new company. Although I am entrusted to take care of the day-to-day operations, I don't intend to stay in that role for long. When the time comes, I shall relinquish it and remain as a passive investor. UOB can take the helm."

"I don't think this is a good idea," T.O said. "I think you should be upfront with the UOB. Otherwise it will destroy the goodwill you have built up with the bank and, as its Chairman is personally involved, your action will leave a bad taste in his mouth. What UOB wants is your connections and your continued involvement. I told you before and I repeat: in a service business you are expected to contribute in order to justify your existence. Besides, Wee Cho Yaw is probably the most powerful businessman, the counterpart of Li Ka Shing, in Singapore. If you ruffle his feathers, you will end up paying the price, of that I am certain. Like the proverb says: 'A young man in a hurry will never reach his destination'. You haven't thought it through properly, have you, Robert?"

T.O.'s advice came too late. It was a done deal. I could not reverse the process. Nor could I reverse my plan for immigration.

≈≈≈≈≈

Cheng Yu Tung was Chairman of Suntec for one year before the chair was rotated, as required under the charter of the company, to Tan Sri.

Tan Sri's style of operation was different to his predecessor's. Unlike Cheng, who looked upon the company as yet another investment, Tan Sri saw it as a vehicle to move his career forward, using it as a platform to deal with government officials not only in Singapore but more so in China which was rapidly opening up to the outside world. He was hands-on in contrast to Cheng's willingness to delegate to others.

In 1988 Tan Sri led the directors to Singapore for a board meeting.

Most of the directors flew on the same Singapore Airlines flight. Many were accompanied by their spouses. Two of the tycoons were there with their lady friends. They occupied two rows in the First Class cabin.

"How can you bring your lady friend along? We have serious business to attend to in Singapore," Li whispered into the ear of his friend. Then he signalled to Richard, his son, to swap seats with the lady friend of one of the two tycoons. "You and I can sit together. Come, Richard. Take over this lady's seat."

"Save the trouble, Brother Shing," replied the tycoon. "I have to think about what I do in my spare time, don't I?"

After the flight took off, Li again initiated a change of seats. He wanted to play cards with the two tycoons. In the end, I changed seats with him and the two lady friends moved up to sit together. The three tycoons were then in one row with Li.

Throughout the flight Richard and I had animated conversations about the good life, the places we had visited, restaurants we had been to and wines we had enjoyed. Although he was still a young man, Richard was westernised, knowledgeable, well-spoken and wise in the ways of the world. From time to time I looked to the back of the plane. The Trio were deeply immersed in their game, guarding their cards zealously to make sure no one gained an advantage by peeping at the hand of another.

In Singapore, seven of us were invited to meet with the Prime Minister. The newspapers were rife with speculation that the government might privatise some of its GLCs (government-linked companies). On the way to the Istana, where the Prime Minister was, we discussed the subjects we wished to discuss with him. Two areas were identified: one was to take part in the privatisation programme and the other was to build a Convention and Exhibition Centre.

We arrived in a convoy – three shiny Mercedes Benz cars, each chauffeur-driven and carrying two of us in the back. I took a front seat in one as there were seven of us. The car numbers and the names of the passengers were provided in advance. At the gates of the Istana, the guards checked the details and waved us on.

The Prime Minister's building was guarded by Gurkha soldiers. Several attendants were at the door to greet us. We were ushered into a waiting room in a wing of the sprawling palace and from there we were whisked into a private lift that took us to the meeting room of the Prime Minister.

There was a long table with the Prime Minister and his Private Secretary seated on one side. We sat opposite them.

"Prime Minister, I hear Singapore may privatise some of the GLCs." Li Ka Shing was the first to speak. "We are interested in taking part even if it means we have to pay more for the companies."

"We don't need your money, Mr. Li," the Prime Minister said with a dry smile.

"Prime Minister, it is like this," said Tan Sri. "We are interested in building a Convention and Exhibition Centre."

The idea of the centre originated from another director. W.H. Chou was a textile tycoon. He had a fertile mind, always bubbling with ideas – a true entrepreneur. Textiles aside, he also dabbled in many other businesses. His instant noodles sold under the 'Doll' trademark were a must-have for underfed and homesick students studying abroad.

The Prime Minister responded favourably to this proposal. "We will identify a suitable piece of land and put it up for public tender," he said at the end of the meeting.

A site of 11.7 hectares at Marina Centre was later identified and put up for public tender. Suntec was successful. Not only did we submit the highest bid but also the design by I.M. Pei, the renowned Chinese-American architect, was judged to be the best.

As he was our architect, we met Pei often. Once he came to Hong Kong to meet the board.

"Mr. Pei, tell me which of all your projects is your favourite," I took the opportunity to ask him at the lunch hosted in his honour.

"Well, Mr. Wang, that is like asking me which one of my seven daughters is my favourite," he replied. After a pause, however, he continued: "The Louvre, perhaps… did you know, in the twelfth century the Louvre was built as a sumptuous palace. It was challenging to convert a palace into a modern museum."

Lee Kuan Yew later wrote:

*In 1988, they proposed building an International Convention and Exhibition Centre, to be called Suntec City, on reclaimed land at Marina Centre which the URA had identified for such a facility, then the largest single commercial project undertaken by the private sector. They got the land by public tender at an attractive price because it was during a recession and we were happy to have them come and invest in an Exhibition and Convention Centre. There were also to be five blocks, originally one for a hotel and four for offices. Unlike other convention centres outside the city centre, the Singapore International Convention and Exhibition Centre is located on a prime site within the city, surrounded by half a dozen large five-star hotels. Therefore, all five blocks eventually became office blocks.*

Suntec City was formed after a re-grouping: ten of the original shareholders of Suntec plus Lee Shau Kee joined as shareholders.

Being the serving Chairman of Suntec, Tan Sri became *ipso facto* the Chairman of Suntec City as well. Chou was his ally in the group. He took over from Tan Sri and became the Chairman of Suntec.

Thus from the very day it was formed, the board of Suntec City was evenly split into two groups. Tan Sri and his Shanghai friends owned 49%. The Trio had 48%. My friend William and I held 3%. Both sides vied to control a development that cost S$1.2 billion alone to build. The two camps avoided open confrontation but, instead, each tried to control the project through a strategy of clandestine manipulation and the use of proxies.

Tan Sri treated Suntec City as his 'family heirloom' and he was determined to stay in control. He had the support of the directors who, like him, were from Shanghai.

The Trio simply considered it yet another consortium project. It was no big deal. At an appropriate time they would find liquidity, such as when the company was listed on the local bourse.

"To these tycoons, it is small money," said Tan Sri as a way of explaining why control to him was important, "but to me it is a lot of money."

Tan Sri was known among his friends as 'the self-flagellating monk'. The man's appetite for work was legendary. It seemed as though he wanted to punish himself with more and more work. He worked all day long including on Sundays. The man's stamina was extraordinary. Work was his only hobby.

In the early days of Suntec, I was a member of his inner circle. After spending a hard day going from one meeting to another, I was relieved to go back to the hotel room and rest. However, he would call in the middle of the night asking to meet in the lobby again because he wished to discuss a new idea that had come up.

Tan Sri was single-minded in his determination to succeed. He was a demanding boss and, to survive in his world, one had to know one's place and demonstrate unwavering loyalty to him. From the beginning, he treated me as a legal advisor and a secretary. He wanted me to stay that way, but I saw Suntec not only as my emigration cushion but also as an opportunity to break out of my professional mould. It was to be my launching pad to be a businessman and, perhaps, get me into circulation with the pack – such was my naivety. It was, therefore, inevitable that we would fall out with each other. It was only a matter of time.

Soon I stepped into Tan Sri's territory. He reacted and I could not blame him. He had a way of dealing with his rivals. He would not confront them. Instead he would clandestinely marginalize them. So my honeymoon with Tan Sri was short-lived. Indeed, it was over even before it began.

After winning the bid, I.M. Pei, the original architect, was discreetly edged aside and instead Tan Sri's son's company, a relatively unknown firm of architects based in New York, took over as project architect.

When I became the Chairman of the Development Committee, Tan Sri did not object because I was supported by the Trio. It was simple to explain: I was their choice of compromise. None of the Trio wished to appoint his own man as they each had to work within certain limitations.

No one could be seen to outdo the others in this delicate tripartite relationship. I was considered to be neutral and suitable for the job even though they knew I was not a building construction man.

They all knew that the role of the chairman was important because every major decision in the redevelopment had to go through him. Nevertheless the appointment did not please Tan Sri. I was perceived by him to have transcended the role he had intended for me. He was conversant with Maoist tactics: retreat when attacked and attack when the enemy retreats.

Tan Sri fired the first salvo. As the Chairman, he could choose to deal directly with individual members of the Committee. Soon decisions were being made without reference to me. I was being bypassed until I was chairman of the committee in name only. My position became pretty much untenable.

"I wish to resign as Chairman of the Development Committee," I told Li Ka Shing.

"It is not a decision to be taken lightly," he said. "Who is going to take over?"

"I know. I propose that you nominate someone."

In asking Li to nominate, I had unwittingly made the mistake of upsetting the delicate balance of power that was held in place for the Trio to work together.

In the end, Albert Chow, the trusted lieutenant of Li, was named. Albert was a quiet man, soft-spoken and composed – not the sort to reveal his inner thoughts. He commanded the confidence of his boss. I had never seen Li challenge any of his decisions, at least in public, and he was knowledgeable in construction matters.

As soon as the new man took over, I was out of Tan Sri's firing line. Life under the Chairman became tolerable again. Not being a property man, Tan Sri had to rely on the skill and judgement of Albert Chow. The fact that he was Li Ka Shing's man made a world of difference to the authority of the chair.

When the tender was submitted, one of the comments made by the Urban Redevelopment Authority (URA) was that our design had encroached on some state land. Tan Sri convened a meeting to discuss the matter. It was attended by Cheng Yu Tung.

"You know, it is like this," reported Tan Sri. "I have successfully negotiated with URA. Both sides made concessions. URA agrees to levy 50% of the premium and as a trade-off we agree to give up 50% of the plot ratio."

Tan Sri beamed. He expected a pat on the shoulder and to be told: "Well done, Chairman."

"Fuck you, Mr. Ong," shouted Cheng. "You don't know fucking shit about properties."

His comment took everyone by surprise. They were stunned.

Ong was the General Manager of Suntec. It was during the days before Suntec City had its own staff, and Ong doubled as the manager for both companies.

I had never seen Cheng agitated before, let alone heard him swear. The man was always gentle and quiet, not the kind easily given to verbal flare-ups. Indeed, I never thought he was capable of expletives. But he was furious.

Although he spoke to the manager, it was plain to see where he was really pouring his scorn: upon the Chairman.

"Your stupid act has cost the company an arm and a leg – S$80 million, to be exact," Cheng continued as he stared at the manager. His mind worked like a computer – his mental calculation ability was awe-inspiring. "Don't you know?"

The manager was flabbergasted. "Ah.... ah... ah..." He was lost for words.

"Don't ah... ah... ah me. You don't even know what I am talking about," exclaimed Cheng. "Now listen to me and listen carefully. Our tender price is S$3,868 per square metre. Across the road, Raffles Hotel pays S$6,000 and at the junction of Orchard and Scott, Wheelock pays S$10,000. Ask yourself – why is our price so low? It is so low because we have to build the convention facility which is our loss-leader. Yet, it keeps the tills in town ringing – for every dollar that is spent at the facility another ten is put into the economy. But the additional floor areas that you have given up are good for building shops, hotels and offices. Now do you see how stupid you are?"

I watched in disbelief. The man's mind was sharp. It was indeed penny wise and pound foolish. No wonder Cheng was upset.

≈≈≈≈≈

"I have spoken to Cheng Yu Tung and Lee Shau Kee," I told Li Ka Shing. "They both agree that the five of us should sign a pact in which we agree to act in concert in all matters relating to Suntec City. The three of you own 48% of the company. William and I own 3% and together we add up to 51%. Are you agreeable?"

"Yes," he said. "But the three of us must have the final say in all matters."

"That's fine with William and me."

I prepared the agreement. It was signed by everyone except William.

William and I had met regularly at Shanghai parties and we became good friends despite our age difference – he was closer to my father's age. We had much in common and talked freely – social gossip, family, work, politics, economy, women… you name it and we talked about it. Anything under the sky, nothing was taboo between us. Normally William was a serious sort of person but, when we were together, he would take off the mask and let his hair down. He became a fun person to be with. We shared many happy moments together.

William was the owner of one of the largest garment manufacturers and he was an astute investor. In the days of Japan's booming economy in the 1980s, his portfolio in Japanese bonds and equities was reputed to be the largest in Hong Kong. He was much courted by investment bankers and was often surrounded by young, beautiful and well-educated lady sales managers sent to provide him with investment advice and procure his business for the company at the same time.

"You know these girls are there to cater to my every whim," said William jokingly. "They carry the kamikaze spirit into business and often they sacrifice themselves in the line of duty and on my account… Ha! Ha! Ha! You know how the Japanese brokers work. They reward loyal clients. Sometimes they tell you what to buy and if you do not make money they think they've let you down and a sense of guilt prevails. Then they send along one of these kamikaze girls to 'atone for their sins' before they find another opportunity to reward you again – either with a hot tip or by giving you an allotment of some hot new shares."

"What do you do with these girls?"

"Well, I won't tell you. You can tell from the gifts I buy them."

"What kind of gifts?"

"I give them jewellery."

"You must buy a lot of jewellery."

"Yes, I do. Jewellery is in my blood. When I was a child, my mother would lay out her jewellery on the bed for me to play with as toys every night. I grew up with jewellery. My hobby is to buy jewellery… I might as well because I have to make my two wives happy. They both love jewellery passionately – just like me."

I could understand what he meant by two 'wives' because, prior to 1976, the Customary Laws of China on marriage were also part of the laws of the Colony of Hong Kong. A man was allowed to have more than one wife provided the couple in the second marriage went through the process, as dictated by the custom, of offering tea to the parents and worshipping 'heaven and earth' together. The law was abolished in 1976. The arrangement was widely accepted by the first wives in those days.

"Which girl doesn't love jewellery?" I interrupted him. "Do you buy it yourself?"

"No, my second wife does most of the buying. She is astute and I let her handle all my money matters. Every time she buys she makes sure she gets two sets, one less expensive than the other. She gives the expensive set to the first wife and keeps the other. That is my way of keeping peace at home… Ha! Ha! Ha!"

"How long have you been with your second wife?"

"For as long as I can remember. You see, we were students together in university. Both of my wives were crowned as 'College Flower' – the title they gave to beautiful and academically acclaimed students at St. John's University in Shanghai. The two girls were also the best of friends. My wife and I got married at about the same time as my other wife met and married her childhood sweetheart. As we were students at the same university, we saw each other often and we went out as couples. We wined and dined and went to parties and social gatherings together. At the back of my mind, I always fancied that girl even after she was married. Then one night, after drinks, I discovered that she felt the same about me. We were consumed by passion and professed our love for each other. We made a solemn pledge that we would both leave our respective spouses and elope. She carried out her part of the bargain and left her husband. But I became faint-hearted at the last minute. I did not leave my wife. We stopped seeing each other until one day we met again quite accidentally in Hong Kong in the 1950s. Our love for each other was reignited and since then we have been together. She is a wonderful woman. I must introduce her to you one day."

That William had his other wife was an open secret in Hong Kong's high society. Every Thursday night, the couple wined and dined in candlelight at the French restaurant Gaddi's at the Peninsula Hotel. All friends of the first wife were alerted. No one would go to Gaddi's on Thursdays. This had been going on for as long as anyone could remember.

That night at Petrus, the French restaurant atop the Island Shangri-la Hotel, I met William's second wife for the first time. One could tell that William was a doting 'husband'. Perhaps the sense of guilt in his heart over not divorcing his first wife and marrying her had never died over the years. He was attentive and loving. He went out of his way to make her happy.

"I can't finish this foie gras," she said.

"Let me finish it for you," said William.

Then the entrée was served. She had lobster.

"The lobster has no sauce," she complained.

"Let me finish it for you," said William.

William ate double portions of food that was high in cholesterol. He was on the heavy side and had a heart condition. At home, a private nurse took care of him round the clock. He also consumed ginseng and bird's nest in large quantities. Every year he spent millions on these health supplements, believing they were good for his general health and acted as aphrodisiacs.

"Robert, when you are in Singapore next time," William said as he gave me S$10,000, "please can you buy me some of the best quality 'blood bird's nest'? Singapore has the best."

"Of course," I said. "I will be there next week."

Bird's nest is an expensive product. It is made of the nest of certain species of small swifts that dwell on cave walls. The birds make the nest from strands of their saliva that harden on contact with the air. Bird's nest is rich in nutrients. It is supposed to be good for the health and is said to improve a man's immune system and blood circulation. When consumed regularly, it improves one's skin, giving it a radiant complexion. It is sought after by women, middle-aged women in particular. The red-coloured nest is especially sought after. It is expensive because it is believed that the colour is caused by the swift 'vomiting blood' to build the nest. It is also believed that these special swifts eat and drink different kinds of food and water, but the truth is that swifts do not 'vomit blood'. Nor is the food and water they take any different. The redness is caused by the nest absorbing minerals from the cave walls – dirty water, chemicals and even poisons. Hence, instead of being beneficial, 'blood nest' can be harmful to humans.

At the end of the dinner, I gave William the act-in-concert agreement which he signed without question. He knew Tan Sri from Shanghai.

In the lobby of the hotel we bumped into Li Ka Shing. He was there for a dinner with family members. I told him that William had signed the pact. Li greeted William warmly and went out of his way to thank him.

The next day my secretary came rushing into my office.

"William died!" she said.

"What did you say?"

"William died this afternoon. His secretary just called."

"I don't believe it. I had dinner with him just last night. What happened?"

"The secretary said he felt unwell when he woke up this morning. He thought it was caused by indigestion. He did not go to work. In the afternoon his condition worsened. His nurse helped him to induce a bowel movement and in the process he had a heart attack. He died."

I burst into tears.

Almost every morning I ran along Lady Clementi's Trail at the Peak. It is named after the wife of a governor who rode her horse on the trail in the early colonial days. The trail is carved out of thick sub-tropical forest that wraps around the shores of Aberdeen Reservoir. A walk there takes one through tunnels of trees. It is one of the most scenic spots on the island.

I was not able to concentrate on anything that morning. I felt compelled to get out of the office. I went walking on the trail. The weather was inclement – wet, dark and cloudy. When I saw freshly fallen white lilies lying among the dead leaves on the trail, I thought of William.

White lilies are symbols of death and are commonly used in Chinese funerals. I was overcome by emotion again and started crying uncontrollably. I bent down and picked up some of the lilies, placing the petals in my two palms held together to form a bowl. Then I rushed to my 'secret garden' which was a clearing located at a drop of some fifty feet below the trail. The clearing was hidden behind thick bushes and trees. Few people knew it existed. Sliding down the steep slope, I landed in the clearing where there was a natural pond into which water cascaded. It was a very private place for me.

As I placed the petals one by one onto the surface of the water, I called out William's name. Then something miraculous occurred. The sun suddenly broke through the thick clouds. It filled the valley with light. When I looked up, I saw a ray of sunlight coming from the side of a tall tree. I followed the light and moved towards the tree. I could not believe my eyes – someone had carved the name 'William' on the trunk under a straight line. The carving was bold and distinct as if it was there to tell me that William had found peace and happiness in the afterlife.

Then the sky closed up again and it began to rain.

At the funeral of William I was surprised that I did not see his second wife there. I was also surprised that the elaborate wreath I had sent was nowhere to be seen. The thought did occur to me that it could perhaps be the first wife's way of showing displeasure at my being privy to her inner secrets – William must have told her what I knew.

≈≈≈≈≈

T.O. had been diagnosed with prostate cancer. He started selling his Hong Kong assets: Smart Shirts to Kellwood International and Cheong Sun to Far East Consortium.

"Robert, I have decided to emigrate," he said. "I have pretty much liquidated everything I own in Hong Kong."

"When are you leaving?" I showed no surprise because I knew T.O. did not have much time left.

"In a couple of weeks. My papers have come through. I am tying up loose ends at the moment."

"Is it wise for you to make this move? Your children are in San Francisco and you will be a stranger in Vancouver."

"You mean I should stay here to die?"

I was somewhat startled by his reaction. Death is a taboo subject in Chinese customs. It is not discussed openly.

"The purpose of life is self-preservation. Even if it means I shall die soon, I am not precluded from planning my future. I have to face 1997 if I remain in Hong Kong. But once I am out, I need not be bothered by it ever again. Peace of mind is what I need most in my current state of health.

"By the way, how are things at Suntec?"

"It gives me plenty of legal work, if that is what you mean. But I have a lot of problems with the new chairman. I don't think he likes me. However he is not the sort to show his feelings. He and the chairman of the smaller Suntec – W.H. Chou – are in alliance. You can just imagine. When the two chairmen gang up and work against me, my position becomes impossible. The new chairman never gives me a straight answer on anything. Instead he marginalizes me through a strategy of behind-the-scenes manoeuvres. He wants to destroy my credibility before the government and the shareholders. It makes me so angry at times that I could easily lose my temper."

"If you lose your cool, you will fall into his trap," said T.O. "Remember the saying: 'Perseverance is as good as gold'? He is the chairman. If you wish to survive, you have to hide your ego, bow your head and get on with life. You have no choice.

"Robert, this may be our last goodbye," he said as we left the restaurant. "Soon we shall go our separate ways. I am sad and I know you are too. 'There is no banquet under heaven that never ends,' as the proverb goes. Let's have a hug together."

Over the years T.O. and I had been more than mentor and protégé. He was like a father to me. We were saying goodbye to each other for the last time. It was sad to see him so thin and looking so pale and frail. A sudden rush of emotion got the better of me. I had to hold back my tears. I was lost for words. I could never thank him enough for all he had done for me – the money to get me out of a bad partnership, the donation that set off a chain of incredible events in Singapore, the advice that steered my career, and the happy times we had had together. Tears came rolling down my cheeks. T.O.'s eyes turned red. We both cried. I felt like I was losing a father and he embraced and patted me on the back to console me. I never knew I was capable of such an open display of emotion.

T.O. took off his glasses, wiped the tears from his face and dipped into the inside pocket of his suit. He took out a picture of himself and gave it to me. It shows a kind and benevolent face. It smiles at me – everything about T.O. is frozen in time.

His last piece of advice to me was: "Suntec City is too big. It is not your game. It is for the big boys. One day there will be a showdown and a victor will emerge. It is naïve to think you can capture it. A snake can't swallow an elephant. You'll be better off if you do what you are best at – service."

Once again, T.O had seen through my raw ambition and warned me not to go through with the plans I had for Singapore.

"To be content with what you have is a gift from heaven," he continued. "Incidentally, you should devote your time to making Lee Kuan Yew the next Secretary General of the United Nations. Work on it." Then he turned and walked away.

# Singapore

In the 1990s, the economy of Singapore was in a rut. After rapid expansion, its economy was registering negative growth. The property market which had ballooned in the previous decade was suffering from oversupply. As building works progressed, Suntec City looked more and more like the big white elephant the locals had predicted it would be. The malls were so big that they mockingly said that the corridors should be used as bowling alleys. It was huge and empty.

"It is joss-stick money for the tycoons – burnt to worship gods," said Ong Beng Seng, a local tycoon, sarcastically. "I know what it is like. I have been through it myself. When you have so much money, you just want to erect the biggest and tallest monument to immortalize yourself, as if it is going to be your last erection."

It was true. Suntec was building a lot of real estate that few wanted. The market was eerily quiet. But by 1995 Singapore's economy was beginning to pick up again. With only two years left before sovereignty of Hong Kong went back to China, it was time for me to leave the city. I never expected to return to live there again – the move was meticulously planned and it was time to take action.

My son, John, was then twenty-one years old and had just graduated with a degree in law from Jesus College, Cambridge. He went on to become a barrister.

We had packed both of our children – John and Gillian – off to public schools in England early, fearful of an uncertain future after Hong Kong's sovereignty was transferred to China. In hindsight, I can only say the move was unwise. It deprived both our children of the warmth of the family at a crucial time of their growth. For John it was worse. He felt like he had been abandoned and he went through hard times as a boarder in an alien environment thousands of miles away from home.

I had always wanted John to go to the Leys School in Cambridge because the school was where Aunt Diana sent her two sons – David and Jeffrey – and I used to visit and fetch them from the school for half-term. The school had left an indelible mark on my mind.

When I plucked John out of his school in Hong Kong he was barely ten. He could hardly speak English. At St. Faith's, the preparatory school for the Leys School, he was often bullied by the local boys. One spat on him from the upper bunk bed and said, "This is for your mother." He had the first fight of his life. He became inward-looking, building walls and insulating himself from the other students. For years he lived in a cocoon, in his own world.

He had this phobia about going back. At the end of a long holiday, he inevitably developed a high fever and would often be seen kissing and saying goodbye to the furniture at home in Hong Kong. During half-term, when Elaine was there to care for him at our house in Cambridge, he would place his palm on hers and ask her to bring the sewing kit. "Let our palms be sewn together so that we never ever have to part again."

One time he was in the house at St. Peter's Street, Cambridge, all by himself. Mrs. Kvan, his guardian, lived next door. He went into our bedroom and opened the wardrobe. When he saw Elaine's long coat hanging there he burst into tears.

Elaine cried every time she thought of these incidents and when she recounted the story to the other mothers they would all cry with her. It was heart-wrenching. She made a point of seeing the children on average once every five weeks – when the children returned home to Hong Kong during the long holidays such as summer, Christmas and Easter, and also at half-terms. Public schools in England break midway through a term to allow local students to return home to their families. The break, known as half-term, is short and typically lasts less than a week, too short for the children to make the long journey home to the Far East. Instead, many of the mothers travel to England to be with them. They are called 'half-term mothers'. Elaine was one of them.

John blamed me for his unhappiness. He sent me a letter when he was ten:

> *Dad,*
>
> *I was happy, so happy when I was at home. I don't understand why you sent me here. I am now unhappy, so unhappy. Maybe one day when I grow up I can understand it and will forgive you. As for now I want to tell you this: I hate you, Dad.*
>
> *John*

My heart ached. But then, how could I explain to my son at his tender age what 1997 was all about?

Gillian, my daughter, fared much better. By nature she is outgoing. Also, when we sent her away to England, she was older – she was thirteen. She took to boarding school life at Wycombe Abbey like a duck to water, becoming a prefect and captain of the school's tennis team.

She later read history at Trinity College, Cambridge, graduating with a 2:1 degree – Second Upper Class – missing a First by just a whisker.

The children love their mother deeply, a love made stronger no doubt by those half-term days she spent with them in England. They are all devout Christians.

I count my blessings that the children's department in my life is so well looked after. It never distracted me, not even one bit, from my love and passion: my career.

I bought a house at Bukit Timah – a bungalow area in the centre north of the island state – set amidst a lush tropical forest and surrounded by other bungalows and greenery. The Swiss Club was a stone's throw away. The bungalow was built at the top of a gentle slope. Not being a citizen of Singapore, I had to apply for permission to buy. My application was unsuccessful. Tan Sri was also interested in the same house. He pulled strings and got permission to buy it. I ended up buying a smaller house at the foot of his bungalow built by the same owner. Thus Tan Sri and I became neighbours.

Almost as soon as I moved into the house, I felt something unusual about its feng shui – something potent and ferocious. Tan Sri's bungalow looked anything but benign. It was imposing and menacing as if the two arms of the man had my neck in a stranglehold. At times I could hardly breathe.

In Singapore it does not simply rain. At times it pours cats and dogs. The geography of the house was such that water flowed from all directions into the low land at the entrance to the house. From the geomancy (alignment of elements, earth, water and buildings) standpoint it is good because water denotes money and is auspicious. True. I never had it so good. It seemed as if all things – money, fame and people – were arriving from all directions to enrich me. My enterprises thrived and the rewards were rolling in.

Then the menaces came.

One day in the garden I saw a baby monkey perched on the fence separating our two gardens. The area was infested by monkeys because the nearby tropical rainforest was their natural habitat.

I knew the adult monkeys must be nearby. To protect myself, I removed a tennis racket from its cover. The move was interpreted by the monkeys as menacing – I was about to attack the baby.

Before I knew what happened next, I was suddenly surrounded and pounced upon by at least a dozen monkeys that descended from the trees. They gnashed, clawed, bit and attacked me viciously. I screamed and ran out of the front garden looking for help, with the monkeys in hot pursuit. A passing taxi came to a screeching stop. The driver got out, went to the boot of the car, took out the jack and came to my rescue by beating the monkeys into a retreat.

But the incident was not forgotten. Whenever I was in the garden, the colony of monkeys would get excited, jumping, screaming and gnashing at me. I became so fearful of these animals that I asked the police for protection. The police gave me Jacob, an Alsatian dog. Jacob was a reject from his class of canines trained to be police dogs. He stood taller than me. Jacob was a one-man dog – my dog. When I swam in the pool, he would pace up and down along the edge to make sure I was safe and he would accompany me whenever I was in the garden. The monkeys were in awe of Jacob. None ever dared to descend from the trees after Jacob arrived.

One morning I took a dip in the pool and went upstairs to prepare for work. As usual, Jacob followed at my heel. When I left, the canine turned his attention to Ning, the daughter of Lucy, our long-serving maid from the Philippines. Ning was the lowest in the household pecking order from Jacob's perspective. Ning did not like being followed and pushed Jacob away – a move that enraged the dog. Without warning, he pounced on Ning and got her by the throat. Lucy heard the scream and came to her daughter's rescue. She pulled Jacob by the tail but could not disengage him. Ning was bleeding badly. Then suddenly the dog released the daughter and in a frenzy went for the throat of the mother instead. Jacob would not let go while the daughter lay in a pool of her own blood, barely conscious and gasping for air. Lucy was at the point of dying from asphyxiation when Ning regained consciousness. By a sheer stroke of good luck, a basin of water lay nearby. The daughter, gathering her last ounce of strength, struggled to get up and managed to pour the water onto Jacob. The startled dog let go of the mother. Both mother and daughter survived after being rushed to hospital.

Jacob was taken away and put to sleep. I was heartbroken. With Jacob gone, the monkeys came down again. These animals continued to regard me and me alone as their enemy. Other members of the household were spared. I was their target and I lived in fear of another attack, made worse by the malaise of the violent acts that almost took the lives of Lucy and Ning.

Another menace loomed in the bushes. One day as I walked in the garden something from the tree dropped on my head, slid down one shoulder and fell to the ground. I looked down and checked what it was. It was a small snake. I quickly stepped on it with all the might I could gather.

The gardener from next door came at my beckoning.

"What kind of snake is this?" I asked him. "It is not dead yet – it is hissing and its tail is still wiggling."

"Oh… man… sir," said the Indian man, shaking his head. "This is a baby king cobra. You know they are very dangerous. One small bite and the venom will kill you within half an hour. These cobras eat other snakes. The parents of this baby must be in the bushes of the garden. Be careful, sir, it can kill."

"What can I do to prevent the snakes from getting inside the house?"

"You can spread sulphur in the garden but sulphur is easily washed away by rain. Singapore rains are heavy. You may want to think about keeping a couple of geese in the garden. These birds are ferocious. They attack snakes."

"Don't I know it," I said, remembering my goose experience at Golders Hill Park in London. "I've been through it myself."

With Lucy's near-death experience still fresh in my mind, I was afraid to venture out into the back garden again. Then I heard strange stories about the house next door.

"What do you mean that the house next door is unclean?" I asked Lucy.

"Sir, it is haunted."

"How do you know?"

"The maids there told me. They see things there. We sometimes talk through the fence."

That the whole of the Swiss Club area is 'unclean' is well known to the locals. During the war, the area was used by the Japanese to execute prisoners. Singaporeans are superstitious. And there is something about the dark of the tropics that seems to breed ghost sightings. Weird stories were often related to me by the locals and visitors alike about ghosts they had seen there. I did not believe these stories but I can tell you what I experienced myself. I was on my way home one afternoon.

"Where to?" the taxi driver asked. I saw the flag was down and the 'For Hire' sign switched off.

"Bukit Timah," I replied.

"Sir, I am going off duty. I can take you there because it is on the way to Clementi," said the taxi driver whom I had flagged down on Orchard Road. "I have to fetch my son from school. Then I have to return the taxi. Where in Bukit Timah do you wish to go?"

"Kampong Chantik near the Swiss Club."

"Oh, I know that area well," said the Malay. "There is a reservoir at the top and from there one can look down into the 'gully of durian trees'. You know spirits live in these trees. Durian fruits never drop except after midnight... never during the day. Otherwise these fruits can kill if dropped on people, you know?"

"I know the reservoir well. I walk my dog there in the morning. But I have never seen durian trees there. Where are they? I would have noticed these trees if they are there. I love durians."

The area is pretty desolate and it is as close to countryside as one can get in urbanized Singapore.

The taxi drew up outside my house. After paying the fare, I was about to get out when the driver turned and looked at me.

"I will show you where the durian trees are."

"Oh, never mind. Don't you have an errand to run?"

"Yes, I have to pick up my son from school. You know, I can see ghosts under these durian trees. I am not joking. I am serious. It happens in the full moon."

"You're lying. I don't believe in ghosts."

"No, sir, I am serious. See how the hairs on my arm are standing up," he said as he raised his left arm from the driver's seat. "I wouldn't lie to you. You can see it for yourself. Today is the fifteenth of the month. The moon is full. I shall pick you up at midnight and take you there. Are you coming?"

"Okay, I'll wait for you at the door at midnight. By the way, what is your name?"

"Ashraf."

He arrived just before midnight. He was dressed in black and had a black scarf tied around his head – he looked like a ninja toy soldier.

We set off towards the reservoir. It was a cloudy night, dark except when the moon broke through occasionally. At the top of the reservoir I felt uncomfortable. I was in the company of a stranger. He had dark skin and was dressed in black; at times I could see only the whites of his eyes.

"You see those durian trees." He pointed to the shadows of what appeared to be trees moving in the wind in the gully below.

"No, I don't see anything. It is so dark here I can't see a thing. I don't feel comfortable. Let's go back."

'This is a set-up,' I thought to myself. A sudden rush of fear got the better of me. 'It's a stick-up. The guy is going to rob me – but wait, he knows where I live. I can't be expected to carry a lot of cash at this time of the night when I am so close to home. Besides, Singapore is safe and if he has bad intentions he certainly doesn't have to take me up to this desolate place at this time of the night. He can simply rob me at home. No, I don't think so. This whole episode looks too spontaneous for me to read anything sinister into it.'

"No… wait a minute," said Ashraf. "I see things moving there. Look, do you see those shadowy figures and flashes of dim light moving under the trees?"

I got goose pimples all over me. I could see Ashraf was excited.

In between the breaks of the moon, I could vaguely see what appeared to be flickers of light, silvery in colour. Then I saw silhouettes of something floating among the trees.

"Now I shall receive the spirits," he said. "Come, come, come… spirits of the unknown. Ashraf Abraham commands you to enter his body and talk to him… na, na, na, na."

"I don't feel well." I interrupted Ashraf. "Let us go now. I don't feel comfortable here." The sense of fear that gripped me had intensified.

"Yes, yes, yes… that is right," Ashraf muttered again. His speech slowed into a slur… gibberish, totally incoherent. He began to sweat profusely. His face was twisted and contorted as if he was in great pain. He assumed a threatening air. The muscles were standing out on his face and his eyes protruded in a frightening stare. Words spilled from his mouth yet what was said did not appear to come from his mind. It seemed to be from another person and was accompanied by a chilling change of voice.

The beginning of the malady was a fit of grief, anger and mourning. He alternately talked and laughed. He walked a while. Then he sat and rolled on the ground. At times, he leapt about, contorting his body and twisting his neck. Then he chanted verses. After that he talked gibberish and seemed to have acquired unusual strength. He tore his clothes into rags. These mad spells returned at intervals and increased in frequency and intensity as I watched in horror. I was absolutely terrified.

It seemed as if the session lasted forever but in fact it was only a few minutes. Then he returned to 'consciousness'. I was greatly relieved when the melodrama ended.

"What happened?"

"I don't know," he replied. "What did I do? Who tore my shirt?"

"It seemed as if a demon entered your body. You behaved as if you were possessed. It was frightening. You grew powerful and tore up your shirt while chanting verses."

"Can't you tell? It was the spirit that entered and took control of me. The month of July is Ghost Month. It is the month when spirits are released from hell to roam our world again. As a lawyer, you should know – no one buys or sells property in the month of July."

Ashraf walked me back to the house. I invited him inside. The experience was so unique and sensational that I felt compelled to reward him. I gave him S$300.

These strange events seem to reflect those turbulent years I spent in Singapore. My journey through Singapore was perilous and full of mystique – it was unreal.

It had not occurred to me that the happenings that night might have been staged for my benefit until I went to New York that year.

"Sir, do you want a shoe-shine?" an elderly black man asked as he approached me on Fifth Avenue. I was in a suit, and my hair was gelled and combed back to give me the look of a tycoon. The Americans got the impression I was a businessman from Japan. It was during the days before the rise of China as an economic power and the Japanese were generally better treated than the Chinese in posh shops and restaurants in New York because they were thought to be richer than the Chinese.

"How much?"

"Just five bucks."

No sooner had I put one foot on the shoebox than I felt a pair of hands clamped onto my shoe so tight that I could not pull free from the shoe mount. Then we were surrounded by four big black youngsters so tall that they blocked out the skyline above us. I was panic-stricken. I felt as though I was about to be robbed but I was not sure.

Suddenly the shoe-shine man took a piece of polishing cloth from his box and started to hit the men who had gathered. The action caused the men to scatter as he continued to chase them. It all happened very quickly. I was so relieved that I dipped into my wallet and handed the man a twenty-dollar note as a gesture of appreciation for his brave act – he had stopped a robbery.

As I left, I turned and saw he was with the same group of young men. They were joking and larking as they shared the take. Then I noticed the same act being repeated over and over again with other victims who had stopped like I did.

I connected the shoe-shine experience with the night at the reservoir. Ashraf obviously had an accomplice who worked with a torch down in the gully that night when I was frightened out of my wits.

# THE CRESCENDO

We lived in Singapore for three years – from 1995 to 1998. The Australian architect had created a unique house split on five levels – a garage in the basement, kitchen and the servants' quarters on the ground floor, sitting room, library and family dining area on the first floor, a formal dining room and two bedrooms on the second floor, and the family and master bedroom taking up a whole floor at the top. The garden at the back had a swimming pool surrounded by lush tropical greenery – fruit, coconut trees and tropical plants. The front garden had a large terrace overlooking the circular ramp for vehicular access to the main door. The clever architect managed to bring the 'outside' into the 'inside' and vice versa. It was a tropical paradise and a delight to be there.

The house was made for entertaining. We entertained frequently and extensively – the rich and famous in Singapore, from Hong Kong and elsewhere. Those were the days of wine and roses and Shanghai parties in Singapore – footloose, head light and champagne flowed. It was the crescendo of my life.

In hindsight, my life there during those years can only be described as illusory: the 'fireworks' and then the 'poof'. I went on an ego trip. The 'rush to fame' did earn me the fireworks and 'fifteen minutes of glory' but at some cost.

I learned how pillaging, philandering, power and greed can destroy us all, and worse, one's family, and how the relentless pursuit of wealth can all come crashing down.

I love the children's story about the butterfly coming down to talk to the caterpillar and asking why he is rushing to eat his way to the top of the tree. "Nature will call you whenever it's ready," said the butterfly.

"What do you know?" was the caterpillar's reply. "You've never been a caterpillar."

I got close to Cheng Yu Tung when he became Chairman of Suntec and later when we formed Sunnet, an investment company, in which he was chairman and I was vice-chairman. Sunnet was extremely successful in its investment strategy, buying into the Western recession on the back of the Eastern boom – acquiring stakes in New York's Four Seasons Hotel and Los Angeles' Beverley Wiltshire when the U.S. market was depressed, and in Singapore's Amcol Holdings when its controlling shareholder, Dato Kang Hwi Wah, got into trouble with the law. It paid handsome dividends each year to its shareholders. I was in his good books.

Each year Cheng travelled overseas to inspect his many businesses. He took me along and included me in the entourage that travelled with him. In 1996 we went to Malaysia to meet Agong – the 'king' in Malay language.

"We have to show deference to Agong," said the private secretary to the king. "His Majesty, Azlan Shah of Perak, is the current King of Malaysia."

"This morning we will tee off with His Majesty," he continued. "I have arranged for Dato Cheng Yu Tung and Dato Kang Hwi Wah to be on the same flight (golf team) as His Majesty. After golf, His Majesty has graciously invited all of you to dinner at his palace. Please remember, when you speak to His Majesty, you should speak from a lower level; that is to say, your head should never rise above His Majesty's. The ladies have no problem as His Majesty is a tall man. The men should bow before His Majesty. Have a nice day."

At the Club, the Royal Selangor, we enquired about the green fees.

"Don't worry – when Agong plays, the Club pays," said the Indian club secretary with a smile. "Enjoy your game."

At the palace, seating was arranged in a crescent on one side of a round table; that is to say, no guest was allowed to sit with his back to Agong. Every guest had to sit facing the king.

It should have been a solemn affair but somehow the day's events had endeared us to each other. Barriers and protocol gently melted away. Agong must have played well. He was in a happy mood. It lifted the spirits of everyone present. At dinner, the fine wines that Kang had brought to the party were drunk. When the alcohol took effect, hearts became lighter and soon the guests began to mingle. It was akin to a Shanghai party in Hong Kong. The guests sang and made merry. A lady high on alcohol lost her inhibitions. She approached and swung her arms around Agong and invited him to dance and sing. Agong, handsome, tall and dignified with his silvery hair and ruddy complexion, got up and obliged. For once, the strict protocol of the Royal Palace was forgotten.

The visit to Malaysia, organized by Kang Hwi Wah, was such a roaring success that in Johor Bahru – the region closest to Singapore – Dato Huhyiddin, who was then the Chief Secretary and now the serving Deputy Prime Minister, closed his eyes and made a sign with his hand to indicate he would approve and sign anything if Cheng and his group, New World, should decide to invest in his state.

"Sign, sign, sign…" he muttered and gesticulated half in jest.

≈≈≈≈≈

Each year Cheng Yu Tung organized a golf trip with all the embellishments that one might expect for royalty. The 'royal family' – Cheng and his family – was surrounded by its entourage. In between rounds of golf, the group played a card game called 'Dig the Big Brother'. The golf and the card game took up all of Cheng's spare time when he was not chasing the buck.

Cheng owned over a hundred and thirty hotels around the world – New World, Renaissance, Stouffers, Ramada (outside the U.S. and Canada) and Panda – and the itinerary would be planned around stays in his stable of hotels. It was Cheng's idea of a perfect holiday – business and pleasure combined.

Many in the group were hangers-on, so-called because it seemed as if these people hung around him for one purpose and one purpose only: to outwit and make money from Cheng. Cheng, of course, knew what they were up to but he loved nothing more than a good challenge and proving he was better by winning. He thrived on competition. It was important for him to outplay and outwit his competitors even if they were his closest friends.

In golf, the strokes – the handicaps – were negotiated so tightly there was little room for error. The hangers-on often met to plot a common strategy against Cheng. For instance, instead of playing eighteen holes, they would concede more 'strokes' in exchange for Cheng's agreement to play an extra nine holes. Being an older man, he was more likely to get tired after the first eighteen; thus the hangers-on would gain an advantage. So the plotting and manoeuvring continued in a never-ending game of wits. It was all in the spirit of competition and Cheng loved it. No one could beat him.

He proved himself to be superior, outsmarting and outwitting the hangers-on time and time again. One by one they got into trouble. A solicitor who gambled with him eventually became a fugitive from the law but not before he had plundered millions from his clients. Others became bankrupt and disappeared. One tried to commit suicide on his own yacht. The hangers-on each enjoyed fifteen minutes of fame as members of Cheng's inner circle. Even as they disappeared, new ones arrived on the scene to replace them.

The stakes were big. In golf, players were divided into two leagues. Cheng's friends – not just in golf but also in the card game – played in the first league while the lesser ones, like me, played in the other league behind them. However, what mattered more was one's status and standing in society.

When the U.S.A. was hit by recession, Cheng Yu Tung bought some properties from a tycoon in New York. The two met whilst in Hong Kong and Cheng entertained his business partner to a round of golf. The visitor was told that the betting was $50,000 per hole.

"I will play $200," said the visitor.

"You go behind," said Cheng.

The tycoon ended up playing with Cheng's employees at the back.

In the U.S.A., Cheng had just bought the Stouffers chain of upmarket hotels that included The Mayfair of Washington D.C. He wanted to see for himself what his staff had bought for him. Everyone was excited, from the chief executive down to the bellboy. It was not every day that the boss paid them a visit.

At the five-star hotel, I could not help but notice that, throughout our stay, the same manager was working tirelessly, running all over the place. He never seemed to stop and was always there to cater for Cheng's every whim.

"Do you always work so hard?" I asked out of curiosity.

"Wheels off," he said.

"What do you mean?" I asked.

"It means we are on high alert throughout the stay of Cheng Yu Tung," he replied. "We will not relax until wheels are off… you know, when the plane takes off."

The next morning – a Sunday – I met the manager again in the lobby. He was surprised and disappointed to see me instead of Cheng. He had gone to great lengths to arrange for Cheng to visit the White House. Over the years he had personally met and was known to congressmen, senators and a few presidents including the incumbent, President Clinton and the First Lady, Hillary. The Mayfair was a landmark in the capital, frequented by politicians. It was through this office that he was able to secure a slot for the new owner of the hotel – Cheng Yu Tung – to see the inside of the White House, the Oval Office, the Press Room and the ancillary offices. He was looking forward to his time when he could be one-on-one with Cheng, the owner. But that morning Cheng was more interested in playing cards with his friends. He asked me to go instead.

The two of us entered the side gate of the White House without hindrance. I was surprised the marine on duty let us past so easily as I did not see the manager giving instructions to anyone to call the White House to inform them that I would be attending instead of Cheng. He must have done so but not in my presence.

Accompanied by a guide who met us at the gate, we entered the building through a side door, past security and through a general office before arriving at the Press Room and from there we moved through a foyer into the Oval Office. We were then guided through a passage into the outside of the Oval Office where the Rose Garden is. The narrow passageway with columns on one side links the working area of the President to where he lives. At that point a guard hurriedly ushered us out as Hillary Clinton was about to arrive in the same passageway on her way to the library.

The next day, the party left Washington for Las Vegas. While in Hong Kong I met a representative of the Las Vegas Hilton at a dinner that Cheng gave. He was a Chinese sent by the hotel to take care of the logistics when Cheng and his party stayed there. Gamblers from Hong Kong of Cheng's calibre were much sought after by all the major casinos in Las Vegas. They offered freebies and all kind of perks to attract not only the gamblers but also members of the entourage, families included.

In the Las Vegas Hilton we were told by the manager in his signed letter of welcome that our stay was free with certain exceptions.

"I heard during breakfast that Cheng and his friends lost US$5 million in the casino last night," I said to Elaine in our room. "They decided it was cheaper to play each other than in the casino. They now play in a suite instead."

"Yes, I heard that too," said Elaine. "This morning, the manager was in the lobby to greet us. He looked cheerful. He confirmed that everything during our stay is free."

"Did you say 'everything'?" I asked. "I thought we had to pick up our own telephone and laundry bills. Also the French restaurant is not free."

"Yes, everything – nothing is left out," she insisted.

For the next couple of days we played golf during the day and in the evenings we watched the many shows that Las Vegas is famous for. Cheng and his other friends preferred to play cards against each other, emerging only to have a quick bite to eat when they were hungry.

Elaine played mahjong – a Chinese domino game favoured by women – with Mrs. Cheng and other wives in Cheng's suite, the Presidential Suite.

"You know I was playing mahjong with Mrs. Cheng," Elaine told me one night. "It was after midnight. Suddenly it went all dark. We raised a hue and cry. Then we realised her husband had returned from a session of gambling. Yes, he went to each and every room in this massive suite to turn off the lights. Can you imagine: a man as rich as he is and the Hilton is not even his?"

"Frugality is a virtue," I replied. "That's why Cheng Yu Tung is so rich."

≈≈≈≈≈

"Robert, this evening I would like to dine with you alone," Kang Hwi Wah said to me the next morning. "I'll make a reservation at the French restaurant for 7.30 p.m." Kang was my neighbour in Singapore. His house at Binja Park was a stone's throw from my house. I had introduced Kang to Cheng Yu Tung. This time we were in Las Vegas as Cheng Yu Tung's guests. It was holiday time. Members of the entourage gambled, golfed and ate together. It seemed odd that Kang wanted to dine with me alone.

"Why does Kang want to eat with me?" I asked Elaine. "He knows I'm here with my family."

"He's got something to discuss with you. You know he was charged with corruption."

"I know, but isn't that a thing of the past? He was acquitted by the court."

"Yes, he was found not guilty by the District Court. He may have something else on his mind."

At the restaurant, Kang looked pensive and solemn.

"Did you know I am going back to Singapore tomorrow?" he asked me.

"But we've only just arrived," I said. "You haven't come all the way from Singapore just to spend one day here, have you?"

"I have unfinished business to attend to."

"I suppose it must be urgent if you have to leave straight away."

"Yes, I have to go back to face the music."

"But you've been acquitted by the court," I said, instinctively knowing he was referring to the case. "Why do you have to face the music?"

"No, the government appealed. I am informed that judgement will be delivered the day after tomorrow. This is why I have to cut short my trip."

"Oh, I see. Are you confident?"

"No, I'm not. I will probably be sent to prison. This may be the last time I see you outside prison for a while."

"I am sorry to hear that. I can only wish you luck."

"Thank you, but I wanted to see you about two matters."

"What are they?"

"At golf today I played against Cheng Yu Tung who partnered this young man nicknamed 'The Whiz Kid'... what is his proper name? You know, the young chap who plays with Cheng."

"Law Siew Fai," I prompted him.

"Why is he called 'The Whiz Kid'? He seems to be close to Cheng despite the age difference – in fact he could be Cheng's son. Do you know him? Tell me about his background."

"He's not called 'The Whiz Kid' for nothing. This young man comes from an extraordinary background. He dropped out of school after he was accused of theft when he was barely fourteen. He became a street boy and earned his keep by washing cars. But he is smart and savvy and he joined a firm of estate agents as a messenger. There he worked his way up, learning the ropes quickly. This was in the days before the government introduced licensing requirements for the trade. Then he became a broker. He was so good at it that he soon got promoted. He was made the manager in charge of the sale and leasing of luxury apartments. This gave him the platform to rub shoulders with the rich and famous. He traded in properties himself and made his first pot of gold – some $7 million. His major break came when he befriended Cheng Yu Tung. Cheng sold him a shopping mall at Chungking Mansions. Shortly afterwards he flipped it. This time he hit the jackpot. He made a whopping $540 million profit. He has never looked back since. He is now a billionaire, a tycoon and, for all I know, a celebrity in his own right. He is not known just for his wheeling and dealing but more for his playboy lifestyle. The press love to report on his deals and, of course, the gossip that has surfaced about his private life. He is certainly not shy of publicity. He thrives on it. He is married yet he lives as if he is single. His name is linked to some of the most beautiful women in town, mostly starlets. He is basking under the sun of success. He earned the nickname 'The Whiz Kid' – not bad for someone who was in the gutter just a few years ago."

"That's interesting," said Kang. "You know we gamble big. At the eighteenth hole, my partner and I were leading. Shadow Creek Golf Course looked spectacular at sunset, wandering creeks, glistening waterfalls and graceful gardens coming together to form a landscape that was simply stunning. The Kid asked if we would agree to 'double or quits'. We agreed. It was quickly becoming dark. Both my partner and I teed off into the middle of the fairway. Cheng had a good tee shot too. The Kid's went horribly wrong. He sliced the ball so that it drifted terribly to the right, up the slope and disappeared into the bushes. I couldn't help but rejoice at our good fortune. I thought that we would win for sure... millions were at stake. It was a lot of money."

Kang paused a moment and took a sip from his glass of wine. Then he continued.

"Darkness came even faster than I thought. The Whiz Kid made a mad scramble up the hill trying to find his ball. He could not, and he paced frantically up and down where he thought the ball had landed. However it was plain that the ball had disappeared into the bushes. Cheng shouted and asked his young partner to go back to tee off again instead of wasting more time because it was getting dark. Eventually he gave up. We thought he was going back to tee off again. We were surprised when he joined us at the fairway at the very spot we were standing. He appeared to still be searching. Suddenly he jumped up and down with joy, shouting, 'Here's my ball. I found my ball!'

"The ball was exposed on the edge of the fairway. It just couldn't be. If it had been there originally, we would have been the first to notice it. We were standing on the fairway all the while near the spot where the ball was. From the way the ball sliced and the direction it went, the ball could not have landed there. It was cheating.

"The Kid's team went on to win the last hole," Kang went on. "I was flabbergasted. No, that would be an understatement – I was shattered and disgusted."

"I'm sorry," was all I could say. "You also mention a second matter."

"Ah, yes. I want to plan long-term for my company."

"I thought that was done. Cheng Yu Tung has bought a substantial stake in the company through Sunnet, a company we run together. He is Chairman and I am Vice-Chairman."

"I know, but I am thinking about something rather bigger, something more spectacular like—"

"Like getting Suntec City to take over the company," I said excitedly. "This can be achieved by swapping shares between Suntec City and Amcol – your company – and, in the process, Suntec City becomes a controlling shareholder of Amcol which is a listed company. It is like reversing the assets of Suntec City into a listed company. That way Suntec City gets a 'back-door' listing without having to go through the tedious process of having to apply to the Singapore Stock Exchange."

'This is the chance I've been waiting for,' I thought to myself. 'It's two birds with one stone: the shareholders get liquidity and the Chairman would be marginalized. It sits neatly with the act-in-concert agreement… maybe, just maybe, with the support of the Trio I can head the listed company…'

"Exactly," exclaimed Kang. "Can you work on it, Robert? I'm willing to relinquish control. I also think this is what the government wants."

Kang Hwi Wah was a flamboyant self-made magnate. In the early 1990s, Amcol Holdings, a company controlled by him, was one of Singapore's hottest stocks. The electronics and property group was valued at S$818 million. It was a stock considered safe enough for pensioners. Many Singaporeans pinned their livelihood on its dividends. The government considered the stock politically sensitive. It would not allow the company to go under.

When Kang first got into trouble with the law, he began his search for a white knight to bail him out. He offered a substantial stake in the listed company to Li Ka Shing who, in his halting Cantonese, he described as 'The Great Bear'. But Li had too much on his plate. He declined. The offer was moved to the next one down the line and Cheng's company acquired a sizeable stake.

The next day Kang flew home. He was charged with receiving S$1.5 million in kickbacks for influencing the reduction in the price of a warehouse that was sold by the Bank of China to his group. It was also alleged that, because of the kickback and some other 'under-the-table' rebates, the price of the property was reduced. Kang's style of doing business, whilst common in neighbouring countries, did not go down well in squeaky-clean Singapore.

The appeal by the prosecution was successful. The verdict of the District Court was overturned and Kang was imprisoned. I had a premonition that this would happen. Indeed, Kang had told me in so many words. I was saddened by the missed opportunity in the sense that Kang could no longer be in the driver's seat, steering his company to an amalgamation with Suntec City – my cherished objective.

≈≈≈≈≈

After a few days in Las Vegas we flew to Palm Springs. At the airport two private jets provided by the Hilton Hotel awaited us. There were no more than twenty of us as some members of the group had returned home to Singapore and Hong Kong. Half of my family flew in one plane and the other half flew in the second. The two planes arrived within fifteen minutes of each other. We stayed at Stouffers Esmeralda in the desert of Riverside County, California – another luxury hotel in the chain that Cheng Yu Tung had bought that year.

Palm Springs is built in the desert. The sky was blue and cloudless, the air dry and crisp. It was not too hot when we were there in the early spring. Stouffers Esmeralda is a resort hotel. It is upmarket and delightful and, of course, being there with the new owner the staff went out of their way to make sure we were comfortable. We spent the day under the sun either at poolside or golfing on courses created out of the desert. The green of the golf course contrasts well with the burnt earth. It was a sight to behold. Our stay was made all the more enjoyable as I was there with my whole family – Elaine and my two children, John and Gillian.

≈≈≈≈≈

On Queen's Road Central back in Hong Kong someone tapped me on the shoulder from behind. I turned. It was 'The Whiz Kid'.

"Big Brother," said the Kid. "You must look after me."

The young man was smartly dressed. His hair was short and neat, well greased with a parting on the left. His complexion was ruddy. He was well groomed and looked every bit the tycoon he was. He had a glow that only a happy man could radiate. He was clearly the picture of a very successful person in the prime of his life. There had been a lot of news about him in the papers. If it was not about a mega-deal like yet another takeover of a listed company or paying top dollar for a landmark property, it was something about his juicy private life – this actress or that model he had consorted with.

"How are you?" I asked, overwhelmed by his friendliness.

"Oh, not too bad… not bad at all," he said jokingly. "I have recently bought a few acres of land on the other side of the border. In my spare time I gather together chicks. I 'dig' and smoke opium to pass the time."

I burst out laughing. It was funny the way he said it – like a joke with an excellently timed punchline. I went along with the flow of the conversation. "When your pickaxe gets blunt from 'digging', I shall lend you mine. You must look after me too."

It was a light-hearted exchange of pleasantries. It was amazing how he humbled himself. He was never a stiff-necked snob. He carried no chip on his shoulder but was natural and genuine. It was this side of his character that endeared him to everyone. He was just plain likeable. That was the thing about the Whiz Kid. Being a solicitor, he knew I was constantly involved with all kinds of deals and some of them could benefit him.

"Did you hear this?" Elaine asked me one day. "It just came through on the news."

"What?"

"Whiz Kid tried to kill himself. He locked himself in the cabin of his yacht, sealed the windows and burnt charcoal. He was in a coma when he was found. He looked half dead on the television."

Just before the market had crashed, the Whiz Kid went on a buying spree, acquiring properties and listed companies. It seemed as if his funds were inexhaustible.

He led the life of a playboy. The women around him were like lanterns on a merry-go-round. He owned more than a dozen expensive cars – Ferrari, Rolls-Royce, Porsche, Benz, BMW… you name it and they were there in his collection. His yacht was the venue for lavish parties which he threw regularly to entertain tycoons and his girlfriends.

Then the crash came. His fortune changed. Overnight his wealth evaporated into thin air. He lost $600 million on forfeited deposits alone. His creditors went after him and writs were flying all over the place. He was in dire financial trouble when he tried to kill himself.

Although miraculously he survived, he was never the same again. Abandoned and ignored by his friends, he would frantically look for ways to get their attention. He gave interviews and revealed sordid details of his secret relationships with actresses, models and tycoons, using bold and filthy language.

He said he gave one beauty queen half a million dollars a month to be his mistress. He displayed pictures of himself in a wet kiss with a Singapore actress. Another well-known actress was described as possessing 'breasts that split to two sides' like a number 8 Chinese character. Yet another had legs the size of elephant trunks.

As he continued to spill the beans, some of the actresses and models he had had affairs with called him up voluntarily. On the surface they wanted to find out how he was. The truth was that they were more concerned that he might have taken videos of them in bed together. And, if he had, the girls were willing to go to great lengths to retrieve these potential time bombs before it was too late. It made him feel he was coming back from the wilderness to a station in life to which he was more accustomed.

A tycoon friend took pity on him. For old time's sake, he gave him a couple of million which he squandered just as quickly as he had received it.

In desperation, the Kid turned to the media again, revealing more unsavoury secrets of the tycoons and girls. He was hoping once again that he would get the attention he deserved and they would give him money just to shut him up.

He must have hit the lowest point in his life. His wife had divorced him. He was declared bankrupt. His friends had abandoned him en masse so he was alone and friendless. It was then that he increasingly turned to drugs as a way to escape the harsh reality of life.

A boil filled with pus and the size of a tennis ball appeared on the left side of his neck. His face was drawn, haggard, greenish and pale – the look of a drug addict. When he yawned one could see the whites of his big round eyes. He looked hideous. He was delirious most of the time, a far cry from the smug, confident and dapper young man he once was.

A local magazine sent him to Paris ostensibly to get treatment for the lump on his neck but the true purpose was to sell magazines. Accompanied by a staff writer and a girl who posed as his girlfriend, his sojourn in Paris attracted a wide readership. During his trip, pictures were taken of him with the beautiful girl and sensational articles were written about his 'last tango in Paris' – the public loved nothing more than a 'rags to riches' story – but then, bang! The bubble of the self-made billionaire and darling of the media burst. It became a 'riches to rags' story. The world came crashing down, sending him back to where he came from – it was just the kind of stuff that Hong Kong is made of and the crowd loved it. They called for more… and more.

It was the end of the road for the Whiz Kid. He became even more isolated. Dejected and lonely, he took refuge in Macau. There an old friend nicknamed 'Market Wai' took care of him. He put him up at his hotel and provided for him.

Then one day the police came. The Kid was arrested on drug-related offences – he was accused of supplying prostitutes from China with drugs. He pleaded guilty as charged – drug trafficking – but somehow escaped a custodial sentence.

After the incident he left Macau and went to a small town near Canton. He dabbled in real estate. He tried to get into the gambling business only to be let down by a client who disappeared after running up a gambling debt of $2 million. Old habits died hard. He remained a hard gambler and womaniser. His substance abuse got worse.

"Whiz Kid died." Elaine was again the person to break the news to me. "He died of a heart attack."

I was taken aback and saddened by the news.

The night before he died, he ate his usual midnight dinner with friends after a night of hard gambling and God knows what else. The next day he went to a firm of lawyers to sign off some papers on a property he had wanted to give to a local girl. While he was there, he suddenly passed out. When the ambulance arrived, he was already lifeless. The police did not suspect foul play. He died from natural causes – a massive heart attack.

≈≈≈≈≈

It was late in the evening when I returned from work to the house in Singapore. Li Ka Shing had telephoned me that day and told me he was visiting Singapore. He wanted to see Suntec City. I invited him for dinner and he accepted.

"Guess who's coming for dinner," I said to Elaine.

"You are so excited – who?" she asked with a smile.

"Superman Li!" I exclaimed excitedly. "Next Thursday at 7.30 p.m."

"Is he coming alone? What should I prepare?"

"Yes, he is. He says he eats simply and prefers congee with vegetables and tofu – nothing fancy. He doesn't want the usual big dishes such as shark's fin and 'big fish and big meat'. He just wants a simple home-cooked dinner, nothing too oily, in our home."

Elaine is a good cook. Cooking is in her blood like many of her compatriots from Canton, the largest city in southern China. They say in Chinese: "Live in Soochou, die in Kweichou and eat in Kwangchou." Soochou is China's Lake District. It has the best climate and scenery. Kweichou is known for its redwood that makes the best coffins. Kwangchou (Canton) is best known for its many culinary delights.

Elaine often cooks for small gatherings. When we entertained a bigger group, she would either get outside catering or supervise the domestic staff, one of whom, Lucy, was an excellent cook. She made the best spaghetti in town, always al dente.

"We can't just give him tofu, can we? It is not every day that Bill Gates comes for dinner. I shall prepare the usual for a guest of his importance. But I shall use less oil. I can steam a fish."

"But you can't get good fish in Singapore, not like what we get in Hong Kong. Fish in the tropics doesn't taste good."

"The local catfish is good. You like it. Shall we dine upstairs or downstairs?"

"Of course, the formal dining room," I replied. We used the formal dining room only for large parties. Ordinarily, the family ate in the dining room downstairs.

"But won't that be too big for just three of us?"

"No, I want this occasion to be remembered. How shall we set the table?"

"I will use a good centrepiece."

"We can use the pair of crystal swans," I added.

"Yes, they're elegant," she said. "I shall place a pair of candelabras at each end of the table. In between, I can use flowers to add colour."

"What about the glasses?"

"We can use the crystal, the longer stemmed and cylindrical globe for white, the wider globe for red, champagne flute between water tumblers and perhaps a small sherry glass on the side."

"It sounds good. We can do a combination of West and East – setting in Western with courses one after another and serving in Eastern style using our fine china and fine ivory chopsticks."

"But does Li drink?"

"He doesn't drink at lunchtime but he does drink at dinner. I saw him drinking at the dinner party Wee Cho Yaw gave."

"I know, I was there too," Elaine said. "It was the dinner Wee hosted for the shareholders of Suntec at UOB's penthouse."

"That's the one. It was a big party. It's not every day that 'Hong Kong' comes for dinner, even for the largest retail bank in Singapore. I remember Wee drank a 'salute' toast to Li who was sitting next to him. They both emptied their glasses. Then Wee asked the waiter to fill up

Li's glass with more gin. The waiter made a mistake. He filled Wee's glass with gin and gave Li water instead. Wee was so busy talking that he didn't notice the mistake. Then he turned and proposed another 'salute' drink to Li. As he drank, he grimaced. He knew the waiter had made a mistake. Nevertheless he emptied the glass. Yes, a whole glass of gin! Then he turned and gave me the thumbs-up sign and praised me – his way of saying 'thank you' for bringing Hong Kong to Singapore and to his party. Li spoke in Teo Chow while Wee spoke in Hokkien. They had no difficulty in communicating with each other. The two dialects must be similar." (Teo Chow and Hokkien are both coastal areas in the southern part of China, between Shanghai and Hong Kong).

"Yes. I remember how the party became rather rowdy when the alcohol took effect," Elaine said. "Almost everyone left their seats and they were drinking, talking, laughing and joking – just like a Shanghai party. It must have been Singapore's social event of the year – the time when Singapore and Hong Kong met."

The following Thursday, Li arrived punctually at 7.30 p.m. He was very disciplined and seldom late, and would chide others for being tardy.

He was dressed in a blue suit with an open-necked white shirt. It was rare to see him without a tie. He walked in with his usual swagger, beaming as he entered through the foyer and up a set of steps that led to the enclosed courtyard.

"Robert, this is just a small gift for you." He handed me two presents, one bigger than the other, both beautifully gift-wrapped.

"Oh, you shouldn't, Mr. Li," I said meekly. "You are always so generous. I have received so many gifts from you that I am embarrassed."

"This is nothing. They are for Elaine and you." He had remembered the name of my wife. I was surprised and impressed.

"Can I offer you something to drink? Dry sherry?"

"No, I don't drink. I will take a tea instead, please."

"Welcome to our humble home," I said as I toasted Li.

"You have a beautiful home," Li remarked as he raised his cup to my glass in salute. "Can I look around?"

"Certainly." I turned and whispered into Elaine's ear, "Remove the glasses."

The galleried dining room was entirely lit by candles. A pair of chandeliers hung from the ceiling. The cathedral-style window was hung with opulent curtains, beige with dark blue turn-ups. A collection of oil paintings adorned the mahogany wall panelling. An antique cherry wood long dining table stood in the centre of the room complemented by a collection of different antique English chairs and an array of side tables. In the candlelight, the room came to life, glowing in harmony and creating an ambience that was intimate and relaxing.

"Wow, Robert," said Li. "Your dining room is bigger than mine."

"Mr. Li, you are so modest. Compared to you, I am a pauper. If it is true then the only explanation is that houses are cheap here and you have chosen to live in the same modest home for over thirty years. Everyone knows."

Elaine and I sat on one side and Li on the other side of the long table.

"Did you know I come from a family of scholars?" Li was in a relaxed mood as he recounted his childhood. "My father was a schoolmaster. He took us to Hong Kong when I was twelve. Sadly, he died just a year later, leaving my mother to look after me and my two siblings. I was the eldest. I quit school and sent my mother back to China. I told her not to worry about me. I would get a job, work hard and support her. I promised her that I would one day bring her back to Hong Kong."

The candlelight flickered. Li's eyes turned red.

"I worked as a salesman in a plastic factory. I was paid commission based on the business I introduced. I worked hard – sixteen hours a day, including Sundays. I went out of my way to keep my customers satisfied. From the time an order was placed, I made sure it was executed properly. I made them happy and they placed more and more orders with me. At sixteen, I was earning more than the manager who was over forty years old. One day, the owner pulled me to one side and told me that the manager had complained. I assured the owner that from that day onward I would not take home a single cent more than the manager.

"Then I left and set up a factory of my own, also making plastic goods – flowers, combs and soap boxes. I exported to France at a time when the country was reviewing its policy on tariffs. The duties I paid were withheld by Customs. Then, in the 1950s, the import duty on plastics was abolished. France returned the duty I had paid – a whopping $5 million windfall in all. It was a lot of money in those days. It was my first pot of gold.

"My landlord was greedy. He just couldn't stop raising the rent. So I bought a factory building. That was how I started in property."

Our conversation then turned to Hong Kong and the imminent transfer of its sovereignty to China.

"Do you know?" Li said. "I was invited by Deng Hsiao Peng, the Paramount Leader, to see him in Beijing in the early 1980s. The night before the meeting I went to the Forbidden City and there, under its wall, I paced up and down. I kept asking myself: shall I tell him what he wants to hear or shall I tell him the truth? In the end I chose the latter. I explained to the Paramount Leader what I thought would be the consequences if China was to take back Hong Kong. He listened attentively but told me politely in the end that the decision was made and it was irreversible. China would take back Hong Kong. It would become a special administrative zone governed by its own people. Investors could set their minds at rest."

The dinner lasted well into the night. Courses of cold starters, abalone, shark's fin soup, steamed fish, chicken, vegetables, fried rice and dessert were served. It was a delightful dinner and Li was a wonderful guest to entertain.

"Look what Li has given us," I told my wife after Li had left. "It's a pair of dress watches. Gosh, they must be expensive. I've built up a collection of these expensive watches from his gifts over the years."

"You must be close to him," she said.

"Don't be silly. I am only as close to Li as I am useful to him," I replied cynically.

Over the years he had given me platinum and gold watches, a solid platinum pen and golf sets when I was useful to him compared to a selection of fruits when I was less useful. Only one gift was constant however – the generous hamper that arrived every Christmas.

# THE ESTABLISHMENT

"Dr. Goh, please follow me," said the maître d' of the Chinese restaurant in Singapore's Shangri-la Hotel. "I have a table for you."

The restaurant was popular and it was a Saturday. A long queue had formed outside.

"Thank you, captain, I prefer to wait in the queue like everyone else," said Dr. Goh.

"But, sir, I am sure others in the queue won't mind if you are given priority," the maître d' insisted. Those queuing looked approvingly at Dr. Goh.

"Please go ahead," one said.

"No, thank you, I prefer to wait like everyone else," he insisted as he turned to me to carry on the conversation from where we left off. He had been expounding on the theory of how human weaknesses such as greed, ego, self-deception, complacency, laziness and cowardice can be controlled through what he considered 'forces of coercion'. It gave me a rare insight into the way the great mind of Dr. Goh worked.

I greatly admired Dr. Goh Keng Swee. He had met Lee Kuan Yew while studying at the London School of Economics. When Lee became the Prime Minister of Singapore, Dr. Goh played many roles under him including stints as Minister of Finance, Minister for Interior and Defence, and Minister for Education. When I first met him, Dr. Goh was the Deputy Prime Minister. He was widely credited as the architect of Singapore's financial system.

Lee Kuan Yew, Dr. Goh Keng Swee and Lim Kim San were three of the most senior 'Old Guards' who transformed Singapore from a backwater to a thriving metropolis: from Third World to First World. Lee, the Prime Minister, is commonly known as the Father of Singapore.

Ever since John Tung's unsolicited donation, I had managed to be in Dr. Goh's good books. I saw him often at the MAS (Monetary Authority of Singapore) which he headed at the time and for a while after his retirement from politics.

I greatly cherish memories of Dr. Goh and was pleased when his daughter-in-law Tan Siok Sun, who wrote his autobiography (*Goh Keng Swee, a Portrait*), sent me a copy with a handwritten note: *My little portrait of an extraordinary man known to you.*

Dr. Goh was indeed an extraordinary man. Sadly, in his old age and with his hearing impaired, we saw less of each other.

Dr. Goh passed away on May 14th, 2010. The former Prime Minister, Lee Kuan Yew, delivered a moving eulogy at the funeral that started with the statement: "It was my good fortune to have strong men around me." Indeed, Dr. Goh was a strong man.

≈≈≈≈≈

The first time I saw Lim Kim San was at a wedding. Wei Chi, the youngest daughter of Wee Cho Yaw, the leading banker and Chairman of UOB, Singapore's largest retail bank, was getting married to David, Aunt Diana's second son. Aunt Diana took me by the hand, ushered me to the top table and introduced me to the guests there one by one; she was always that kind aunt who would go out of her way to shower kindness on me. I did not know who Lim Kim San was then. But I remember the speech he gave. He spoke without notes and with all the confidence that one could only expect to find in a seasoned public speaker, like a politician.

The next time I saw Lim Kim San was at a dinner given by Lee Kuan Yew who was then the Senior Minister. Elaine and I arrived early. I asked the chauffeur to go around the block. Then, much to my dismay, the car was caught in heavy traffic. As the minutes ticked away, I became increasingly anxious. The last thing I wanted was to be late. After all, it was not every day that one got invited to a dinner by none other than the Senior Minister. When Lee retired as the Prime Minister he remained an M.P. and was appointed by the Cabinet to be Senior Minister. The next Prime Minister, Goh Chok Tong, also retired to become Senior Minister in like manner.

We were the last to arrive. Seating in the lounge was arranged in a U-shape. The Senior Minister was sitting in the middle. As I had arrived late, the Senior Minister signalled for me to take the seat next to him, the only one that was still available. Elaine took a seat further away. Mrs. Lee was there. A distinguished-looking man with thin silvery hair, a round face and ruddy complexion sat next to the Senior Minister. Although I did not recognize him as the man who spoke at the wedding, I thought he looked familiar.

"Kim San, why did you make the speech in English?" Lee Kuan Yew asked, referring to a speech Kim San had made earlier.

"You also make important speeches in English," interjected Mrs. Lee before Lim Kim San could answer.

Lim smiled and remained quiet.

I did not know that Lim was one of Singapore's 'Old Guards'. He ranked in the same league as Lee Kuan Yew and Goh Keng Swee. He served the nation with distinction in various positions such as Defence, Communications, Environment, HDB (Housing Development Board), MAS, Public Services Commission, Port Authority and so on. To crown it all, he was also the serving Chairman of Advisors to the Elected President.

But there was more than just being 'Old Guard'. He was close to Lee Kuan Yew. The two men clicked from the very beginning. Through the years together, they formed a relationship in which they made up for each other's shortcomings and were enriched by each other's talents: Lee, an aspiring politician with a First Class Honours degree from Cambridge and Lim, a practical man who never went to university but excelled as a savvy man-of-the-street. Lee Kuan Yew and Lim Kim San were a perfect fit, an example of how two people at opposite ends of the spectrum could complement each other so well.

Lim Kim San and I sat at the opposite ends of the long dining table set up in the lush surroundings of a central courtyard. We were too far from each other to exchange any meaningful conversation.

In hindsight, it was inexcusable not to know a man as important and whose influence was so ubiquitous as Lim – second to none except Lee Kuan Yew and, perhaps, Goh Keng Swee. As the Chinese saying goes: 'How can you not see the Mountain of Tai when you are not blind?' I cursed myself.

≈≈≈≈≈

Tan Boon Teik was Singapore's Attorney General when I first met him. Over the years we befriended each other. I suppose he thought I was able to deliver; I made good on my pledges. I delivered the donation from John Tung; I delivered the lawyers; I delivered the tycoons.

He was willing to do me favours. It was through his introduction that my daughter, Gillian, got into Wycombe Abbey, a top-notch public school for girls in Oxfordshire. His daughter, Sui Lin, went to the same school.

Boon Teik also introduced me to Dr. Peter North. Dr. North was the Principal of Jesus College, Oxford. He wanted to raise money for scholarships to enable students from China to study at Oxford University.

"I shall introduce you to the people who I think can help you," I said to Dr. North. "But, before I do, I would like to share some thoughts with you on why they donate.

"It's the same everywhere," I continued. "People donate for a purpose, either to enhance their reputation or they want something, such as gaining the admission of a son, daughter, grandchild or someone close to the donor into Oxford. You must play on this psychology when you appeal for donations."

Dr. North nodded. He did not seem to be a die-hard academic. He was pragmatic, practical and businesslike. He was ready to play along, so to speak. "I understand what you mean," he said.

Indeed, I too had an axe to grind, an ulterior motive. I was hoping John, my son, could go to Oxford – a vicarious way to get pleasure out of something I had not been able to achieve myself.

When John went to St. Faith's, the preparatory school for the Leys School of Cambridge, he was hardly ten. The Leys School has a good record of its students getting into Cambridge. But one cannot apply to both universities in the same year, so in that sense Oxford and Cambridge are mutually exclusive, not to mention the unspoken requirement that the application must be recommended – a letter of reference from the headmaster of their school to certify he or she is indeed of Oxbridge material. Although A-Level subjects matter – most, if not all, applicants are expected to get straight 'A's anyway – they are by no means conclusive. What matters more is the interview. If an applicant comes across brilliantly he may be made an unconditional or a low-threshold offer; that is to say, he would most certainly get a place even if he gets less than the norm of three 'A's. The system gives the panel the ultimate power to pick and choose who they want for the university.

It is not uncommon for Oxbridge hopefuls to prepare for the interview by employing tutors to drill them on how to answer questions. But brilliance is after all in the personality, and if an applicant does not possess the requisite attributes then no matter how much coaching is given to him he will not shine through enough to get an offer.

But Dr. North was not just anybody. He was the principal of an important college in Oxford – Jesus College. He was an internationally renowned legal scholar, having chaired many statutory bodies such as the Independent Review in Northern Ireland. He was also chair of the Oxford Inquiry, established to review the running of the university.

Both reports when published were widely known as 'The North Report', demonstrating the kind of clout Dr. North possessed.

I was not wrong in assuming that, if I assisted Dr. North in raising funds for Oxford, my son would be treated less harshly in the interview and he would be made the usual conditional offer – three 'A's in the A-Level subjects.

I advised John to apply for Oxford against his wishes. Having spent years going to school there, he was sentimentally attached to Cambridge. In the beginning, there were occasions when he was bullied at school. He would tell the waiters at the Indian restaurant in Castle Street and they would stand up for him. Every half-term, when John was out of school, he stayed either with his guardian or at the family house next door to the guardian's. The restaurant was nearby. He was taken there to eat often. Over time, he and the waiters became friends. They saw John grow from a small boy to a young man. At times he would ask for permission from the guardian to wander off on his own to visit his friends at the restaurant. The waiters often volunteered to collect John from school when it broke up for half-term, with the permission of the guardian. John would point out to them the boys who had bullied him. Those Indian waiters demonstrated in no uncertain terms they were there to protect John and acted like his godfathers. No one dared lift a finger against John. Meanwhile, John grew up and made friends. He no longer required others to protect him.

John's guardian, Mrs. Kvan, was Danish. Before retiring to Cambridge, she taught history at a top girls' school in Hong Kong – Diocesan Girls' School. Elaine went to the school with Sabre Kvan, her daughter, and the two became best of friends; they often had slumber weekends together either at Sabre's or Elaine's home. It was through Mrs. Kvan that Elaine bought the adjacent house for use during half-term.

Dr. North's appeal for funding yielded instant results. Funds for many such scholarships were raised. There were many donors willing to support such a worthy cause, giving scholarships to brilliant students from Beijing's prestigious Tsinghua University to undertake post-graduate studies at Britain's best-known university. It was also considered to be politically appropriate at a time when the two countries were poised to embark on a new stage of their relationship given the imminent return of Hong Kong's sovereignty to China.

What surprised me most was an offshoot in the drive to raise this funding for the scholarships. Sir Run Run Shaw pledged £10 million to Oxford to start a school which would be named 'Sir David Wilson's School of Oriental Studies'. Sir David was then the serving governor of Hong Kong.

I knew Sir David through Sir Run Run. He was my teacher of '*tze kung*', an ancient exercise that uses breathing to control and regulate the flow of '*tze*' (vital energy) in the body. It is an exercise that I practise on a daily basis religiously. Those who practise '*tze kung*' believe that control of one's breathing gives one strength, vitality, inspiration and good health, and that improper breathing is a common cause of ill health.

Sir Run Run and I saw each other often on social occasions. Every time we met he always asked me the same question: "Robert, how are you getting on with the '*tze kung*' I taught you?"

I always avoided a direct reply. He knew I was not truly dedicated to '*tze kung*'. Then one day he called.

"Robert, have you started? You promised me that you would start when we met last time."

"Yes, I have started, Sir Run Run." I lied out of deference to him but I knew that I could postpone it no longer. I had to start immediately, and certainly before the next time we met.

Much to my surprise, an hour later Sir Run Run showed up at my office unannounced. He walked straight into my room and said, "Show me."

I was speechless and embarrassed that I had been caught red-handed lying. Sir Run Run just smiled. I had not taken him by surprise. He just wanted to prove a point with me. "Don't lie," he said.

The following week I flew to Mauritius to visit a friend who had recently relocated his factory to the island state to take advantage of the quota-free exports to E.C. countries. This friend was a doctor by training but he never ceased to amaze me with the array of machinery that he had invented to automate his sizeable knitwear operation. What I did not know was that Singapore Airlines provided only one flight per week out of the island.

The Royal Plaza was the most exclusive hotel on the island. With the turquoise sea, the private beach of fine powdery sand and its opulent interiors, the hotel was exquisite. However, I was stranded and bored to tears. It seemed as if I was the only guest in this incredibly beautiful hotel.

So I started the '*tze kung*' because I had nothing better to do.

The technique is as follows: I imagine a table-tennis ball that rests two inches below my navel. As I inhale, I do three things simultaneously – tighten the rectal muscles, pull in my stomach and inhale. As I exhale, I relax the muscles. I continue to concentrate on the table tennis ball. Each time I inhale, it moves up from the tip of the spine to the head (the big circle) or the chest (the small circle); then it descends down through the tip of the nose (the big circle) or from the chest (the small circle) and back to the resting place – the navel. As the process repeats itself, I chant:

> *Breathing Out –*
> *Touching the Root of Heaven,*
> *One's heart opens;*
> *The Dragon slips into the water.*
> *Breathing In –*
> *Standing on the Root of Earth,*
> *One's heart is still and deep;*
> *The Tiger's claw cannot be moved.*

Then, one day, about a week after I had started, the pieces suddenly fell into place – it clicked. It began with a purple cloud that gathered at the top of my head. As the '*tze*' entered my head, the cloud 'exploded' in the shape of a mushroom akin to an imaginary atomic explosion.

"Hallelujah," I exclaimed in jubilation. "At long last, I've mastered '*tze kung*'. It's a marvellous sensation. I can't describe it. Oh, it's wonderful… so wonderful."

Sir Run Run was delighted when I described my first '*tze*' experience to him. He knew he had finally got me started – I was probably his first disciple. I know this because, over the span of some thirty years – that is as long as I have now practised '*tze kung*' – I have not once been successful in turning an aspirant into a disciple. Scores of them have wanted me to teach them, ladies in particular, because they can all see the power of '*tze*' on my face – robust with a glow that can only be explained by the mystical power of '*tze*'.

Without a religious-like conviction, one can never fathom let alone master the art of '*tze kung*'. Had it not been for Sir Run Run's tenacity, the wonders of '*tze kung*' would have eluded me. Sir Run Run is a perfect example of how beneficial '*tze kung*' can be to one's health and well being. In November 2011, a group of close friends celebrated his birthday – his 104th.

It was some time during the winter of 1991 when Sir Run Run took me to Government House to demonstrate '*tze kung*' to Sir David Wilson. I had by then been doing '*tze kung*' for many years. He obviously considered me his prized disciple. "By learning to control your breathing, you can influence the regulation of your heartbeat, blood pressure, circulation and digestion," explained Sir Run Run as I demonstrated the movements to Sir David. "By squeezing air in and out of the head and lungs using muscles of the rectum and stomach when you breathe, you will move the '*tze*' (energy) to different parts of the body and, in the process, the tissues can be repaired and cleansed efficiently. The movement also increases the oxygen intake into the lungs so that it nourishes and energises the body as you inhale and expels poisons from it as you exhale. Breath is life and if you breathe well you will live long."

Run Run's donation pledge to Oxford was widely reported. Tan Boon Teik, the Attorney General, was very pleased. He was proud that he made the introduction even though in the end, for reasons unbeknown to me, the donation was never made.

"My son in Oxford has just won a Boxing Blue. My daughter has been accepted into Cambridge this year," said Boon Teik. "I know your son is taking his A-Level subjects. Has he decided which university he is going to apply to?"

"John tells me that his first choice is Cambridge."

"Robert, if your son doesn't apply to Jesus College, Peter North will feel insulted. Are you fetching your children from school in England this summer?"

"Yes, we are."

"Then why don't you call on Peter?" he continued. "He wants to see you in Oxford."

It was a pleasant summer's day when we arrived at Jesus College, Oxford. Dr. North resided in the Principal's Lodge that was at the heart of the campus.

"Come, it's such a fine day," he said. "Let's drink champagne together."

The roof of the Principal's Lodge commands a spectacular view of the college. It overlooks the lodgings of the college amidst the many lofty structures surmounted by spires.

After a pleasant lunch in a dining room adorned with curious wainscot engravings, we moved to the drawing room where coffee was served. The carved mahogany panelling gave an air of luxury. It was set in three tiers with ovals placed vertically. With the passage of time, it had faded to a unique antique greenish-brown colour. The lintel was elaborately carved on the inside with a decorated cartouche and cherub's head. It was a most engaging feature of the college. Christopher Wren, who built St. Paul's Cathedral, was commissioned to design the ceiling for this remarkable room. When the work was done he asked to be paid in kind – his portrait to be painted. Today, the painting still hangs on the wall of the dining room. Against a backdrop of gothic windows and adorned by a concert piano and chests from medieval times, I could not believe how opulent and beautiful the room was. The aesthetics took my breath away. It was so awesome that I cried. No other room except the Temple of Abu Simbel in Egypt has affected me the same way.

"What a beautiful room," I exclaimed. "This room has no rivals. It's simply unique." Dr. North smiled and nodded.

"Young man, I look forward to seeing you at the interview this winter," said Dr. North as he ruffled John's hair affectionately when we said goodbye.

It was close to Christmas, late into the night, when the telephone rang. I was woken up.

"Is that you, Robert?" a voice asked.

"Yes, it's me. Who's calling?"

"Oh, it's Peter North here," said Dr. North.

"Oh, hallo, how are you, Peter?" I expected him to give me good news.

"I sat through the interview. John did well—"

"Thank you." I cut him short, thinking that John had been made an offer – the usual three 'A's for an applicant who had passed the interview.

There was a momentary silence before Dr. North spoke again. "John is what we in Oxford terms call a 'first-class reject'."

"What?" I exclaimed. "He was not made an offer?"

"No, I am afraid not."

"You know he could have applied for Cambridge. His tutor thought he stood a good chance. I am sorry I've let my son down. In my effort to help, I have messed up his chance with Cambridge. 'First-class reject' – thank you for telling me, Dr. North."

"I am sorry."

"But you're the principal. You asked John to apply to Jesus College. Everyone knows how influential you are."

"I am sorry, Robert." He apologised again.

"Thank you for giving me this wonderful Christmas gift," I said sarcastically as I rang off.

I could not sleep at all that night. Elaine was disappointed as well.

I told John. He might have been disappointed but he did not show it, at least not on the surface.

"Just as well," he said.

I never saw Dr. North again. He went on to become the Vice-Chancellor of Oxford University and was knighted by the Queen.


## ALIVE IN THE CROCODILE PIT

*When God wants to destroy someone, He first makes him crazy*

Suntec City was built according to the principles of *feng shui*. It is shaped like a left hand. A huge man-made fountain resembles the palm, and the five buildings – one short and four long – resemble the fingers; hence, the name 'Five Fingers Mountain'.

A Five Fingers Mountain is also featured in the folklore *Journey to the West*. It is there that the Monkey King is incarcerated by the gods for his sins. He is only set free when he agrees to accompany a Buddhist monk on his pilgrimage to the West to obtain the book of enlightenment. The monk travels with his three protégés and a dragon prince who acts as his horse. They have agreed to protect the monk as he travels. The journey is perilous and fraught with danger.

The Monkey King is born out of a piece of rock. The gods use a brilliant light to trace his every movement. He is clever, brave and, at times, mischievous. On one occasion, he makes trouble in Heaven. The gods send an army to subdue him. He manages to defeat the army single-handedly. He does it by using his many powers, including the power to clone himself many times by pulling hairs from his body and blowing them to become his doubles. He is also able to transform himself in seventy-two different ways. His somersaulting allows him to travel long distances by leaping.

He is controlled by the monk through a headband he wears which he cannot remove. Only the monk can. By chanting a spell, the monk can tighten the band whenever the Monkey King needs to be disciplined.

My journey through Singapore was fraught with danger. It was as perilous as the Monkey King's journey to the West. The monk took the shape and form of the Chairman.

I was overly optimistic that I could control Suntec City – a bold attempt that was an act of heroism mixed with a dash of madness. Tan Sri considered Suntec City his possession and a vehicle to advance his career. He would fight tooth and nail to keep it. Cheng Yu Tung made no bones about it. It was just another consortium project. He did not wish to be bound together, in his words, "for a hundred years". On the surface, Cheng had the support of Li Ka Shing and Lee Shau Kee – two of Hong Kong's richest tycoons – but, behind the façade, the alliance was falling apart and the act-in-concert agreement was rendered less and less relevant.

There was intensive rivalry between Li Ka Shing and Lee Shau Kee. Both of them vied to be Hong Kong's richest. At times they were at each other's throats. The difference between Number 1 and Number 2 is huge. The former gets all the attention; when prime ministers and politicians visit, they ask to see him. He also gets to see them when he travels overseas. He gets all the media attention. He is sought after by money men such as the head of Goldman Sachs, Morgan Stanley and other top international bankers and financiers. Deals are often presented to him on silver plates together with all the finance he needs. He gets the first bite of the cherry, so to speak – the right of first refusal – before the same deal is passed down the line to the next person.

Being first therefore means everything. The two fight bitterly for the top spot. Once there, the victor guards the privilege jealously. He will do anything to ward off challenges and attempts to unseat him.

For as long as one could remember, Li Ka Shing was untouchable in that Number 1 slot as Hong Kong's richest man. He basked in the sun. But at times his pre-eminence was challenged.

"Mr. Li, I need your approval on this matter," I said. "I have already spoken to Colin Lam and—"

"Don't mention that name to me," interrupted Li. "He is a…" He muttered something.

"What? Mr. Li, I am talking about Colin Lam, the right-hand man of—"

"Yes, I don't want to hear that name," retorted Li.

"What happened?"

"Okay, I will tell you. Did you know Yeung Chi Wan?"

"Yes, I did. He was the owner of Miramar Group. He died recently, didn't he?"

I knew Yeung through his long-time mistress who was a successful businesswoman in her own right. She owned chains of restaurants and boutiques. She was a woman about town. Everyone knew her.

She used to describe how romantic her lover was. Every time they met, Yeung would reserve a room at the French restaurant in his hotel – the Miramar Hotel – and order flowers, red roses, to fill the room. There they would dine by candlelight. Yeung was generous to a fault.

"Yes, after he died we had reached an agreement with his family," Li continued. "Larry Yung and I would each take fifty per cent of the shares to be sold by the family."

Larry Yung was once the richest man in China. He headed CITIC, a giant state-owned conglomerate that is listed in Hong Kong.

"Then Lee Shau Kee came along and said he too wanted to be included in the deal. Larry Yung and I agreed to carve out ten per cent each from our stakes and gave twenty per cent to him. He agreed. For all intents and purposes it was a done deal – my word is my bond. I then left the execution part to Victor, my son, to handle.

"Unbeknown to us, Lee Shau Kee reneged on the agreement. He went behind our backs and offered fifty cents more per share to the widow. He succeeded in snatching the company from us. When the deal was made, he walked out of the room rubbing his hands gleefully saying, 'Victor, I am sorry. I am very sorry. I've let you down.'"

I could see that Li was still fuming as he recounted the incident.

After taking over the Miramar Group, Lee Shau Kee was propelled into the Number 1 spot. Li Ka Shing was unseated. Indeed, that year *Forbes* rated Lee Shau Kee the fourth richest in the world, behind only Warren Buffett, Wal-Mart's Waltons and Bill Gates. Being the richest man in Hong Kong raised his profile beyond all expectations. Politicians and international financiers flocked to him in droves. He was sought after by the international media. They overwhelmed him with interview requests. Fame on an international plane gave him even more recognition at home. He went on to hold the coveted Number 1 spot for a while before Li caught up again and displaced him.

The two men became antagonistic to each other. However, in business as in politics, there are no permanent enemies or friends. It all depends on what serves the interest of the party at any given point in time.

It is strange how the human mind works. When one basks in the sun of success, one thinks the sky is the limit. After all, Li Ka Shing had started from scratch and within a short period of time he had been propelled to the top. In a capitalistic society like Hong Kong, nothing is impossible. The important thing is to get on the track. Anyone can then be launched into the orbit of tycoons, me included. I could not forget the incident with Cheng Yu Tung that happened in or around 1995 when I had moved to Singapore.

"Big Brother Tung," I addressed Cheng Yu Tung by his nickname one day when I called on him at his office.

"Big Brother Robert," Cheng returned the courtesy.

It took me by surprise. How one addresses a person is determined by the pecking order – one's position in society. In the hierarchy of things in Hong Kong, one must be senior enough before one can address Cheng as 'Big Brother', let alone be addressed back by him in the same fashion. He will never call someone below him 'Big Brother' unless that person is a close personal friend. This mode of address is reserved for his equals such as 'Big Brother Li (Ka Shing)'. Most people call him 'Mr. Cheng', and those who work for him, 'Lo Chun' – Commander-in-Chief.

I was surprised Cheng addressed me in that manner and it was not just him; of late, I had noticed others in Hong Kong had also begun to call me 'Big Brother Robert' – a phenomenon that was as strange as it was welcome.

It went to my head. "Could it be that I have arrived?" I naively asked myself.

"What are you trying to prove?" Elaine asked me. "Can't you be satisfied with what you have? There is already so much on your plate. What more do you want?"

"That's the way I am. This is my way of getting even with my past… all that discrimination I suffered as a child just because I was poor. It wasn't even my fault. I couldn't control how I was born, could I?"

"Yes, once upon a time, life did short-change you but it's all over now. You should be at peace with yourself. You told me yourself: nowadays when you think about the past you can no longer shed tears no matter how hard you try. What does that tell you? It means the past is over… yes, behind you. It is no longer there to haunt you. There is nothing more for you to avenge. What more do you want?"

"Revenge sees no bounds. I want to be repaid for all those lost years when I suffered at the hands of poverty. I couldn't see it as a child but now it's clear. Instead of boosting my confidence, you are always there to dampen my enthusiasm. Don't you like to see me moving ahead? All wives do… except you. I am sick and tired of your attitude. Why are you always so negative?"

"End of conversation," Elaine retorted. "I am not going to argue with you any more. It is not the past that consumes you; it is the raw ambition… this screw-the-world, get-even-with-the-past… avenge this and get even with that… it is all part of your ego trip. I don't think I can talk to you any more. Why can't you be happy and content? There is so much bliss around you… our family, children, friends… yet you choose to ignore them and always strive for more of what you can't get. This will prove to be your undoing. One day all that pillaging and philandering will come crashing down, and take the family with it."

"You may be right. But at the moment I am surfing on a good wave. I don't know where the wave will carry me. But if I don't try I shall never know. Maybe one day I can control Suntec. Who knows?"

"What control? The shares you own are negligible. How can you control Suntec? T.O. has warned you before: 'A snake cannot swallow an elephant.' My advice to you is: if you sleep so close to the elephants you will get squashed."

"The corporate world is full of examples of 'small' controlling 'big'. Take the example of Jardine Matheson. The two brothers, Henry and Simon Keswick, together own less than three per cent of the stock, yet they control a business empire that is worth US\$30 billion. David Li's shareholding is equally minuscule yet he rules the roost at the Bank of East Asia. This is the route all tycoons take to become who they are. You use 'OPM' to grow 'MOM', I'm not wrong in thinking big, am I?"

"What is 'OPM'? What is 'MOM'?"

"Other People's Money and My Own Money – you use money that belongs to others to grow your own."

"How can you do that?"

"It's easy. When one is in control, opportunity knocks. There are all sorts of ways one can enrich oneself. For instance, if a good deal comes along one can either give it to the company or keep it for himself. If he decides to keep it, he can use a company that he controls to buy and hold the asset. He places it through incubation until the value goes up. He sells it back to the company. He makes a profit in the process."

"Is that legal?"

"Yes, it's done all the time. The astute businessman won't do anything that is illegal. Oh, no, that would be foolish. There is no law, for instance, that says he can't make his own investment even if he heads a listed company. Yes, he may be required to declare an interest but in real life it is not always done. If he does anything illegal, he may get caught and thrown into prison. No, he won't take such a risk. He won't do anything that he can't get away with. Yes, the criterion is always: can I do this and that and get away with it? It's all worked into the risk and reward formula. I have seen it all."

"But to control big with small you must be good enough—"

"Are you saying that I'm not good enough?"

"No, but don't you think Suntec is too big? Even if you overcome Tan Sri you may just be there to warm the seat for the 'king' who will come later. In the meantime, he uses you as a foot soldier to test the water, until he is ready to step in and claim the crown. Do you want to fight a war that you can't win and, even if you do win, the spoils are not yours?

"Do you remember the Chinese parable of a seabird and a giant clam? The two are locked in a life-and-death struggle. The bird has its eye set on the clam's meat. As it pecks, the clam closes up and traps the beak of the bird inside. Neither is prepared to give way. While the tug of war continues, a fisherman comes by and harvests both. It is anyone's guess who that 'fisherman' is."

"You haven't answered my question," I reminded her. "So you are telling me that I am not good enough, aren't you?"

"You said it. I didn't."

"I have to try, haven't I? I've already achieved early success."

"What early success?"

"Don't you know? Ever since I made it known that I had arrived on the back of the act-in-concert agreement, I noticed a visible change in the attitude of the management. Suddenly they listen to me. It has not happened before."

"I don't think your hour of glory is going to last. T.O. has warned you before. If you step onto Tan Sri's turf, he can and will make life difficult for you. Who are you? At best you're just a messenger for the big boys. Please know your place, Robert. It makes no sense to act bigger than you actually are. It's your ego at work again."

"But the big boys support me."

"Don't fool yourself. On the surface, maybe. Below the surface, it's self-interest that drives them. Suntec is just too big. It's not for you. Know yourself, please, Robert."

"Please don't be so negative. Even if I am wrong, let me enjoy my moment of glory. Can't you see? I am basking in the sun. I am the 'ambassador'. Everyone who comes through wants to see Suntec – walk the mall, visit the column-free hall so big it could hold three jumbo jets next to each other, the kitchen with its state-of-the-art equipment, the fountain that has entered the Guinness Book of Records as the largest in the world. It is called the 'Fountain of Wealth' because it is said to generate good '*tze*' (air) and people are queuing up just to touch the spouting water. They even sell the water by the bottle, like London fog. I've never had it so good. It's the best time of my life. I am at my prime. Can't you see?"

"Let me warn you. It's just vanity, pure and simple. You can try if you want to but it is going to end the same way. Mark my words. You will not succeed."

"I should at least try and see whether or not I can get there. You may not know but my maternal grandfather tried. He succeeded for a while. Then he fell from a dazzling height. He lost everything – a lifetime of greed came crashing down on him. So what? At least he tried. He got his fifteen minutes of fame. It was his life. And this is my life."

"At least you know what you are up to. For the sake of the family, I wish you luck. But I don't think it is wise for you to tell the world at large that you have the support of the Trio to take control of Suntec. This kind of talk can create problems. It's foolish."

"Well, you may be right. But how else can I establish my authority?"

"This is like talking to a brick wall. I've had it up to my neck. I need a rest. Let's change the subject. Almost every day there is someone passing through. I am sick and tired of entertaining."

"Isn't that wonderful? It is a great feeling. But you can't deny it's good for business. I hit the jackpot and it's big. Shouldn't you be happy too? Remember you have a stake in it."

"I am just a simple housewife. I am not ambitious. My family comes first. Fame and fortune mean little in my world. Look at what success has done to us. You're seldom home; I don't know where you are half the time. At times I don't even know whether you are here in Singapore or still in Hong Kong. What kind of life is it for me? Money isn't everything, you know. I need peace of mind. I yearn for the old days when you were a struggling solicitor, when family values came first and friends were truthful. Nowadays, when I look around, it is nothing but falsehoods – false values, false sense of grandeur… false this and that. Yes, it's phoney… do you understand? Is it worth it? For the sake of the family, answer me. Is it worth it?"

"Of course it's worth it. I just love it. I work hard. I play hard. My life is exciting. By the way, next week we have been invited to dinner with the President and the First Lady – 7 p.m., next Thursday, at the Istana."

"But Dad and Mum are arriving from Hong Kong the same day. I have arranged a dinner at home with the children."

"I have accepted the invitation. You don't say 'no' to the President of Singapore, do you? The family dinner can wait. What about Friday?"

"But Friday night we have been invited to a concert at the Victoria Theatre."

"If that's the case why don't we have lunch instead – either Friday or Saturday? But please clear it with my secretary beforehand."

≈≈≈≈≈

At the Istana, I was surprised to find there were no other guests, just the four of us – the First Couple, Elaine and me.

"Nanyang Girls' High School is my old school," explained the First Lady. "The school wants to raise funds to build a new wing for the boarders. Robert, can you help?"

"Mrs. Ong, I'm only too glad to try," I replied, "but I don't carry much weight, I'm afraid. My appeal may fall on deaf ears. I tell you what, I have an idea. I'll draft a letter for you. Please write and sign it on your letterhead and send it back to me. You can then leave the rest to me."

In the letter that arrived I was asked to approach certain named tycoons. No one could refuse the First Lady. Bingo! It was easy. Almost all the tycoons I approached with the First Lady's signed letter made a donation – some so large they made local donors uneasy.

"Robert, you have spoiled the market for Singapore," one of them chided me. "We don't do things the way you guys do in Hong Kong, you know? It sets a bad precedent."

The First Lady was nevertheless happy – the wing for the boarders at Nanyang Girls' was made possible by the donations.

I was in the good books of the President and the First Lady. We saw each other often both in Singapore and Hong Kong.

"We both live so simply and healthily it boggles my mind even to think about how we can both end up with cancer," said the President.

Sadly, both of them died not many years later; in fact, not long after Ong Teng Cheong's term as the President of the Republic ended.

≈≈≈≈≈

In the early 1990s, Hong Kong entered a new era. Its industries had moved north, out of the Territory. China's involvement in international trade became more intense. Hong Kong's integration with the mainland accelerated. Service industries filled the vacuum left by the departing factories. Interest rates were low and unemployment was low despite the changes. It was a boom time for Hong Kong. Not even the imminent return to Chinese rule could affect the mood of optimism. It was as if the casino was about to close; the punters wanted to play the last hand.

Singapore was doing well too. It proved the theory that Hong Kong and Singapore always work in tandem: they go up and down together, seldom one without the other, at least in recent history.

The struggle for control of Suntec entered a new phase. It was a well-known fact that I had impinged on Tan Sri's territory. He would have none of it. Soon he started plotting and fighting back. The process of cleansing began in earnest. The Chairman had his way of dealing with disloyalty and those he considered his enemies. It was never open, always clandestine. Open confrontation had to be avoided. It was just not his style.

Dr. Chua Yong Hai was a government scholar. He spent many years in government before we recruited him as General Manager of Suntec City. There was no denying that Dr. Chua was a good manager. He oversaw the construction of the project. The man was deep and thoughtful, a true professional in every sense. His integrity was beyond reproach. During his watch, we had not had a single claim for compensation despite the numerous construction and other contracts that went out on the project. It was completed on time, within budget and almost entirely trouble-free. One would have expected Dr. Chua to stay on and steer the company into the next stage – market, sales and rent. But it was not to be.

He was seen to 'tilt' towards the Trio. He learned about the act-in-concert agreement. Being a prudent and careful man, he took the trouble to go to Hong Kong to have it verified. The answer he got proved to be his undoing – his kiss of death.

"Robert, I shall from now on follow orders from your side instead of the Chairman," Dr. Chua said upon his return.

Soon Tan Sri knew. It sealed Dr. Chua's fate.

On the pretext that we needed a different man, a marketing and sales person, at the top to take care of the post-construction era of Suntec City, Dr. Chua was given a golden handshake and left the company.

Another man was appointed. He was given the title of CEO. This time Tan Sri made sure we had nothing to do with his appointment. The new man, therefore, owed his loyalty to Tan Sri. He made no attempts to hide the fact he was the Chairman's man. True to his word, he remained loyal to Tan Sri till the end.

Next the knife fell on SICEC (Singapore International Convention & Exhibition Centre). It was managed by a German named Claus Schultz. As the similar Hong Kong convention facility was managed by New

World, Cheng Yu Tung's flagship, it was natural for Claus Schultz to sympathize with our cause and side with us.

He was replaced.

I was a director in the management company, Singapore Convention and Exhibition Centre Limited. To root out my influence, Tan Sri changed its name to East West Exhibitors Limited and left the company dormant. A new company was formed to manage SICEC.

I was removed in one masterly stroke.

After he consolidated his grip, Tan Sri began to play a game of cat-and-mouse, all done with a view to undermine, marginalize, harm and provoke; in short, wear me down until I lost my cool. My career at Suntec took a turn for the worse, and deteriorated progressively until it became pretty much impossible.

"Robert, you are all stressed out," said Elaine. "You have to find a way to put Suntec City behind you or else your health is going to suffer. Do you still remember what Sir Y.K. Pao, the shipping magnate, used to say to you?"

"Yes, I do. He said that a billion is 1,000,000,000. When '1' gets knocked down the zeros that follow don't mean a thing."

"You're like a bird in a cage. The two chairmen take turns to have you removed from the cage every now and then. They take pleasure in each plucking a feather. Then they put you back in the cage. You'd better throw in the towel and leave Suntec once and for all. It's not your game. Admit it."

"That's absolutely true. I am a prisoner of the Five Fingers Mountain in this book, *Journey to the West*. I wear the headband of the two chairmen which they can tighten at will. It is squeezed so hard that the pain is excruciating. I scream and ask for mercy. It doesn't help. I'm doomed."

I was often driven close to losing my temper. An open confrontation was considered an absolute taboo in a struggle set against the background of the imperial palace. In the intrigues of the court struggle, one could manoeuvre and back-stab but one could never lose one's cool – it was the prerogative of the Emperor and him alone – lest one be driven out of the court and into exile.

I remember what T.O. had told me: "Never lose your cool. Once you do, the game is over. Remember the character that means 'forbearance' in Chinese has the sharp edge of a knife pressed against the heart. It reminds you that even under extreme provocation you must forbear. Forbearance is golden. It is the key to survival."

Tan Sri stopped holding meetings of the board. Instead he held meetings of the Executive Committee of which I was not a member. In doing so he marginalized me.

I countered by getting Cheng Yu Tung to appoint me as his alternate on the board – I was already a director but the main duties of the board were delegated to a committee (the Executive Committee) of which only the Trio, Tan Sri, Sir Run Run and W.H. Chou were members. I became a de facto member of the Executive Committee as well as being on the board and could continue attending the meetings of the committee as Cheng's deputy.

Tan Sri reacted by holding paper meetings instead on the pretext that the directors were all busy people and could ill afford the time.

I was again marginalized.

I proposed to Tan Sri's ally on the board, W.H. Chou, that we should ask the government to build a pedestrian subway linking the nearest underground train station, Raffles, to Suntec City. I was asked to go ahead only to be told that we would not tender when the government, pursuant to my overture, approved and put the project up for public tender. It showed me up badly in government circles. In the end, Hongkong Land, a subsidiary of Jardine Matheson, won the tender. Raffles Link was built.

Tan Sri spent more time in Singapore. He was determined to root out his adversaries with all means at his disposal. On the surface he wore a smiling mask but behind the façade he plotted and manoeuvred clandestinely and duplicitously to isolate and marginalize his rivals without being seen to confront them directly. He was particularly careful that he did not affront any one of the Trio in the process. He knew they were more powerful than he was and acting in concert they were deadly. He could ill afford to run afoul of them.

Thus the game of cloak and dagger was played out in full, each trying to undo and undermine the other from behind. Increasingly, it resembled one of the dramas that unfolded within the compounds of the old Forbidden City in Imperial China – full of intrigue and cunning, all aimed to destroy adversaries and advance self-interest.

I became the scapegoat. It was not unnatural that Tan Sri considered me to be a pain in the neck. He had to remove me. The backstabbing and secret manoeuvres intensified. The struggles soon acquired the proportion of either 'you live or I die' – more from my perspective than his – as the sniping and character assassination came almost entirely from him. Being the Chairman, he was powerful and had at his disposal an array of weapons. He also had the Shanghai shareholders on his side. I was mostly defenceless.

But, occasionally, I too found ammunition to fire back. The Trio was with me.

"The Chairman is bad-mouthing you," Wee Cho Yaw came over and told me at a pre-lunch gathering.

Soon the Trio – Li Ka Shing, Lee Shau Kee and Cheng Yu Tung – left their conversation with Tan Sri and came over to join us.

It showed the Chairman which side these tycoons were taking. It was gratifying and I took comfort in the knowledge that the most powerful businessmen from both cities openly supported me.

Then an opportunity arose for me to fire back at the Chairman. After Kang Hwi Hwa was jailed, his business empire began to crumble. His company, Amcol, went into receivership. The government-appointed liquidators began an earnest search for a white knight to save the company. To allow the company to falter was considered to be politically unacceptable. The fact that pension money from retail investors was involved meant the government had to prevent the company from going under.

I remembered what Kang had told me when we last saw each other in Las Vegas. With the blessing of the Trio, but completely unbeknown to the Chairman, we started to negotiate with the liquidators with a view to reversing Suntec City and gaining control of Amcol through a back-door listing.

If we were successful, the Chairman would certainly be dislodged as he would have to face an enlarged group of shareholders. The true value of the act-in-concert agreement would manifest itself. Secretly I was hoping I could play a bigger role in the listed company – controlling Suntec as a proxy for the Trio was what I had hoped for.

But an Indonesian buyer emerged at the eleventh hour, just as we were about to close the deal.

"You should not squeeze us so hard on the pricing," said V.J. Rajah, the liquidator. "We represent the government of Singapore. You must take that into consideration and show us the deference we deserve. If you can't give us more then we will take the deal to the next in line. We've told you that there is an Indonesian buyer in waiting. They are prepared to give us more."

The deal was being negotiated on Suntec's side by a party that was made up of the likes of Henry Cheng (Cheng Yu Tung's son), Colin Lam and Albert Chow (respectively the right-hand men of Lee Shau Kee and Li Ka Shing). They were hard nuts to crack, the toughest in Hong Kong. It was bad enough dealing with them individually but, when they combined, they were formidable and at times downright impossible to deal with. It was no coincidence that the liquidators were exasperated.

We continued to press hard on the pricing. In the end, true to the words of Mr. Rajah, there was indeed another buyer waiting in the wings. The company was snatched away from us.

The Chairman was raging mad.

"How can you convene a meeting of the Board without going through the chair?" he barked at me.

It was the one time when I almost got even with Tan Sri – almost.

But I would have to wait for another time.

# THE PERFECT STORMS

The Hong Kong Club was first opened in 1846. It is located in Central, the heart of Hong Kong. During the colonial era '*The Club*' – as it was simply referred to – was where senior officials and heads of Hong Kong's major *hongs* – conglomerates of British origin such as HSBC and Jardine Matheson – rubbed shoulders and made decisions that affected the livelihood of the people. It was an exclusive gentlemen's club. Its membership was open mainly to white British subjects until as recently as the 1970s. There was nothing in the rules to say that it was off-limits to the Chinese. However, no member nominated and seconded the application of a Chinese other than in exceptional circumstances. If one did so in an act of folly, the application would sit idle, gathering dust. It just would not be brought up for consideration by the Membership Committee. Nor did the Club have any lady members until the door was forced open by the Sex Discrimination Ordinance in 1996 – a piece of legislation that Anna Wu had a hand in.

Then, one by one, domains exclusive to men fell in quick succession. There are no more 'Speak Easies' for men at the Club any more.

"There are women at the Members' Bar," I remarked with some curiosity to an old colonial servant well known to me at the Club. Anna Wu was there with us at the lift.

"Oh, you know," he spoke in a Scottish accent as he sneered and made a gesture of scorn at Anna Wu, "it's all because your partner… you know, this lady…"

Anna Wu smiled as if to acknowledge what she and her colleagues in the Legislative Council had pulled off.

When British rule ended, many of its members returned to the old country. Admission rules at the Club were relaxed. Nowadays, the ratio of British and Chinese members is close to 50:50. Even today, its members are still the most influential people in the city.

To launch a Singapore Hong Kong Club to rival Hong Kong's icon was an idea that I held dear to my heart. The Club would provide a platform for the elite of the two cities to meet, interact, exchange ideas and perhaps invest together. It would play a pivotal role in bringing not only the two cities but also its leading players close to each other 'by a process of harmonization' – a phrase coined in Singapore. The idea of the Singapore Hong Kong Club was warmly received both in Singapore and Hong Kong.

Finally it was possible. The timing was opportune. Everything was ready. Tycoons from both sides were willing.

My next step was to find a guiding light; what better choice than Lee Kuan Yew to be the Club's patron?

I wrote to the Senior Minister. At the same time I asked Wee Cho Yaw to nominate luminaries from Singapore to be elected to its Board of Governors. I was not conversant with the local business scene. I needed Wee's input to find candidates that matched Hong Kong's nominations.

In hindsight, I suppose Wee supplied me with Singapore's list in anticipation that the Senior Minister would accept the invitation to be the patron. Except for one or two, I did not recognize any of the names. I assumed this was entirely normal as I was new to Singapore. Nevertheless, I noticed all of them belonged to powerful corporations such as Singapore Press Holdings which I knew to be publishers of the *Straits Times* and *Business Times*, two of Singapore's leading dailies.

I wrote to all the nominees. Almost everyone replied giving his consent. However, Lim Kim San, Chairman of Singapore Press Holdings, did not reply.

In the meantime, Lee Kuan Yew declined the invitation. Instead, Minister B.G. Yeo, who was then the Minister of State for Finance and Minister for Foreign Affairs, agreed to be the patron.

Chairmanship was to be by rotation between Hong Kong and Singapore. Since the initiative came from us, it was natural that the first chairman would be a person from Hong Kong. As usual, Li Ka Shing was the first to be approached. He declined. Cheng Yu Tung agreed.

Momentum gathered and the Club was all set to go. It was unstoppable. With so many top businessmen on its list of members and the resources that were at their disposal, the Club was destined to succeed.

News of the Singapore Hong Kong Club spread quickly among the elite of the business communities. It was a runaway success. Everyone worth his salt wanted to join even though membership was by invitation only. No one wanted to be left out. It would be a symbol of inferiority if one was not invited. The reaction was overwhelming.

Being new in Singapore, I was not conversant with local customs and conventions and its history. I wish someone had alerted me to the sensitivity of the situation but it was not to be. The intervening events brought me into the centre of a catastrophic storm like none other I had experienced. It created sheer havoc, consuming me from within and in the end destroying me.

While it was acceptable for Lim Kim San to serve under Lee Kuan Yew – this must have been why Wee Cho Yaw nominated Lim to be a governor in the first place – he would not be pleased if he had to serve under another patron, as a matter of protocol. I was oblivious to how sensitive the matter had become once the Senior Minister declined the role of patron of the Club.

It also drove me out of Singapore… all over a lousy, non-profit-making and charitable club that was meant to serve the interests of both cities.

Prior to moving to Singapore and heeding T.O.'s advice, I had worked towards selling my shares in the 'merchant bank' to Suntec of which Tan Sri was then the Chairman. He also wanted to sell his shares – a five per cent stake. The matter was discussed by the board of Suntec and the parties almost reached an agreement – both of us declared our interests. Li Ka Shing did not attend the board meeting but was briefed by his deputy. When Wee found out what we were up to with our joint venture shares he was not pleased. He expressed his displeasure in no uncertain terms on at least two occasions, both times over the telephone, before the launch of the Club.

"I hear that you wish to sell your shares in our joint venture company to Suntec," Wee Cho Yaw said to me. "The 'merchant bank' is a private limited company. You can't sell without my consent. I have pre-emptive rights."

"Where did you get the news that I'm selling?"

"Not only are you selling but also the Chairman is."

"Did the Chairman tell you?"

"No, Li Ka Shing told me."

"But Suntec is also a shareholder of the 'merchant bank'. I don't suppose you would object to the company buying more shares. One day Suntec will get a listing—"

"A listed company holding the shares in the 'merchant bank'?" interrupted Wee. "I won't allow that. You have to sell the shares to us."

"You can't force me," I replied agitatedly. "I'm selling the shares of the holding company. It doesn't go through the Memorandum and Articles of the company. Therefore pre-emptive rights don't apply."

Wee was clearly angry. He hung up on me.

Of late I had been under a lot of pressure. The Chairman's duplicitous manoeuvring drove me to the brink. I had to fight every inch of the way to stay involved. Every time I felt I was under attack, I had to turn to the likes of Cheng Yu Tung for help. I was never able to be one step ahead of the Chairman. I had to ward off blows from all directions, not knowing where the next one would be coming from. Incriminating missives were flying all over the place. Cheng Yu Tung had shown me a copy of a less-than-kind letter that was sent to him as a member of the Executive Committee. On a flight to Beijing, Sir Run Run showed me correspondence that he had received from the Chairman in which he complained about me. As if my corporate woes were not enough, I was also plagued by problems at home. My marriage had hit the rocks. It was a stressful time, career-wise and in my personal life. I lost sleep and I lost weight. Tension was mounting. I was close to a nervous breakdown. I was being driven to insanity. I lost control of myself, at times shaking so badly that I needed drugs to calm my nerves. I shivered even under two blankets in the air-conditioned bedroom of the Singapore house. It was the worst time of my life.

I sat up in bed and stared blankly at the ceiling lights. I knew I had made a mistake of epic proportions. No one could save me. I had offended the most powerful businessman in Singapore – one whose influence was ubiquitous and whose friends included Lim Kim San, not to mention the Trio.

Wee Cho Yaw was the last person whose wrath I wanted to incur. Besides, he had been good to me. He had always supported me. When I struggled against the Chairman, it was he who openly took my side.

At dinner I sat quietly. It seemed as if a hundred things were going through my mind all at the same time. As I ate, a sense of imminent disaster got the better of me. It was the calm before the storm.

I remained pensive, not speaking throughout the dinner. Elaine could only watch me in silence. My mind was caught up in an intricate network of confusing thoughts that evening. I had offended Tan Sri and now this altercation with one of Singapore's most powerful businessmen had happened.

'What if the three of them gang up against me?' I asked myself. I was thinking of Lim, Wee and Tan Sri acting together. 'I am doomed.'

"You know, T.O. was right," I said to Elaine. "He warned me at the beginning. If I did not contribute to the business of the 'merchant bank', a service company, I should sell the shares and get out. Otherwise I would get into trouble with Wee Cho Yaw. He is not a man to be trifled with."

"T.O. is your mentor," Elaine replied. "He has your best interests at heart. He is an intelligent man. You should always listen to him. What's happened?"

"I took the advice of T.O to heart." I was defensive. "Since coming to Singapore I have worked toward the goal of selling the shares."

"You mentioned that before. Did you and Tan Sri not reach an agreement to sell the shares to Suntec?"

"Yes, I don't know why. It may be the pricing. There may be other reasons. Li Ka Shing, astute as he is, does not like the deal. He told Wee

Cho Yaw about the deal when they met at a cocktail reception. Wee doesn't like it either."

"What happened?"

"Wee called me up today."

"Yes, and what did he say to you?"

"He said he would not agree to the shares being sold to Suntec. I must first get his approval. He enjoys pre-emptive rights over the shares. Then I reminded him that Suntec is an existing shareholder. It will eventually go for a listing. That made him uncomfortable."

"Why was he uncomfortable?"

"I don't know. He merely said he didn't like the sound of it. Then, in a moment of frustration, I told him that I did not need his consent as I could simply sell the shares of the holding company. I didn't have to go through the M&A of the joint venture company. That really upset him. He hung up on me."

"That's not a good sign at all. You've ruffled the feathers of Wee Cho Yaw and you will pay the price."

"I know and I'm at a loss as to what I should do."

"You should apologise to Wee before it is too late," Elaine suggested.

I called up Wee to apologise for my recalcitrance. The matter quietened down. He did not press me again. As far as the shares were concerned, we were happy to let sleeping dogs lie. Then one day it flared up again.

"Robert, Tan Sri has agreed to sell his shares," said Wee. "Are you also agreeable?"

"Yes, but at what price?" I asked.

"I'll get my colleagues to contact you on the valuation."

I was later informed that the price would be based on NTA (net tangible asset) value. No consideration was given to the company being a going concern, let alone its goodwill and earning power.

I telephoned Wee and told him that I would not sell on that kind of pricing for my shares. It did not go down well with him. He was upset and hung up on me – the second time that had happened. Our relationship took another turn for the worse.

If it had been up to him, he would not have invited me to the grand opening of UOB Plaza in the Central business district, Raffles Place. I was not in his good books again. But the invitation had been sent out before this latest incident.

UOB Plaza Two is a 531-feet building of 38 floors. It is linked to UOB Plaza One by a podium floor which houses the banking hall. It was opened by the Senior Minister, Lee Kuan Yew, in 1995.

The opening was a grand affair. Local dignitaries queued up to congratulate Wee Cho Yaw. The podium floor was exposed to the elements on all four sides. The weather suddenly changed. It started raining. Before long it was pouring cats and dogs. There was a mad scramble among the guests to run for cover. The venue was at the mercy of the gale-force winds that swirled mercilessly around.

The opening ceremony shifted indoors. When I rejoined the reception line I was soaking wet. After the tirade on the telephone, it was obvious Wee Cho Yaw was not pleased to see me. He took my hand and pulled me forward. The message was clear: 'pass quickly'. To everyone else, it seemed as though he was welcoming me with a smile on his face; however the smile did not extend to his eyes which remained cold as steel.

I knew he was unhappy with me but that was not all of it.

"Robert, I would like to talk to you," Miss Tan, a personal assistant to Wee, said sternly. "Do you know what you have done?"

"What?" I wiped the rain from my face. "What have I done?"

"Do you know you have used the name of Lim Kim San without his authority?" she continued. "He is very angry with you."

I knew exactly what she was talking about. That morning an article had appeared in the *Straits Times* about the Singapore Hong Kong Club. News had leaked out that Minister George Yeo was its Patron while tycoons from the two cities – all named – were members of its Board of Governors. Lim Kim San headed Singapore's list.

I had been worried all day. Lim Kim San had never replied one way or the other when I wrote to invite him to be a governor, despite my many reminders. Wee Cho Yaw would probably have put in a good word for me if I had not upset him over the shares. After all, it was a trivial matter. It was Wee who nominated Lim.

By that time I was aware of Lim Kim San's powerful background. I was horrified to hear that I had offended two of Singapore's most powerful men on top of my continuing saga with Tan Sri.

It was three storms merged into one. It was the perfect storm. And it was the first in a series of other perfect storms to come.

I was in no mood to continue the conversation with Miss Tan. Imagined or real, I felt as if everyone at the reception was cold to me. They spoke ill of me behind my back. I was at a loss as to what to do next. My head was spinning; I was sweating; I was not in my right mind. I knew I was in serious trouble. I hurriedly left the cocktail party in the middle of the worst tropical storm I had seen in Singapore. As I descended the steps I was in a cold sweat, lost, bewildered and scared beyond words.

My roof was caving in. My world was collapsing around me. A sense of utter fear and despondency took hold. I headed home immediately.

If Tan Sri had heard about my plight I could bet my last dollar that he would go and see Wee Cho Yaw the very next day.

The two would seal my fate. I was doomed. Everything I had painstakingly built up over the years came crashing down like a deck of cards.

I wrote to Wee Cho Yaw to apologise for my intransigence. I offered to sell him my shares. He was unmoved.

I remembered the drinking at the Shanghai party. I had refused the 'salute wine'. Instead, I now had to offer to drink the 'punishment wine' which Wee Cho Yaw still declined to accept.

I had to swallow a bitter pill to ensure my survival in Singapore. First and foremost, I had to appease Lim Kim San. I did not know how to go about it as I had no direct access to him.

I related my plight to Tan Boon Teik, the Attorney General. He promised to help. He drafted a letter for me and I signed it. He said he would take the letter personally to Lim Kim San and plead on my behalf.

"Lim Kim San is very angry with you," he said after he had been to see Lim. "He chided me for intervening. You'd better get someone else to speak to him."

I went to see Dr. Goh Keng Swee as a last resort. I showed him the fax in which Wee Cho Yaw had nominated Lim Kim San. Dr. Goh was quiet but sympathetic.

"Can you put me through to Lim Kim San?" Dr. Goh asked his secretary.

"Lim Kim San is on the line," she said after a few minutes.

"I have Robert Wang here with me," Dr. Goh said. "He has told me about the Singapore Hong Kong Club. It was Wee Cho Yaw who nominated—"

Before he could finish the sentence, Lim Kim San interrupted him. Dr. Goh listened patiently. Although I was not privy to the conversation, it was clear that Lim was complaining about me. My 'sins' were being recounted in full. Dr. Goh nodded as he listened to Lim. Occasionally he would clear his throat. The call seemed to last forever.

"It is a small matter... a small matter." Dr. Goh appeared to be agreeing with Lim. "How's your health, Kim San?

"I hope this is the end of the matter," said Dr. Goh after the call. He did not tell me what Lim had said to him nor did he explain why it was to be the end of the matter. I was present throughout the telephone conversation. Dr. Goh must have assumed that his friendship with Lim and the telephone call would be enough to put to rest what he thought was a small matter.

I thanked Dr. Goh profusely and left.

These events took place around the time of the official opening of Suntec. I sent an invitation to Lim Kim San and telephoned his office several times to ask if he would accept. I made it known to him that Lee Kuan Yew would be attending.

"Mr. Lim wants to know whether it is Lee Kuan Yew who wishes Mr. Lim to be present," asked his secretary.

"No," I replied. "We would like to invite Mr. Lim."

Lim Kim San did not reply.

≈≈≈≈≈

The official opening of Suntec was a grand affair. After ten years of construction, the project was finally completed. It was a milestone event that called for celebration. Hong Kong's Who's Who showed up in force: the shareholders, families, relatives and friends. It was a memorable occasion. Amidst the pomp and pageantry, Suntec City was opened by Lee Kuan Yew.

Being the only resident director it was not unnatural for me to organize and coordinate the activities of the directors for the duration of their stay and the programmes were sent to the directors ahead of time for comments.

No comments were received.

The Chairman never indicated one way or another whether or not any part of the planned itinerary was unacceptable. There were meetings, photo calls, sightseeing, golfing, cocktails and dinners culminating in the grand opening. It was a busy schedule.

It became apparent at the outset that the Chairman did not want to participate in any part of the programme. He refused to indicate whether or not he would be at any function in advance, only to show up at the last minute when he knew that everyone else would be there. And when a time was reserved for one activity, he would purposely organize another event to distract the directors from attending my activity. For instance, at the time reserved for a photo call, the Chairman would call a meeting of his own only to relent when he knew the other directors were turning up for the photo call.

His motive was clear: he wanted to sabotage the programme I had planned in order to shore up the Chairman's authority.

In the meantime, the Singapore Hong Kong Club was all set to go. The name of Lim Kim San had been removed from the list of nominees.

The inauguration officiated by Minister B.G. Yeo was to take place the day after Suntec's grand opening. Meanwhile, rumours were flying thick and fast that I had run foul of Lim Kim San and that the launch would be called off.

I checked with Wee Cho Yaw. He said he had given his consent and would attend the inauguration. I really wanted it to be successful. After all the setbacks of the past week, it was the only way I could redeem myself – my reputation, credibility, standing and everything else I represented was at stake. I wagered my whole future on the Club. I worked frantically in the hope that the Club would be launched successfully.

If I failed, it would be the end of the road for me. I would have to return the joining fees to all those who had been invited to join. It would mean a loss of face – a sign that I had been forsaken by the business elite of both Hong Kong and Singapore.

It was a tense time.

"Minister George Yeo wants to speak to you," Sally, my secretary, told me.

I was gripped by an ominous feeling. A sense of foreboding sent a chill down my spine. I knew the Minister wanted to talk to me about the Club.

"Mr. Wang, I think we should cancel the launch," he said.

"Yes, Minister."

It would have been futile for me to protest. The forces I had to work against were simply too formidable. Some of the most powerful people in Singapore were involved. My heart sank.

But another storm was looming on the horizon.

≈≈≈≈≈

"All you do is complain," I said to Elaine. "Why don't you follow my example and be happy even when times are hard?"

"How can I be happy when I know you keep a woman outside?" she screamed at me. "You don't care about the family, do you? All you care about is yourself and what you can get out of life. You don't care what misery you cause to others in your relentless pursuit of wealth and fame!

"I'll leave you," she continued. "And it's not an empty threat. You're full of shit, Robert!" She left the room sobbing.

I was stunned.

She knew my secret; one I thought I had hidden so well but deep down I knew would blow up some day. That day of reckoning had arrived.

It blew up right in my face. I was torn between the devil and the deep blue sea. Coming at a time of already great distress for me, the timing could not have been worse. It was a double whammy.

"What should I do?" I cried out in despair. "Oh God, please tell me what I should do."

It had been close to two years since it started.

At the funeral service of a local tycoon I had prayed: "Let your spirit descend upon me. Give me your wisdom. Give me your prowess."

It was funny how my prayer was answered. It was as if the deceased had sent me one of his own family members. At the wake, I happened to meet his niece, Nichole. She was young, pretty, well-educated and intelligent, having studied at a U.S. Ivy League university, and recently returned to work in the family business. I was completely besotted by her even on our first encounter. We talked about wines.

"You know, I was at the Waterside Restaurant at Bray on the banks of the Thames," I said, trying to impress her. "I was introduced to this bottle of white Bordeaux – Chateau Lynch-Bages 1994. It was a truly delightful wine, dry, creamy, smooth to the tongue and full of body like the best of a Burgundy white. Yet it cost a mere forty pounds. I have been scurrying around wine shops from Singapore to Hong Kong hoping to buy this white. I can't find any."

"Bordeaux is home to red," she replied. "I never knew it made white. I'll find out more for you. My father is a connoisseur. You won't mind if I call you, will you?"

"Of course not," I said excitedly.

Nichole did not call. Instead, she sent me six bottles of white Lynch-Bages 1994 with a handwritten note:

> *Chateau Lynch-Bages normally produces no white. In 1994 the owner did it for fun. He made 7000 bottles for friends and his own use. Only a small quantity got into the market. I found these quite by accident. Please enjoy it. Best, Nichole.*

I was overwhelmed by her kindness. I started calling her and soon we began to see each other, sporadically in the beginning but quickly becoming regular until finally we were seeing each other almost every other day.

Things came to a head. I began to spend more time with her than at home. I had to lie to explain my frequent absences, knowing full well that my wife must know that I was up to no good.

It was a stressful time. I was mired deep in a triangular relationship. I could neither leave my wife nor my mistress. It was causing indescribable pain and suffering for both of them. Nichole was losing her hair in clumps. My wife was miserable, crying all day long.

There is no doubt that men and women are different in terms of problem-solving: When a man has a problem he will go into the cave alone to try to solve it; a woman will talk to her friends.

Soon tongues began to wag. I was that bad husband who had created so many problems for his wife. Elaine, however, had never confronted me until one day the cat was out of the bag. The paper could no longer wrap the fire. Some kind of ending became inevitable.

In London, while we were there to spend time with the children at our Knightsbridge flat, my wife was weeping again. My daughter, who was then sixteen, saw her agony. She came into my room and hugged me.

"Daddy, why can't you be more conventional?" she asked in tears.

"I can't leave her." I was so touched by her gesture and so overcome by a sense of guilt it was all I could say to her. "If I did, I would have the life of a person on my conscience."

At that point my wife came rushing into the room. "What about my life?" she screamed.

The whole family including my son broke down and cried.

It was a painful time for me as well. I was so consumed by the sense of guilt and stress that I developed shingles. It first appeared in a small patch – strawberry-like bubbles – which soon spread from my abdomen to my back. The pain was excruciating.

As a way to relieve the pain, I went jogging around the Serpentine in Hyde Park. I returned just in time for dinner. I took a bottle of white wine, lay down on the sofa and watched a movie. I got up quickly when the movie ended. I complained to Elaine about a severe headache and asked for painkillers. I went to the toilet. As I urinated I was hit by a sudden dizziness. I passed out just as my wife was giving me the aspirin. Thinking that I had had a heart attack, she started to pound my chest with her fist. An ambulance arrived. At the hospital I was revived and the doctor in the Emergency Room asked me to describe my symptoms.

"I feel this pain in my chest."

I was sent to the Cardiac Ward for observation after tests had been done. There were three other patients on the same ward. One was a young man. His skin had turned black, almost as black as charcoal. The other was so short of breath that he had to get to the window to inhale heavily every other hour. All night long, the patient in the bed next to me was heaving with spasms. It was not a pleasant experience.

The next day a teaching professor of London University came with his students. "How are you feeling this morning?"

"My chest hurts," I replied. "I have a heart problem."

"What do you do for a living?"

"I'm a solicitor. Honestly, I know it is the heart."

"There is a tendency for lawyers to jump to conclusions." The professor spoke light-heartedly to his students, who burst out laughing. "All the test results returned negative. You don't have a heart disease. Your wife hit you hard. That explains the chest pain. It's in the paramedic's report. Hell hath no fury like a woman scorned. Have you wronged her lately?"

I smiled gingerly. I knew I had scorned my wife. No one in the family came to visit me in hospital although it was just an overnight stay. I had not only upset everyone in the family but had also driven Nichole to distraction.

Soon she saw how hopeless the situation was. "If our relationship has to remain a secret then I really shouldn't be in it. I've had it up to my neck. I am leaving you."

With those words she began to distance herself from me, seeing other men.

One night I called her up close to midnight and asked where she was.

"I am having dinner with my father," she said politely. "I shall call you tomorrow. Good night."

I drove to outside her apartment block. There were no lights on in her flat. She was not back yet. I decided to wait. No sooner had I switched off the engine than I saw a Mercedes Benz sports car pull up at the kerb on the opposite side. Nichole got out with a man. Together they entered the building, larking about and holding hands. Both appeared to be high on alcohol. I followed closely on their heels. The night watchman to whom I was well known tried to stop me. I was well aware of what he wanted to tell me, something I already knew and did not wish to be reminded of again. I waved him away with my hand and went straight into the waiting lift.

As the lift door opened, I immediately noticed a pair of men's shoes neatly placed on the doorstep. Nichole had a habit of asking all visitors to remove and leave their shoes in the lobby to prevent spoiling the white carpets. Although I had a key, I decided against entry. However, I put my ear to the door. I could hear the song *Power of Love* being played. There was the sound of giggling and laughter from within. Then it all went quiet. I actually stood listening for the good part of an hour, all the while with one ear applied to the door, and the couple did not emerge into the sitting room again until much later. I knew they had headed for the bathroom. It was a small flat, the one we had used for our rendezvous.

The watchman, sensing trouble, came up to the floor to check what was going on. He pulled me over to one side. "That man has been spending nights at the apartment at least twice a week during the past month," he whispered to me. "You had better leave."

I did as I was told, heartbroken yet relieved. I knew there and then that we were finished. It would be good for everyone, her in particular.

I wrote a note and put it in an envelope together with the key to the apartment. I left it under the windscreen wiper of the smart sports car: *Please inherit this key to the apartment and look after her well. She is a good woman.*

After driving round the block, I returned. I had changed my mind: I did not think the message was appropriate. I removed it from under the wiper. She deserved to be set free, to love again. I owed her more than I could ever pay her back. I was glad I did it.

It was the last time I saw her, although from time to time we met at social functions. She pretended she did not know me. We did not greet each other. She became the most familiar 'stranger' I ever knew. Later I was happy to learn that she had met Mr. Right and they were happily married. I closed my eyes and gave the couple my blessing. It was a soft landing for everyone. A potential disaster had been avoided.

Like the Chinese proverb says: 'If one plants melons, one gets melons, and if one plants beans, one gets beans.'

Another Chinese proverb says: 'Disaster doesn't strike alone.' Yet another perfect storm was in the making.

≈≈≈≈≈

1997 saw a run on Asian currencies. Hong Kong was hit by the crisis that started with the devaluation of the Thai baht. Interest rates in the early part of the 1990s contributed to an unprecedented upswing in property prices. Paradoxically, the imminent return of Hong Kong's sovereignty to China not only did not dampen but also fuelled the speculative fever in the market – from stocks to properties – as if the punters wanted to play their last hand before the casino closed.

When the first Chief Executive of the Hong Kong SAR arrived on the scene, he quickly announced a policy on housing – 85,000 flats would be built yearly to meet demand and deflate the property bubble. Then the Asian currency crisis that had started in Thailand in 1997 spread quickly. The economy of Hong Kong, in tandem with other Asian economies, took a nosedive – wiping out billions upon billions from its market.

2003 saw the deadly SARS (Severe Acute Respiratory Syndrome) epidemic that virtually shut down the place. It made a lasting impression on the city, from the all-prevalent face masks to fear bordering on sheer panic that the disease would spread unchecked in the heavily populated environment. There was no antidote to the disease; of the nearly nine thousand people infected, more than seven hundred of them died.

I left Singapore in disgrace but the rumours would not go away. They continued to spread. One such was that I had been forced to leave because I was a wanted man in Singapore.

As a visitor from Singapore, I did not feel it. But, coming home to live in Hong Kong again, I could see the changes. I felt like a stranger in my own town. Most noticeable of these changes was that Hong Kong had lost its direction and, along with it, its sense of optimism – the 'can do' attitude that was always so much a part of its culture.

There were fewer expatriates. Many Brits had left to return to the old country and others to seek greener pastures elsewhere because fewer jobs were available. Hong Kong had become increasingly like a city in China. *Time* magazine, in an article written on Hong Kong, stated: 'It was not quite dead yet, but it was bleeding. It was not a 'Manhattan Plus'… but something more like a 'Shanghai Minus'.

≈≈≈≈≈

"Call for you, Robert," said Elaine as she handed me the receiver.

"Who would call me so early in the morning?" I asked.

"It's Li Ka Shing."

Coming at this time, the call from Li Ka Shing was ominous.

"Good morning, Mr. Li." I tried to sound cheerful.

"Good morning. You are well, aren't you?" Before I could answer, Li Ka Shing continued. "You know we had a meeting last night. I did not make the decision. He did."

It was unimportant who had instigated the decision.

"Thank you, Mr. Li," I replied nervously.

I knew what was coming. He did not have to tell me more. I knew the Trio had met and a decision had been made to ditch me, and for good reason – I had become an embarrassment to them.

Li wanted to tell me he was not involved, hence his reason for phoning so early – it was just his way of doing business. He wanted to get it out of the way first thing before he began his round of golf.

My fall from grace was complete. I was now persona non grata even among my friends. Some of them were mercilessly cold. They went out of their way to cold-shoulder me. When they saw me in the street, they would look the other way to avoid eye contact. It was almost as if the stigma of me would brush off on them if they stopped and talked. If they did stop, they would look for the first opportunity to get out of a conversation. I tasted the bitterness of being abandoned first-hand… like the way the fallen ones, out of grace or retired from office, were treated by their fair-weather friends from Shanghai during the days of the textiles era in Hong Kong.

Oprah Winfrey, the U.S. talk-show queen, once said: "The lesson taught me to be wary of those who once bowed at my feet. When the winds of change come, they are the ones who will be at my throat." She was right.

After returning disgraced and removed from power in Suntec City, I made a desperate attempt at rehabilitation. I wanted to get back into the power play again with all means still at my disposal.

"Mr. Cheng, about my position as your alternate," I said. "Will you—"

"I don't need a second alternate." Cheng Yu Tung was abrupt. "One could get a billion or even ten billion to manage if one was good enough."

It was like rubbing salt into a wound. Cheng knew I wanted to manage OPM (other people's money). Not only was Cheng telling me that he would no longer appoint me as his alternate on the Executive Committee but he also hinted that I was not good enough to manage OPM. In other words, I could not be like one of them.

Elaine had hinted as much to me. I half believed her. I would have doubted anyone else's assessment, but if it was Cheng Yu Tung who said so, then he must be right. I had always considered him to be the most intelligent and talented Chinese businessman alive. In terms of business acumen, Cheng surpassed all others I knew. He had no peers.

Another thing that Oprah said is also true: "There is just a natural order to things. When you're rising, people are pulling for you as you rise. Once you reach a certain level, and if you go beyond what a person feels you should be, then the opposite happens."

The epic changes bore down heavily on the law practice. Since the 1980s, the firm of Robert W.H. Wang & Co., Solicitors & Notaries, had been one of the largest in Hong Kong, not to mention its offices in Singapore and London. In Hong Kong alone it had a staff of over two hundred, of whom some forty-five were qualified. It occupied some twenty thousand square feet of prime office space in Central, Hong Kong.

Then the company was caught in a perfect storm. It was hit on three fronts: one, the Asian currency crisis; two, abolition of the Conveyancing Scale; and three, globalisation.

In Hong Kong, solicitors enjoy a monopoly on all conveyancing work. Before 1997 the fees were prescribed by the Law Society under a Scale. Work was charged according to the Scale. It would be a disciplinary matter if a solicitor was found to be in breach of the rules. Land is scarce in Hong Kong. Hence most buildings are high-rises.

In the old days, solicitors could act for both parties in what is known locally as 'block conveyancing'. It was therefore not surprising that conveyancing work was lucrative. Often the conveyancing department was so profitable that little heed was paid to the development of other areas of practice. These other areas were often there to dress up the company to show that the services provided were comprehensive, in line with the image of a large firm. By 1997, the firm was heavily dependent on its conveyancing practice. This was unwise, as subsequent events proved.

In 1997, in line with the practice that was already prevalent in other jurisdictions, Hong Kong abolished the Conveyancing Scale. Fees immediately took a severe beating. They plunged to less than a tenth of the pre-abolition levels. The change could not have happened at a worse time. That same year, the economy, in tandem with other countries in the region, plunged into a severe recession. To exacerbate an already bad situation, globalisation hit Hong Kong. The firm lost clients such as Citibank, JP Morgan, Marks and Spencer, Chase Manhattan and Barclays to international and Euro-market firms that set up offices in droves in Hong Kong.

These firms also poached our staff. Our firm became a favourite poaching ground. The firm of Robert Wang was known in local legal circles as the 'training school'. Often no 'examination' was required if a candidate came from the firm. The vetting of and training given to the firm's staff were considered good enough to be acceptable to most if not all firms in Hong Kong.

As if these occurrences were not enough, the government introduced a compulsory pension scheme for all workers in or around 1998. All employers had to make compulsory contributions. A combination of these factors caused the overheads of the company to be stretched to the limit, and to the point that billings could not keep up.

"Robert, the firm is bleeding," said Anna Wu, who was then the Managing Partner. "We are running at a loss of over $1 million a month. Unless something is done, and done quickly, we will soon bleed to death."

"I know. The situation is worrying. I'm losing sleep over it. We are caught in the middle of a perfect storm."

"Yes, we are. As you know, the firm relies heavily on conveyancing work; it makes up fifty per cent of our income."

"Have you thought of cessation?"

I suggested cessation because of the hopeless state the firm was in. Amalgamation with a large firm was no longer possible. Although we had often been approached by top local and international firms for amalgamation in the past, no firm would be interested once they knew we were going south. We had exhausted all means at our disposal to save the firm, not to mention the fact that the practice of law had become a risky business as clients were more inclined to sue solicitors for negligence and firms were more willing to act for them, a phenomenon that had emerged in no small measure as a result of globalisation. Compared to the amount of claims, the fee a solicitor received for his work was minuscule. It was said that a solicitor would 'gain a sweet (the fee) but could lose a factory (damages for negligence)' – it rhymed in Chinese. Risk and reward were not commensurate and the partners were liable jointly and severally without limits.

"Indeed, I have," Anna replied, "but unless we wind down the practice in an orderly manner, a sudden rush to cessation can cause a ripple effect. We are stuck with our fixed costs such as salaries and rents. These obligations have to be met in a timely manner. Once we snap we can pretty much say goodbye to the practice. As we are personally liable, the partners can be brought down. We could go bankrupt overnight!

"Take the premises as an example," she continued. "Since the start of the currency crisis, rents in Central have plummeted. No one would be interested in taking over our lease nor would the landlord agree to an earlier termination. There are no takers in this market at the kind of rent we are paying. To all intents and purposes, we're stuck.

"If we keep the existing level of staffing we can't make ends meet. The recession has dried up the work. Even if work is available, the outside competition is so cut-throat that it can only be done at a loss. If we cut staff, we still have the other fixed costs to reckon with. I've done the figures. Whichever of these two alternatives we take, we will still run at a substantial loss – a minimum of $1 million every month. That assumes the situation doesn't get any worse. It's a no-win situation – either way we're doomed. Do you have any bright ideas? You are always resourceful, Robert."

"We can cut salaries across the board. Yes, no one escapes the axe – partners' drawings included."

"The trouble with cutting salary indiscriminately is that you'll lose good people," she warned. "You'll end up in a situation where the good ones, those who are still profitable, leave and the rest stay. Won't that aggravate rather than improve the situation?"

"I think you are right. Let's carefully consider all our options."

Indecision was the worst way to deal with a crisis of this magnitude. The problem did not go away. On the contrary, it compounded with each passing day.

"Mr. Wang, I just wish to alert you. This month's billings have fallen far short of our expenses," said Alice Yeung, the chief accountant. "Our overdraft facilities are used up to the hilt. HSBC have placed us on the watch list. They request that we provide our accounts to them on a quarterly basis instead of the usual once a year. Our facility with them is in danger of being cancelled. Unless the partners are prepared to dip into their own pockets, I'm afraid we won't be able to pay salaries this month."

"How much is needed?"

"A minimum of $2 million."

"Did you tell Miss Wu?"

"Yes, I did. She asked me to talk to you. She wants you to make the decision."

"If we cut salaries across the board by twenty per cent and the partners do not draw, can we get by this month?"

Alice took out a calculator and started hitting the buttons. "We can scrape through but just barely."

"Please tell Miss Wu that I intend to cut staff salaries across the board by twenty per cent with immediate effect. If Miss Wu doesn't object then I want the practice manager to convene a full staff meeting at 6 p.m. today. I shall announce it myself."

I should have left the task to Anna Wu. She was the Managing Partner. It was unwise for me to usurp her power but in the heat of the moment I was confused, panicky and probably thinking: 'Oh, what the heck. It's urgent. Someone has to make a quick decision.'

It was folly on my part. The move was ill-conceived. It strained my relationship not only with the Managing Partner but also with the rest of the firm, other partners included. The reaction was bad. I was faced with a barrage of questions from some of the most astute solicitors in the business.

"I have signed a contract with the firm," one said. "Now you wish to vary the terms unilaterally. Are you saying that I must accept?"

"No, I am not. I do appreciate that the salary can only be reduced by mutual consent but the situation is critical. Unless I get your agreement, I am afraid the firm will not be able to pay the salaries. We'll serve you requisite notice to terminate your employment. Indeed you may also treat this act as the company's repudiation of your contract. You are at liberty to accept the repudiation and treat the contract as having ended but without prejudice to your accrued rights."

"Are you speaking for all the partners?" another asked. "Why hasn't this announcement been made by Anna Wu? She is the Managing Partner."

Anna Wu quite wisely stood on the sidelines. She remained quiet throughout the proceedings.

"Why didn't you speak up to support me?" I asked as I stormed into her room afterwards. "I thought we'd agreed on the salary cut."

I threw a tantrum. The events of the day had exhausted and overtaken me. I pushed the documents off her desk before I left in anger. In one stroke, I had destroyed a relationship that had been painstakingly built up over some thirty years. We had never so much as raised our voices to each other, let alone quarrelled. Our relationship was always cordial. Anna started the firm with me and together we had built it up so that it was successful and admired throughout the profession, both within and without.

After the incident Anna Wu left the firm.

≈≈≈≈≈

In 1998, I regained the helm of the firm and introduced severe cost-cutting exercises that led to many resignations, among them some of the best and brightest lawyers. The company shrank rapidly. It was only saved from disintegration by the concerted actions taken by the remaining partners. Michael Dalton was a pillar of strength. He stuck through the rough with admirable resilience. He was loyal and faithful until the firm ceased practice.

I often imagined the firm to be that ship caught in a perfect storm. Battered by huge waves, it lost all its engines and was tossed adrift in the open sea completely at the mercy of the elements. Miraculously the ship did not sink. When the storm was over, the ship in its battered state sailed into a calm bay. There, whatever was left of it was sold for its scrap value.

≈≈≈≈≈

I was hit by not one but three storms that year; 1997 will be remembered as an 'annus horribilis' – a horrible year – as predicted by my 'Pak Tze'.

"Any higher bids?" shouted the auctioneer at the annual fund-raising ball for the hospital. "If not, I shall knock down on the bid from that lady on the right. It's a beautiful lady's dress watch – Chopard with happy diamonds. Remember it's for charity. Your money will be put to good use… any higher bid? $50,000 once… $50,000 twice…"

"$50 million," shouted the figure as he entered the ballroom. He did not just walk. He literally burst in. He looked gaunt and unkempt. He was dressed in his pyjamas. The pair of slippers he was wearing looked old and worn out. He raised his right arm and repeated: "$50 million." He approached the stage.

The timing was perfect. The sequence of events was so theatrically executed that those present thought it was a stage act. They recognized him to be none other than the indomitable Mr. John Tung, a past chairman of the hospital board. The pyjamas he wore made him look so comical that everyone burst out laughing, thinking that it was part of a skit.

"It's Mr. John Tung, our past chairman," shouted the auctioneer. He could not believe what he was hearing or seeing. Like everyone else, he was astounded.

The ball chairman and directors quickly stood up and left their seats on the stage, descending the few steps to meet John Tung. He was a well-known philanthropist. Over the years, the donations he had made to the hospital were exceptional. As the major benefactor of the hospital he was much respected.

As the rush of activity subsided, he was ushered onto the stage and to a seat in the centre.

"I donate $50 million." John Tung quickly rose from the seat, grabbed the microphone and announced his bid again.

"Wow!" the guests let out in unison as they turned and looked at each other in disbelief. Only then did they realise it was not an act.

John Tung had gone a bit cuckoo of late. His character had changed overnight. From being a man of few words, he suddenly became loud, nagging and talkative. He seemed to have lost his inhibitions. He ceased being the composed, disciplined, authoritarian and reserved person he always was – the kind that could, for example, remain silent throughout an aerial tour conducted by his realtor of the acres upon acres of farmland he purchased in Texas.

"What's your name?" John Tung demanded to know as he crossed the road to meet a young man he had spotted that morning. "You're David's son, aren't you?"

"Oh, Uncle John, it's you," the young man said in surprise.

To him, Uncle John, as the head of the extended family, was an elder who came from another planet, high and mighty and a man of vast wealth. He seldom spoke when the family gathered. He certainly had never spoken to him before. Yet, this time, Uncle John had crossed from the opposite side of the road just so that they could talk. It seemed strange. And he was dressed in his pyjamas.

"How much do you have in the bank?" Uncle John asked. "I can help you make money… lots of money. Now, just tell me…"

"Erm… er…" The young man was perplexed and bewildered. He never expected such a question, yet he did not wish to be discourteous to Uncle John.

"Tell me… tell me quickly," Uncle John persisted impatiently. "Just tell me. I want to make money for you."

"About a hundred thousand dollars," the nephew replied nervously.

"Give it all to me. Let me short-sell IBM for you."

Recently, John Tung had been behaving outlandishly, telling everyone to sell IBM if they owned the shares and, if they did not, to short-sell IBM as if he had an axe to grind against the giant company listed on the New York Stock Exchange.

Mrs. Tung and I met at the Landmark shopping mall in Central, Hong Kong.

"How are you?" I asked her.

"I'm fine but John is not well."

"I meant to ask you about him. He is asking me to short-sell IBM shares. What has IBM done to him?"

"I don't know." I sensed she was reluctant to tell me more. "He is telling everyone to short-sell IBM."

"But there must be an event or a chain of events that pushed him towards this sudden change of personality," I prompted her again, indicating at the same time that I was aware of his condition.

There was a momentary silence.

Finally she answered: "Since you already know about his condition then I will tell you. A few years ago, John invested as an angel and provided venture capital to this young start-up in Silicon Valley. They started a factory there to make disc-drives which were IBM-compatible. Then IBM suddenly changed the design of the machines they made. In the process, the company's products were rendered IBM peripherals. Davong, the company, went into liquidation as a result. John lost a lot of money. He blamed IBM for his losses. He began to nurture a deep-seated hatred against the company. Then one day he snapped. He just went berserk. He short-sold IBM shares as his way of getting back at the company. He did succeed for a while. He pushed the share price from a high of US$104 to $98. Now he is telling everyone he knows to also short-sell IBM.

"He behaves strangely. I took him to a specialist and he was diagnosed as suffering from what is known as 'agromania' – an intense desire to be out in the open. It distorts his personality completely. He acts in an irrational but irresistible manner for a belief – he thinks he possesses special powers and he is invincible."

A few days later, John Tung appeared at my office unannounced, still in his pyjamas. He had many days' growth on his chin. He looked as if he had not bathed for as many days. His legs were swollen.

"Did you short-sell IBM?" he asked me.

For a couple of weeks now, he had telephoned incessantly, telling me each time that I should short-sell IBM shares.

"Look at me," he continued before I could answer – which was just as well because it saved me the embarrassment of having to tell him that I had not. "I possess special powers. I don't need to sleep. All I have to do is draw circles in the air."

He demonstrated how he drew circles.

"The special power gives me the energy. Can you believe it? I don't need to eat. Nor do I have to sleep. I'm sustained by the magical power. I possess supernatural strength. Now, let me show you. Just stick out your index finger."

I did as I was told. Using two fingers, his thumb and index finger, he gripped my finger. I could feel it. It was not firm. I could easily pull free.

"Now pull… pull," he commanded.

I made a feeble attempt to pull free from his grip.

"See? You can't pull free. I possess special powers. You can never free the finger unless I let go. Look, I am just using two fingers."

I made a vain attempt to pull free again.

"You see. You can't pull free, can you?"

I smiled and nodded.

"Now, Robert, I want you to call up this hospital and speak to Dr. Wong of the Cardiology Department. Tell him I wish to donate $50 million to his clinic."

He passed me a calling card. I asked my secretary to put through a call to Dr. Wong. Then I went outside.

"Patricia, just tell me through the intercom that Dr. Wong is busy. Don't call Dr. Wong just yet," I whispered into the ear of the secretary.

"What has taken so long?" John Tung asked impatiently. "I want to speak to Dr. Wong myself."

Even before the secretary came through the intercom to tell me that Dr. Wong was indisposed, John Tung had all but forgotten about the call.

"I am going to fly…" He was talking gibberish. Then he turned and left. I followed closely behind him to make sure he got into his waiting chauffeur-driven car safely. I was amazed that he knew where his car was.

"Mrs. Tung, your husband has just left my office," I advised her on the phone. "He wanted me to call one Dr. Wong. He wants to donate $50 million to his clinic."

"Robert, I'm glad you called. You must help me. My husband has gone crazy. He is doing strange things. He has been walking into institutions pledging to donate to this and that. Can you stop him? Can you apply to the court for a restraining order?"

"He's my friend. He's been good to me. I can't in my right mind let him down at a time when he needs help, Mrs. Tung, I am sorry, but I can't act for you."

"Please, Robert, you must help me," she pleaded. "To restrain him does not mean we want to hurt him. We both love him. It's for his own good. He needs medical care. His mind wanders from one thing to another.

"T.O. would have asked you to do the same for John," she continued. "Next he thinks he can fly."

"Yes, he told me he could fly just this morning."

"You see. Unless we stop him, he is going to jump out of the window."

We successfully applied to the High Court. An insanity order was granted against John Tung.

With his wings clipped, John Tung returned to earth. He quietened down and became his usual self again, except perhaps more withdrawn.

"Robert, John wants to see you," Mrs. Tung telephoned me about two months later.

On his deathbed John Tung looked skeletal, reduced to skin and bone. He stared at me blankly. His eyes were round and intense. He did not speak but signalled to me. I held his hand. He squeezed it. I embraced him and patted his shoulder gently. Tears came rolling down his cheeks. We both cried.

It was his donation that had sent me on my 'Journey to the West'. That unsolicited S$3 million donation opened many doors for me – access to officialdom, the tycoons, the Singapore practice, Suntec City and all the rest of it.

John Tung died shortly afterwards.

"Like a rocket he went up and up," explained Mrs. Tung. "Then the rocket ran out of fuel. It succumbed to gravity, dropping back to earth."

Mrs. Tung never failed to amaze me. When her husband was alive, she was always quiet and submissive, never the sort to make waves. She was just a housewife. But after her husband died, she took control of his vast business empire. She assessed each of the senior members of staff before giving them the businesses one by one, according to her judgement as to who was capable of carrying on the good name of her late husband.

She honoured all the donation pledges of her husband, even when they were made during a time when he was out of his mind, including the two large donations that were pledged to the hospitals.

The couple were childless. They had always lived simply and frugally. She willed the entire fortune to one hospital group. None of it went to relatives.

The image of Mrs. Tung – tall, elegant, graceful and well-educated – lingers. Like Mrs. Liu, T.O.'s wife, they came from a world apart. Ladies like them are few and far between in today's world.

≈≈≈≈≈

All day long I had been feeling uneasy. I had not heard from T.O. for weeks. All the while I had been thinking about his PSA levels, worried that the prostate cancer would catch up with him. I had a premonition that morning when I called.

"Mrs. Liu, it's Robert here," I said. "I hope it's not too late…"

"Oh, Robert, I am so pleased you called. I was just about to call you myself. Please can you come immediately? T.O. has been asking about you. He wants to see you."

My heart sank. It was not in the character of Mrs. Liu to impose such an obligation on others, no matter how close, not even her own children. A chill ran down my spine. I knew T.O. was dying.

"I'll go to the airport immediately." Tears filled my eyes. I felt this compulsion to be there, to be next to him, by his deathbed as he transcended this world into the next. I owed everything to him. He was more than a dear friend. He was like a father to me. It was my filial duty.

"Elaine, please pack our suitcases. We are going to the airport. T.O. is dying."

While at Hong Kong's airport, a call came through from Mrs. Liu. "T.O. has died. I will let you know the funeral details. I'll call you again."

I burst into tears.

I went straight from the airport in San Francisco to the funeral home where his body lay. Only Mrs. Liu was there in the chamber.

"T.O., Robert is here to see you. He's come a long way. I know how much you wanted to see him. He's here. You can now rest in peace. I shall leave the room so Robert can say goodbye to you."

I went down on my knees. I held his hand and stroked his silvery hair gently and affectionately.

"Goodbye, T.O., my dearest friend, my teacher. I'm eternally grateful to you. Thank you for all that you did for me. Thank you from the bottom of my heart. I love you like a father. Thank you."

The funeral service took place at San Francisco's Grace Cathedral. It was a solemn and dignified occasion. Margaret and Robert, their children, were well-known in the local community. Friends and relatives filled the cathedral. I delivered the eulogy like part of the family.

"T.O. was more than a friend. He was like a father to me. He taught me many things. He taught me the value of life, how to stand upright and proud with my head held high; why one should make gains only by one's intelligence and never by unethical means; why everything in life has a price except one's integrity; why one's attempt to preserve life should not be at the expense of one's principles; why true wealth comes from within; why one must not make a mistake of basic objectives; and why a man's success in life is not measured by the wealth he has accumulated but more by how he has raised his children – and, in the latter regard, T.O. considered himself to be extremely fortunate."

# THE COMEBACK

"Robert, you have fallen from so high to so low," said Sir Run Run.

Sir Run Run was there for me at the lowest point of my life. He single-handedly shored me up when I was all but abandoned. Rumours had it that I had done something wrong and the tycoons had decided to distance me. He went out of his way to give me assistance in disproving these rumours. He made certain that I was seen in his company and at the functions he hosted.

The dinners he gave were the stuff that legends are made of. No one could refuse an invitation from Sir Run Run. Hong Kong's elite were frequent guests at his villa at the top of Shaw Studios. As an entertainment mogul, he enjoyed access to the latest of all the good films. Whenever an award-winning film was available, it would be shown in his private theatre at the villa before it was released generally.

The parties that he gave were unique. Guests would arrive in their chauffeur-driven limousines. To get to the main entrance, the cars would have to go up a long ramp in single file. Sir Run Run's personal assistants and a team of ushers would be at the door to welcome the guests who were led into a foyer to meet the host, and then into an area reserved for pre-movie cocktails before being ushered into a spacious private theatre. An oil painting of four ladies in Chinese costumes playing flutes, by the famous artist Chen Yi Fei, hung in the foyer. Once the movie had started, Sir Run Run would take leave and return to work. He would reappear later to join the guests in the opulent dining room filled with splendid objects and adorned with chandeliers and paintings. There, the guests would be treated to a sumptuous dinner catered by the Peninsula Hotel.

Sir Run Run entertained regularly. His villa was a place where friends, senior officials and heads of Hong Kong's major corporations rubbed shoulders. Being seen there was Sir Run Run's subtle way of telling Hong Kong at large that I was not persona non grata as far as he was concerned and not a fugitive from Singapore as the rumour mill had it.

But he did not stop there. He also went out of his way to help me restore my shattered reputation in Singapore, where he was well known.

"You know Tan Boon Teik, Singapore's Attorney General." I telephoned Sir Run Run on the day I returned from a Beijing trip with the Attorney General. We had been there to meet with China's Minister of Justice to discuss how Singapore lawyers could practise in China. "He and his wife are in town. Do you think you can join us for dinner this evening? I really have to quell the rumours that are circulating in Singapore about me."

"Of course, Robert," he said. "I shall be there."

That dinner did much to tell Singapore that I was still in the good books of Sir Run Run Shaw, a leading figure in both cities.

During a time when I was low and all but abandoned, Sir Run Run did so much to show me in a good light that I once wrote to him: 'I would like to kneel before you and thank you for all that you have done for me during my darkest hours.'

We were travelling with Sir Run Run on his annual 'pilgrimage' to China. The chartered Boeing 727 was used as a 'taxi' to ferry members of the entourage. At times the plane made two or more stops a day, landing at airports that in some cases were so remote they were not accessible by commercial flights.

Every stop was neatly planned. As the plane landed it was the same routine. A welcoming party comprising local officials and dignitaries was on the tarmac. As Sir Run Run and his wife, Lady Mona, descended the steps, the waiting students began to chant in chorus: "Welcome, welcome, many welcomes…" Dressed in colourful local costumes and lined up neatly on one side of the red carpet, they danced and waved. Flowers were presented to the leading ladies. Group photographs were taken below a banner that read: 'Welcome Run Run Shaw and Mrs. Shaw'. A fleet of vans, each marked with a number, lined up neatly. A local guide and driver stood to attention by the door of each car. Everyone knew their place and it was as if the whole routine had been rehearsed. My group always took the Number 5 bus.

Everywhere we went, the traffic was held up to ensure we passed freely and quickly. It was the standard reception meted out only to heads of state.

Everyone recognized Sir Run Run. He was universally respected, admired and even worshipped.

He is a leading philanthropist. Over the years, he has donated $3 billion to education. The secondary schools he has built in diverse parts of China provide education to some two million students. His name appears on many buildings as a mark of respect for his generous donations. He is a household name throughout China.

"I know why you donate," I teased Sir Run Run once.

"Why?" he asked, beaming a broad smile.

"Giving is the cruellest form of taking. Like the proverb says: 'Throw away a brick to entice a piece of jade' – that is why you give."

He smiled. He was inscrutable. I was wrong.

Many years later, seeing how healthy he was, I tried again.

"I know why you donate."

"Why?" he asked, again smiling.

"For longevity. I can see how they put you up on a pedestal and worship you and I can also see how happy you are."

He smiled. He neither said 'yes' nor 'no'. He remained inscrutable. I was wrong again.

Many years later, I saw all those schools that had been made possible by his donations. I tried again.

"I know why you donate."

He looked at me. This time he did not say anything.

"You transcend your own generation. You donate so that future generations of Shaws can benefit."

He smiled. He nodded approvingly. He remained inscrutable. He did not say I was right.

Then one day, out of the blue, he confided in me.

"You know, Robert. I was born in Ningbo. My brothers and I used to peddle hand-rolled peep shows in the streets of Shanghai during our teens. I went with my elder brother, Run Me, to Singapore and together we started the Shaw Organization.

"In those days we used to mix with people like Tan Kah Kee. We played mahjong at a beachfront house on Saturdays. Others who were there included the likes of the Aw brothers, Boon Haw and Boon Par, who made the Tiger Balm ointment. Boon Par, the younger brother, obtained the secret formula when the master he was apprenticed to died in Rangoon. Boon Haw, the other brother, was a marketing genius. He designed and developed a car in the shape of a tiger. It was used to distribute ceramics in the streets of Singapore. The tactic worked and Tiger Balm became a familiar trademark.

"Tan Kah Kee never failed to fascinate me," continued Sir Run Run. "He was a man of extraordinary fortitude, enterprise and acumen. He started a business of his own in pineapples before he expanded into rubber plantations. Then he made a brave move. He switched into rubber manufacturing. It proved to be his mettle – an uncanny ability to sniff out opportunities and take risks. The move established him as one of the most successful Chinese businessmen in South-East Asia.

"He was extraordinary as a philanthropist. Most would give a fraction of their wealth but Tan gave all of it while he himself lived frugally, subsisting on a diet of rice and vegetables. He gave until he went bankrupt in 1936, when the world price of rubber plummeted in the years of the Great Depression. Tan Kah Kee Rubber was taken over by the bank HSBC. One day a bank representative came to inspect it. He saw this young man covered by a rubber sheet. It was apparent that he had worked all through the night. The inspector was so impressed that he returned and made a report to his superior in which he recommended that the bank should let this young man take over what was left of Tan Kah Kee's business. The young man eventually took over. His name was Lee Kong Chian. He later founded Lee Rubber and Overseas Chinese Banking Corporation

(OCBC). Today, OCBC is rated as the safest bank in the world. He also married Tan Kah Kee's daughter.

"I shall follow in his footsteps. My children are well provided for. Tan Kah Kee used to say: 'Wealth would impair the ambition of the wise and increase the folly of the foolish'. Our children can make their own fortunes. There is no need to be their slaves."

I know what philanthropy has done for Sir Run Run.

"Robert, my life is perfect," he whispered into my ear. He was ninety-seven that year.

≈≈≈≈≈

By sheer coincidence, the collapse of the Thai baht took place almost on the exact date that sovereignty of Hong Kong was handed over to China – 1st July 1997. It heralded the Asian financial crisis. In October that year, the Hong Kong dollar, which is pegged at 7.8 to the U.S. dollar, came under siege. Hong Kong's inflation rate had been consistently higher than the U.S.'s for years. The peg took away Hong Kong's fiscal tools. The Monetary Authority spent US$1 billion to defend Hong Kong's currency regime. The peg was maintained.

The stock market was volatile. It dropped by 25% within a few days in October that year. In order to protect the peg, the government raised overnight interest rates from 8% to 23% and, at one juncture, to as high as 500%. The Monetary Authority was aware that speculators such as George Soros, who had recently emerged victorious in the siege he laid against the British pound sterling, were taking advantage of Hong Kong's currency regime; when the net sales of the local currency occurred overnight the bank rate would automatically go up and this hike in rate would then exert pressure on the stock market the next day. On the back of this vicious circle, the speculators were able to short-sell and make money. It was as risk-free as getting money out of an ATM machine.

The political fortunes of the Financial Secretary, Sir Donald Tsang, were on the wane at the time. He had condemned those analysts who spoke ill of Hong Kong as inferior "second-rate analysts" and went on to predict that "the crisis would be over by Christmas". He declared war against the speculators.

The fight was all over the newspapers on 15th August 1998, a Saturday, when we arrived at Hong Kong's swanky new airport at Chek Lap Kok which was designed by Sir Norman Foster of Britain. The currency war had just started. The government had made known its declared objective. It would not stop until the speculators were beaten off. It ended up buying $120 billion (US$15 billion) worth of shares in component companies of the Hang Seng Index. The government ended up owning 10% of HSBC, for instance.

I was surprised that year to find Sir Donald in the group for Sir Run Run's annual trip to China. A Boeing 737 plane had been chartered. It took us to different parts of China, often landing at military airports that were not open to commercial flights.

Throughout the trip, Sir Donald maintained a poker face, although I could see him talking constantly on his mobile phone. It was hardly a holiday for Hong Kong's Financial Secretary. All the while, he was doing battle with the international financiers who were laying siege to Hong Kong's currency. I could not help but admire him for his determination and tenacity and the way he batted for Hong Kong. When we arrived at the courtyard of an old temple, we were treated to a folklore performance. He suddenly turned his head.

"I am so pleased that I came," he said as our eyes met. "There is no more squabbling."

Wherever we went, Sir Run Run was warmly received by the dignitaries who were there – party secretaries, provincial heads, mayors and even a minister or two. Sir Donald said little. He kept to himself, constantly checking the latest situation on his mobile phone.

The next day we arrived at the peak of Mount Wudang in Hubei Province. The Tianshu Feng Monastery is the most famous in Taoism.

The temple was built in 1430. In the compound there is a room named the 'Change Luck Chamber'. It was out of bounds to visitors. The door was locked. No one thought that members of Sir Run Run's entourage would want to 'change luck'. However, a banker's wife asked for the door to be opened for her. She obviously wanted her luck changed in the middle of the Asian financial crisis. Everyone had been affected, the rich in particular.

"I want my luck changed too," I told the monk who unlocked the door for the banker's wife, giving him a $100 note. "Please explain to me what I have to do."

"Go inside," said the monk enthusiastically. He was obviously pleased with the tip. "Place your arms around the column. Turn anti-clockwise – remember it must be anti-clockwise – and shout aloud in your own words how you would wish to change your luck. Remember, turn anti-clockwise. The lady before you turned in the wrong direction."

Just as I was about to enter, I saw Sir Donald come up from behind. I deferred to the Financial Secretary and his wife, Selina.

"This is Hong Kong's Financial Secretary," I told the monk. "What he does affects Hong Kong. Please make sure he does it right. Please lead the way."

Elaine and I followed closely behind the couple as we were ushered through a narrow passage into a hall. It was so dark that I could not see my fingers. In the centre of the dark room, I could feel a column so big that at least ten people could wrap themselves around it with room to spare.

"Wrap your body and arms around the column," commanded the monk. "Shout out loudly and clearly how you want your luck to be changed. Those behind shall then repeat, also loudly, after the leader. Don't rush. Say your words slowly and clearly."

"Change luck. Change luck," shouted the Financial Secretary. "Go away, speculators. Go away, speculators."

We repeated the same verses in unison at the back. Then, at the end of the ritual and when everyone else had left, I sneaked back into the dark chamber unnoticed, not even by Elaine. With my arms wrapped around the column again, I shouted, "Change luck. End my ordeals. End my streak of bad luck. Get the devils off my back."

From the temple we later visited a cave. The cave was deep, tranquil and peaceful. A poem was inscribed on a wall. It had been written by a general surnamed Wang, a historical figure. Wang led an army in a campaign and in between the many battles he came to the cave. Struck by the serene environment and its beauty he wrote:

*Pleased I am to lay down arms*
*Such serenity fills me with wonderment*
*The gentle breezes and tranquillity are my divine gifts*
*In the cave, I find my heavenly kingdom.*

"You are in a similar situation," I remarked to Sir Donald. "You find peace in the middle of a fight to the death against the speculators." He smiled hesitantly. I was also thinking of my own battles.

On the bus, a lady in the group asked aloud: "Can someone translate what is written on this chit for me?"

At the temple she had wanted an answer to a question asked of a Taoist god. The monk asked her to kneel before a statue of the god. She was given a bamboo container in which there were many sticks, each marked with a number. She prayed while shaking the container until one dropped to the ground. She matched the number of the fallen stick with a chit. It was the god's answer to her question. Not being conversant with Chinese, she wanted someone on the bus to translate it into English.

"This chit says: 'Have you nothing better to do when you come and ask the fairy a question, the answer to which you already know?'" said the translator.

Everyone on the bus broke into laughter. It was somewhat cruel but then no one knew what she had asked of the god.

The ritual that was carried out at the 'Change Luck Chamber' that day changed the fortune of Sir Donald. He was widely praised for winning the currency war against the speculators and for his handling of the economy. Then, in 2001, he became Hong Kong's Chief Secretary after the sudden resignation of Anson Chan.

He never looked back. He went on to assume the office of Chief Executive of Hong Kong in 2005 when his predecessor, Tung Chee Hwa, suddenly resigned for health reasons.

It was amazing. It also changed my fortune. Not only did my law practice stabilize, but green shoots began to appear in my career. I was ready to take on new challenges.

Events that took place and the rapidity at which they occurred in Suntec City also took me by surprise. While Tan Sri was quietly and happily ruling the roost, the unexpected happened. Out of the blue, an offer was received to buy what remained of the offices and the shopping mall in Suntec City.

In line with the 'no vote' and 'no confrontation' culture of the company, no formal board meeting was convened to consider the offer. Behind what appeared to be a friendly façade, the two camps – one led by Cheng Yu Tung and the other by Tan Sri – feverishly plotted and manoeuvred to try to beat each other into submission.

One such tea meeting took place at the Hong Kong Club.

"I think we should stay the way we are," said Dr. D.S. Li, a supporter of Tan Sri.

The motion was echoed by all of Tan Sri's supporters. It was apparent they had talked about it before the meeting and reached a consensus.

"It is a good offer," said Li Ka Shing, who had made a rare appearance. "We should accept it unless there is a better deal."

"Well, it's like this," said Tan Sri after much ado. He realized it was futile for him to try to maintain the status quo. "The offer is a combination of cash and units. There is no telling whether the units, when listed, are worth what they are said to be worth. Our CEO has informed me that another purchaser is prepared to make us an offer that is all cash. It is superior to the current offer. Why don't we wait until that offer comes through? We can then compare the two and make a decision."

The meeting ended inconclusively, much to the consternation of those who wanted a definitive answer that afternoon.

"I've not seen you this happy for a long time," said Elaine. "What's up?"

"I'm thrilled to bits. We've received an offer to buy Suntec City for over S$2 billion."

"Wow, that is good news," she exclaimed. "Is the offer made through you?"

"No, it came through Li Ka Shing and Cheng Yu Tung."

"Is the price good?"

"It's fantastic. We are just selling what is unsold in Suntec City. The jewel in the crown, the Convention Centre, is not included."

"The shareholders are pleased, are they?"

"Not everyone," I told her. "Tan Sri has been taken by surprise. He is trying to ward off the hostile bid. He tried to rally the shareholders to his side. At a gathering of shareholders today, several of his allies on the board, including almost all the directors from Shanghai who traditionally support him, spoke out against the deal."

"Why are they against it if it is such a good deal?"

"It's not a question of dollars and cents. It's about who controls Suntec City."

"Tan Sri is in control, isn't he?"

"No, not any more if it is sold. He's been getting complacent. It's all quiet on the Western front as far as he is concerned. He holds no more board meetings. Even the annual general meeting is now done on paper. He probably thinks inaction is the best way to ensure his continued rule. Well, he is wrong. Someone has worked behind his back and now this offer has arrived. Rest assured it has not come out of the blue. It must be the culmination of months, if not years, of meticulous planning."

"You think it is Li Ka Shing's work?"

"Yes, but the other two, Cheng Yu Tung and Lee Shau Kee, must have also agreed. The offer was first conveyed to me through Cheng Yu Tung. He seems to be the driver. Li is taking a back seat. He's happy to let

Cheng spearhead the whole exercise. Lee Shau Kee, as usual, is on the side of Cheng Yu Tung. I'm not surprised."

"The three of them add up to forty-eight per cent. It's still short of the majority."

"I was asked to speak to William's son. He confirms he will abide by his late father's wishes and honour the act-in-concert agreement."

"What position do you take?"

"It goes without saying I will also adhere to what I've signed. I don't care who is going to take over as long as it is not Tan Sri. You know how much I have suffered at his hands over the years. I'm still not out of the woods yet."

"Aren't you home and dry? Isn't it a done deal?"

"Not really – both sides shy away from a vote. Instead they plot and manoeuvre. It is a constant tug of war. Neither side is prepared to give way. It's a stalemate."

"Who's got the upper hand at the moment?"

"It's difficult to tell. The gathering ended on the note that Tan Sri be given time to find another buyer who can better the offer that is currently on the table. I think he is just buying time."

In the ensuing weeks, Tan Sri and Wong Ah Long, the CEO, frantically searched the market to find a buyer who could come up with another offer. An overture from a firm called ERGO was indeed received. But the so-called 'offer' when received had many strings attached to it. It was half-baked at best – a far cry from the conclusive offer that was already on the table.

Tan Sri, in a desperate attempt to keep his position, wanted the fund to take over the shares of those who wanted to sell so that he could continue to control the company.

Then the unthinkable occurred: civility ended and acrimony began. The old taboo was broken. Confrontational tactics were employed. Li Ka Shing's side accused Tan Sri of trying to 'divide and rule'. Hitherto, it was unheard of that the parties would openly confront each other. It was just not in the culture of the group.

The move must have taken Tan Sri by surprise.

Another informal tea meeting was notified to all shareholders. Again it took place at the Hong Kong Club. It was hardly to be expected that Tan Sri and his supporters would be there. It was intended to bulldoze a decision, one way or another, on the back of the act-in-concert agreement. Tan Sri did not attend although he sent along his alternate, one Miss Chen. As the meeting started, it became increasingly apparent that the group that gathered that afternoon favoured the offer that was already on the table. One of Tan Sri's supporters broke rank and crossed over to support the Trio. He was the nephew of W.H. Chou – he had replaced his deceased uncle as a director – even when his father was vehemently batting for Tan Sri, his friend.

Miss Chen saw the writing on the wall. She excused herself and left the room, apparently to take instructions from Tan Sri. She returned to say that Tan Sri had been consulted. He would also agree.

I could not believe it when it was all over. I was thrilled beyond words.

That night I went out to celebrate on my own. I did not return home until 3 a.m. I wanted to celebrate this momentous event alone. As I walked the streets and crawled from one pub to another, I was completely overtaken by emotions as image after image flashed across my mind of those fateful years when I was incarcerated at Five Fingers Mountain. Finally, sadness gave way to joy and jubilation – it was one of the happiest days of my life.

≈≈≈≈≈

The origin of the Lunar New Year goes back thousands of years. It is the most significant festival for ethnic Chinese all over the world, wherever they may be. It is a happy occasion when people take a break from work in order to be together with family and friends. It involves a series of customs and traditions, one of which is to pay elders respect by visiting them at their home or workplace.

During the Lunar New Year, people of all ages look renewed – new clothes, new haircut, and new this and that – and display a feeling of triumph.

I telephoned Li Ka Shing.

"Kung Hei Fat Choy," I said. "May the Lunar New Year bring you good health."

"Thank you, Robert. Have you left out something?"

"Oh, yes, Mr. Li, may you continue 'long into infinity'."

Since the time I had first wished him that his personal status quo should continue 'long into infinity', Li had come to expect me to greet him the same way every Lunar New Year.

I took the cue from his licence plate. The Mercedes sports car that he drove every morning from his house at Deep Water Bay to the golf club – a few hundred yards, at the most – bore the registration number '199' which in Cantonese denotes just that: 'long into infinity'.

I also visited Tan Sri to greet him with '*kung hei*' or 'congratulations'. It is traditional for 'friends' to congratulate each other by uttering auspicious greetings on family, money, health or longevity.

We had a good conversation as if we were old friends. Then he saw me to the lift lobby.

"You're more intelligent than me," he said.

"How can that be?" I replied. "The level of intelligence determines one's success and you're way, way ahead of me. I am no match. You're not comparing apples with apples." At the back of my mind I was thinking: 'Not me. Someone else, maybe.'

Superman Li's right-hand man is now the Chairman of Suntec REIT – the new owner of Suntec City. As for mortals like me, I had to find a way forward, a new niche to continue my career. I found it in a back street in Kowloon.

I dare say Mauro and Monica are the most stunning couple I have met in my life. It is no exaggeration to say that with his piercing brown eyes he looks like Napoleon; and she is a European heiress of culture, elegance and class. Ever since we met on a holiday in the Philippines over thirty years ago, we have been friends. Over the years the friendship has developed to be like family. Of all our friends, none are dearer to our hearts than Mauro and Monica.

They say the world is made up of two kinds of people: the Italians and those who aspire to be Italians. I certainly fall into the latter camp. Mauro and Monica are the reason I eat spaghetti at home. I want my pasta to be cooked *al dente*, just like the Italians eat it.

Mauro's main business interest was in textiles – Chinese hand embroideries – and his company was one of the largest Italian importers. His company eventually became established at D'Aguilar Street, a popular address for dealers in that industry. He saw the potential in the backwater that was Lan Kwai Fong. While real estate prices in prime Central locations were rising beyond his means, Lan Kwai Fong's real estate was a fraction of the price. This was due largely to the fact that the steep slope in the area made it hard for people to reach and, indeed, until Mauro opened his delicatessens, there was nothing to climb up for.

Undeterred, Mauro picked up a number of premises there and turned them into outlets for his imported Italian delicacies and upmarket Italian clothes. T.O. redeveloped the old buildings and sold him these properties in the late 1970s.

The delicatessen and ensuing restaurants became a big hit with locals and expatriates alike. More and more people started to find their way up to Lan Kwai Fong. They showed up during lunch and for drinks before and after dinner.

Others started to see the potential in this area. Gordon Huthart started a popular nightspot called Disco Disco and it became the place for movie stars and celebrities. More people recognized what Lan Kwai Fong could become. Canadian developer Allan Zeman opened a restaurant called California. Through the tireless efforts of Zeman, Lan Kwai Fong became an area to be reckoned with – so much so, the Government eventually stepped in to make it viable in many ways like repaving and sprucing up the street.

Since that time Lan Kwai Fong has blossomed. There is no mistaking the area. During the weekend, countless expatriates and locals can be found crowding the brick-paved streets, more often than not with several alcoholic beverages in hand. Neon signs dangle overhead in a style like classic Hong Kong postcards. The noise resembles the loudest of rowdy block parties. Lan Kwai Fong has become a unique and phenomenally successful haven of bars, restaurants and outdoor cafés.

What started as a handful of restaurants and nightclubs has morphed into a beehive of night entertainment, all the result of one man's dream – Mauro's – and another man's vision – Allan Zeman's – and the eyes of a city upon it.

In the process, the value of properties shot through the roof. It went up eightfold during the ensuing ten years according to a survey made by C.B. Richard Ellis, even during a period of time when the overall property market was riding a roller coaster.

Meanwhile Mauro pointed me to a quaint little side street in Tsim Sha Tsui tucked away behind Kowloon's Nathan Road.

"Robert, I think Minden Avenue has the potential to be developed into another Lan Kwai Fong," he said. "You should pay attention to the street and see what you can do with the properties there. It has the right configuration – narrow, quaint and cosy. It's well served by public transport – bus and underground – not to mention the many pedestrian subways that will soon run below it. The area is now run-down. No one wants to buy there. It's your opportunity."

I was somewhat sceptical and also not sure if I could trust my own nose. I wanted a second opinion. What better way to test the water than to bounce the idea off the tycoons? Much to my surprise, everyone responded positively about the street.

'I can't be wrong if so many great minds all think alike,' I thought to myself.

"I thought my tycoon days had ended," I said to Elaine. "A new twist of events have got me right back into their midst. I'm in circulation again."

"What's happened?"

"You remember the basket of properties I purchased in Tsim Sha Tsui?"

"Yes, what about it?"

"Unbeknown to me, it consists of units in old buildings that are targeted for demolition."

"So, what's the big deal?"

"Much to my surprise, I discovered a couple of real gems in the basket. One is the only property along the entire street that is not already in the pocket of Cheng Yu Tung," I said excitedly. "Cheng has built his portfolio of properties up painstakingly over the years, one by one, a cumbersome process known in the market as 'hammering nails'."

In land-scarce Hong Kong 'hammering nails' is a good way and, at times, the only way to obtain land in prime locations. But one has to be patient. Buying too many and too quickly will jack up the price.

"Cheng has spent $3.8 billion over the years to buy up these properties. He has ended up owning the entire street... well, nearly, except for this one which has somehow slipped through his fingers. Whether or not he owns this last unit makes a huge difference to the deal he is now negotiating with the authority. The government is spearheading the renewal of the area and offers joint redevelopment rights to all the owners. The value of his stake – and, hence, the percentage in the joint venture – depends on whether he owns the 'units' or the 'parcel of land' along the street. I reckon his portfolio is worth at least a couple of hundred million more if he buys my unit. Then he can claim a value based on the price of the parcel of land as opposed to the aggregate value of all the units he owns."

"Well, have you talked to him?"

"Yes, I did. He's obviously very eager to buy this remaining unit and he's been chasing me almost every other week asking me to sell."

"And are you selling?"

"Yes, I mentioned a sum which I worked out to be half of his expected gain – about $200 million – if he could participate in the redevelopment as owner of the parcel of land as opposed to the owner of fragmented units. And he told me to fuck off."

"You are holding him to ransom."

"Yes, that was exactly what he said."

"Did you talk to Mauro?"

"Yes, I did. He advised me to go soft on the price. The crash is on the way."

"What crash?"

"The property market has reached its peak. He thinks the bubble is going to burst soon, what with the currency crisis in Thailand and the government's pledge to increase housing supply by building 85,000 units per year for the next few years. A crash seems inevitable."

"Are you going to heed Mauro's advice then?"

"I don't know. I'm still negotiating with Cheng. I regret I didn't use a go-between. It's embarrassing to have to negotiate directly with him. I don't wish to ruffle his feathers... no, not so soon after my disaster with Wee Cho Yaw. Mauro also told me that the area is destined to be the next Lan Kwai Fong. That's why I'm somewhat reluctant to sell. You know how property values there have gone up over the years. It's staggering... absolutely staggering."

"Yes, you told me that Cheng went and took a look at the street – Minden Avenue – not once but three times and agreed the street has the potential to become another Lan Kwai Fong."

"I took him there on a Sunday from his house at Repulse Bay. He was alone. I asked him about his bodyguard. He told me it was his day off. Then I jokingly said that if someone wanted to kidnap him, he could do it on a Sunday when the bodyguard was not working. It's very unlike Cheng to be so relaxed. Normally he is never careless.

"Not only did Cheng say so, but also Li Ka Shing was so convinced about the street's potential that he actually asked me to buy – 70% his and 30% mine. Li will put up the money for me initially and I will have up to nine months to repay him."

"But it sounds like a really big investment. Where can you get that kind of money?" Elaine looked worried.

"You don't understand. Once Li is there, I can find back-to-back investors easily and, in doing so, I come up with what I think I can afford and get the rest on the back of OPM. Now do you understand?"

"Well, if you say so," she said grudgingly.

"I have another bit of good news for you. You know in the same basket there is an another unit that is also the only one that has not already been acquired by Sun Hung Kai, in another old building."

"What, you hit the jackpot again?" she exclaimed.

"Yes, I'm like the phoenix rising from the ashes – as many have before me and as thousands will afterwards. Except this time it's straightforward. I simply negotiated a deal with Raymond Kwok to get into a joint venture with Sun Hung Kai to have the old building redeveloped into a hotel. I shall call it 'The Minden'. You can't beat the location – it's right in the heart of Hong Kong's tourist hub."

"Wow, the lucky star shines on you again!"

Sun Hung Kai is the largest property developer in Hong Kong. The family wealth of the Kwok brothers is in the same league as the Trio.

It is truly amazing. No matter which way I turn, I always seem to end up back in the midst of the rich and famous, just as my 'Pak Tze' predicted.

"Do you remember A.C. Chao?" I said.

"Didn't he take the same ship as your father when he came to Hong Kong in the 1940s?"

"Yes, he and my father shared the same bunk bed on the ship. No sooner had they boarded than the Japanese imposed a blockade, banning all ships from leaving Tsingtao. In the dead of a moonless night, the captain decided to take the chance and run the blockade. The ship's engine was started and the anchor stealthily pulled up. As the ship began to move slowly through the calm waters, it was spotted and the soldiers opened fire. The captain pushed the engines to full throttle and moved full speed ahead. The ship took a few direct hits but managed somehow to limp its way to Hong Kong.

"Chao went on to become a successful entrepreneur, owning factories in Indonesia. He died this year at the ripe old age of ninety. A few years before he died, he donated his fortune to Ningbo. Hundred of millions were involved. He was hands-on and managed his philanthropic deeds right down to the last detail, making sure the money went to the intended beneficiaries – schools, universities, research institutions and the like. You know, he was always a modest man, mean to himself. He lived a spartan life. Indeed, few knew he was that rich. It took everyone by surprise that he had that kind of money to give away. I really admired this man. He was a true son of Ningbo.

"I am sure he did it because he believed that it was the sacred duty of every son who made good in life to repay the native land by 'building bridges and repaving roads' as the old saying of Ningbo goes. Fallen leaves go back to the soil to enrich the roots. What that man did was admirable. It stirred my heart and I want to emulate it."

"So what do you want to do?" Elaine asked.

"I have this burning desire and it gets stronger as I grow older. I want to give to Ningbo. I could, for instance, build a school in Zhou Shan and call it 'Ting Sau Middle School'. 'Ting' was the middle name of my father and 'Sau' is the middle name of my mother. In a modest way, I shall follow in the footsteps of so many of my clansmen before me. Our children are well educated. They both went to Cambridge and have a good head on their shoulders. They can make their own fortunes. There is no need to be their slaves."

"I couldn't agree more."

"Yes, I came to this world with nothing. I shall depart with nothing."

# EPILOGUE

Each family has its own reunions – a way to remind each other of where they came from and where they are headed. Everyone has a story to tell. As each generation passes, experiences are shared by those who come from behind. They learn from the mistakes – the 'sorrows' of the elders are the best gifts for the young – rejoice over success, cry over sadness, lament over losses... and life continues, thus passing the torch from one generation to another. Yet, they continue to make the same mistakes. Greed, ego and self-preservation always get the better of reason. Lessons are supposed to be learned, yet they never are. History always repeats itself.

As the band played, relatives gathered for tea in the luxurious lobby of the Peninsula Hotel on the Bund in Shanghai. I noticed the changes in the lifestyle of some of my relatives. A couple of the young relatives are successful by any standard. They drive expensive cars, own properties and appear to lead enviable lifestyles. But I know they will make, and learn from, the same mistakes along the way – falling by the wayside, getting up and rising to fight another battle rather than giving up and sinking into oblivion.

If I have to remember any lessons in life, I shall remember just one Chinese character that my mother always taught me – 'Forbearance'. T.O. constantly reminded me that 'forbearance is golden'. But it was my mother who told me that behind every cloud there is a silver lining. If only I could have forborne the moment, then the brush with Wee Cho Yaw could perhaps have been avoided and, along with it, a chain of catastrophic events – Lim Kim San, abandonment by the Trio, flight from Singapore, the perfect storms and so forth. The irony was that, in the end, I sold the shares to Wee based on the valuation he wanted – net asset value – anyway. I should not have fought a battle that I had no hope of winning. A little bit of forbearance on my part could have saved me from the disasters. Yet, on the other hand, to be able to forbear is an outward manifestation of one's intelligence. I am a firm believer that one's success is determined by the level of one's intelligence. It seems logical because decisions are constantly made throughout one's life and they are cumulative in the sense that the more correct decisions one makes, the more successful one is likely to become. I can only go so far on the back of my own intelligence – a far cry from the likes of the Trio. It was folly for me to think otherwise.

History has a habit of repeating itself in families. My grandmother's pathological addiction to gambling destroyed her family and left her own daughter destitute; pillaging and philandering can cause everything to come crashing down; my grandfather once thought he had the world at his feet, only to find out when he jumped to his death his world was in fact no more than six feet below him. The glory that lasted fifteen minutes and poof!... it was over. The billions upon billions that the characters in this book have amassed that they cannot take with them when the time comes.

Of all the sad stories, none is sadder than the life of my aunt, Ting Hai (Siaw Ko). I was glad that my father had bought the house for her daughter in Zhou Shan – it was the least he could do to atone for the 'sins' of his parents, my grandparents. Yet, at the same time, they must know that good fortune is not always a gift from heaven. In the volatile world of today, it can just as easily be lost if one does not strive to improve and reinvent oneself along the way.

Yet my aunt's story had a happy ending. My heart leaps with joy to witness how well her descendants have done in life. Her eldest son, my first cousin, Chun Shin, turned out to be a top engineer. He was sent by the Central Government to build the city of Shenzhen, located in the Pearl River Delta, bordering Hong Kong. Today, Shenzhen is a boom town, thriving and prospering with a GDP to rival Shanghai's and quickly catching up with Hong Kong. Chun Shin's son is a successful entrepreneur who presides over a large printing business. It proves yet again that children can make their own fortune. There is no need to provide for them – Li Ka Shing started from nothing.

Yet there is something inexplicable that is written in the stars – be it the 'Pak Tze' of a man or the fortune of a country. As a Chinese, my generation, living in Hong Kong and Singapore, has been the most fortunate… no wars or natural disasters of significance and a background of steady growth. And we enjoy personal freedom unheard of for most Chinese of the past. Or perhaps, during their time, poverty was so abject that they never had the opportunity to think of such niceties. Survival was their priority.

When I went back to Hing Yip Road in Shanghai, I found our house had been demolished to make way for a hotel. As I sat in the lobby of Hotel 88 at Xin Tian Di, I stared at the well that once stood in the courtyard of the lung tong house that my father bought with five sticks of gold. Memories of the house came flashing back: the 'tram' I built with my grandmother's help; her bound feet; how she dressed me up and taught me how to bang the waist drum on that summer day in 1949 to welcome the soldiers; the night soil… and, of all the memories, none more poignant than that morning when we left the house and the struggle between my grandfather and my mother that followed at the train station.

Little did I realise that I was setting off on a truly amazing journey.

Being born poor was my greatest gift from God. I would not have had it any other way. I mean it… yes, I really do and, in that sense, I feel sorry for those who are born rich. They will never have my life experiences. They are deprived and always will be.

T.O. used to say: "Suppression is the mother of utility." I had been deprived as a child but got back my ounce of satisfaction as I grew up.

And Sir Run Run Shaw used to tell me: "Robert, you are a very lucky person."

It is true. I have always been blessed, and never had any major setbacks in my life. Yes, I went through a hard time in 1997 when not one but three storms hit. But it was all psychological. My ego was bruised – I became less popular and, perhaps, less respected than before. But that was about all. It was just a psychological disadvantage and much of it was a figment of my own imagination. It was true that people in the business world, realistic as they always are, deserted me for a while when I was down. But it was just a temporary state of affairs. As soon as I was back on my feet and appeared to be doing well again, they returned. This is the way the commercial world works: there are no permanent enemies or friends, only what suits and is advantageous at any given point in time. My friends – as if I had any as I was always so engrossed in business – did not abandon me. I did not do anything that sullied my reputation. The only thing untoward that I did do was step on a few toes that I really ought to have avoided. I was merely trying to forge ahead in my career. Nothing I did was catastrophic. I did not steal, cheat or rob, after all, and they all knew that.

Come rain or shine, my family was always there for me. Despite that little blemish in our relationship when I went astray, Elaine and I have had a happy marriage, one that is made in heaven. She is a good wife and I am, although not the best of husbands, a good provider. I never forget she married me for what I was – when I was down and poor, as a student and later as an articled clerk earning a pittance barely enough to support the family. She had to work as a secretary to supplement the meagre income I brought home in those days. After paying rent that took up most of our joint income – you know how expensive rents are in land-scarce Hong Kong – there was little left. Making ends meet was a problem we had to face at the end of every month.

Times were hard when John, our first child, was born in 1973. By the time Gillian, our daughter, was born five years later, things had already improved beyond recognition. I was a successful solicitor, the senior partner in an up-and-coming firm, the envy of the profession. My lifestyle had changed dramatically.

As a couple we were popular, sought after by the rich and famous. There were numerous society balls and other functions where Elaine was invited to give out prizes and I to give speeches. Then, of course, I must not forget those unique Shanghai parties we attended. We basked in the limelight, known and accepted by Hong Kong's elite – the upper echelon of society.

We are a happy family. Every summer we holiday either in Sardinia, Italy, where our best friends Monica and Mauro keep a sumptuous villa in the prestigious Porto Rotondo (the Round Port), next door to the villas of celebrities such as Shirley Bassey, the singer, and Claudia Cardinale, the Italian actress; or in our own second homes in Hawaii, Cambridge, London and Singapore. In Hong Kong we had two residences: one on the Peak and the other on the beach. We now live in a beautiful penthouse by the sea. I feel there is nowhere else I would rather be each time I am home.

My son John is a barrister. He works and lives in Singapore. He took over my share in the Singapore firm – Robert Wang & Woo LLC – and became the firm's managing partner for a while but he hated management. He decided after two years that he had had enough. After giving away his shares, 60% of the firm, for free to my partner of close to thirty years, Woo Tchi Chu, he has now joined another firm so that he can dedicate all of his time to what he loves most – litigation.

It proves to be true what Tan Kah Kee, the great philanthropist, once said: "Our children can make their own fortunes. There is no need to be their slaves." I was upset that my plans for my son did not work out the way I had hoped. I have come to realise however that I must let my children live their own lives and find their own equilibrium.

John is a devout Christian and his wife, Flower, works for the church – the Methodist Church in Singapore – and is in charge of its children's ministry. David, their first child and my first paternal grandchild, was born on 4th July 2011.

My daughter Gillian works in finance. She is married to Dennis, her childhood sweetheart from her Cambridge days. Dennis is a surgeon by profession and works in a hospital. Gillian has just given birth to her second child, Evan.

Our first grandchild from Dennis and Gillian is now two and a half years old. Nate Nate, as we call him (short for Nathan), is not only the love of Elaine but also mine. He is just beginning to talk.

"Mummy has told you not to eat so many jelly beans," Gillian barked at him one day. "Give me all the jelly beans you're holding in your hand."

Nathan reluctantly surrendered the sweets. As he handed them to his mother, he noticed something black on the floor. Thinking he had dropped a black jelly bean, he picked it up while Gillian was not looking.

"Thank you, sweet Jesus." He looked up to the ceiling and shouted in jubilation as he quickly put it into his mouth. Upon realising it was his most hated liquorice flavour, he spat out the jelly bean just as quickly and mumbled as he clapped his little hands together in prayer: "Oh no, not this one, Jesus. Please give me another."

We burst out laughing.

I bought him a large cup of strawberry ice cream sprinkled with M&M sweets.

"Nate Nate, don't eat so much ice cream," said Elaine. "Ice cream is going to make you fat."

"No, ice cream makes Nate Nate grow tall," he corrected his grandmother.

We see Nathan and Evan whenever possible – a couple of times a week – and we look forward to seeing David more in Singapore when he is a little older.

Whenever a grandchild is born, I get a new sense of hope as if a new tree has taken root; one day that tree will grow strong with many leaves, providing shade and cover for the family. I always think: "Who knows? One of them may grow up to be another Li Ka Shing."

And so, dear friends, the story of the Wang family will continue like any other family with its highs and lows, its tears and its songs of joy

– and each family, each generation will produce its one 'black sheep' that will try to break the mould and achieve the impossible, conquer the mountain, walk on water – but each will learn, sometimes the easy way but more often the hard way, that God will never allow just one man one chance, one way to build his own tower to heaven. Or will they ever learn?

In hindsight, it is uncanny that my life has always been sealed in the 'Pak Tze' that my mother had written when I was sixteen, during a time when my life was mired in poverty and so vastly different from that which I later went through. Yet so many of these predictions have come true that it lends credibility to the belief that God has a hand in what we do – our destiny is preordained from above and, according to the Chinese, it is at the moment when a newborn cries for the first time.

The 'Pak Tze' also predicts the year of my death. I am certain like so many other predictions it will prove to be accurate. I cannot say I do not entirely welcome it. When the time comes, I want my tombstone to be inscribed:

HE CAME FROM NINGBO. HE DIED IN HAPPINESS.

## ABOUT THE AUTHOR

Robert Wang was born in Ningbo. Shortly after his birth his parents moved to Shanghai by crossing the Hangzhou Bay at the mouth of the Yangtze River and from there eventually emigrated to Hong Kong.

He is a solicitor by training and, like many of his clansmen from Ningbo, an entrepreneur at heart. He founded the firm of Robert W.H. Wang & Co., Solicitors & Notaries, in the late 1970s and grew it to be one of Hong Kong's largest, with offices also in Singapore and London.

He is an Honorary Fellow of Queen Mary of London University, his alma mater.